MALPRACTICE and Other Malfeasances

by Stanley M. Rosenblatt

Not since the publication of Louis Nizer's *My Life in Court* has there been so fascinating and graphic a volume on courtroom procedure and legal pyrotechnics as this collection of the most spectacular cases of a brilliant trial lawyer.

This book deals with jury trials in the civil field of law, with emphasis on the cases involving medical malpractice. Negligence or malpractice trials are real battles, in contrast to the rigged contests in the criminal court forum. There, the adversaries are usually an overworked and inexperienced assistant prosecutor and a seasoned criminal lawyer (who is nearly always a former prosecutor). If the defendant is poor, he will be represented by a public defender who suffers from the same disabilities as the prosecutor.

In civil law it is the injured person's (the plaintiff's) lawyer who goes up against the mammoth corporations, insurance companies, hospitals and government bodies. These outfits hire the best legal minds in the country, and you will meet the cream of them in these chapters.

Stanley M. Rosenblatt recognizes the courtroom as one of the last competitive areas on the American scene. It is not mediation, or arbitration, or negotiation. It is literally combat, with great sums of money at stake. The author has been involved in some epic

cases. Four of the cases here described represent medical malpractice. Others deal with police malpractice, industrial negligence and other types of negligence resulting in injury and, sometimes, death. In the medical malpractice action brought as a result of the death of Mr. Rosenblatt's investigator, Jerry Burke, Mr. Rosenblatt achieved one of the highest settlements in courtroom history: $1,200,000.00

The cases in this book tingle with suspense. The author has relived these courtroom moments with a skill equal to his ability at the bar.

• • • • •

Stanley M. Rosenblatt is one of the most accomplished trial lawyers in the country. Practicing in the Miami area, Mr. Rosenblatt views the courtroom as an arena where he will battle for his clients against the giant corporations or insurance companies which he feels has wronged them. His record of favorable verdicts is spectacular. Yet, he maintains, his primary aim in writing the book was not to relive triumphs but to demonstrate and demonstrate again the soundness of the jury system. As he himself has written: "...the jury system is far from perfect but it is the best thing we have to avoid corruption and favoritism in civil litigation."

LYLE STUART, INC.
120 ENTERPRISE AVENUE
SECAUCUS, N.J. 07094

ISBN 0-8184-0234-2

Malpractice and Other Malfeasances

Also by Stanley M. Rosenblatt

The Divorce Racket
Justice Denied

MALPRACTICE
and Other
MALFEASANCES

Stanley M. Rosenblatt

LYLE STUART, Inc.   Secaucus, N.J.

Published by Lyle Stuart, Inc.
120 Enterprise Ave., Secaucus, N. J. 07094
Published simultaneously in Canada by
George J. McLeod Limited, Toronto, Ont.

Address queries regarding rights and permissions
to Lyle Stuart, Inc.

Manufactured in the United States of America

LIBRARY OF CONGRESS CATALOGING IN PUBLICATION DATA

Rosenblatt, Stanley, 1936-
    Malpractice and other malfeasances.

    1. Trials (Malpractice)—United States.   I. Title.
KF226.R6   346'.73'033   76-50668
ISBN 0-8184-0234-2

To Jerry J. Burke—
    Friend, Trial Partner, Inspiration

Contents

Introduction   9

I   *Linda Powell v. Dr. Lewis Fagan*
Malpractice and Perjury   13

II   *Gus Burgel v. Red Wing Carriers*
Explosion and Paralysis   85

III   *Elease Morris v. St. Francis Hospital*
The First of Two Unnecessary Deaths   131

IV   *Jerry Burke v. Dr. Marshall Kessler*
and Parkway General Hospital
Jerry Becomes the Biggest Case of All   153

V   *Antoinette Boatman v. Osteopathic*
General Hospital
Malpractice and the Duty to Make a
Decision   181

VI   *Johnnie Lee Williams v. The Sheriff of*
Miami-Dade County
Professional Negligence by the Police   209

VII   *Richard Adams and Michael Robinson*
v. the Miami-Dade County Jail
More Police Negligence   239

VIII   *Arthur Dillon v. Miami-Dade County*
The Value of a Father's Love   259

IX   *Sears's Shocking Sewing Machine*
Caveat Vendor—Caveat Emptor   275

X   *Nobel Vega v. City of Miami Beach*
My Flamingo Park Becomes a Defendant   289

IX   *Olga Scarpetta v. Nick and Jean DeMartino*
The "Baby Lenore" Case   303

Epilogue   347

Introduction

I went to law school because I wanted to become a trial lawyer. The study of law in matters of real estate, taxes, contracts, and corporations never held any interest for me. The only things that intrigued me about the "law" were the challenge and psychology of the courtroom.

The famous trial lawyers I knew about were criminal lawyers, so I assumed they were the best. I eventually learned that this assumption was almost totally erroneous. In general, criminal lawyers aren't even in the same league as negligence or personal injury attorneys.

Negligence or malpractice trials are real battles in contrast to the rigged contests in the criminal court forum. There the contest is generally between an over-worked and inexperienced assistant prosecutor and a seasoned criminal lawyer (who is nearly always a former prosecutor). If the defendant is poor he will be represented by a public defender who suffers from the same disabilities as the prosecutor. Ninety percent of all criminal convictions are obtained on "bargained" pleas of guilty. The "copping" of pleas mechanism is the only thing that keeps our so-called "criminal justice system" from crumbling.

It is the injured person's (plaintiff's) lawyer who goes

up against the mammoth corporations, insurance companies, hospitals, and governmental bodies. These outfits hire the best legal talent in the country. I am convinced that Greater Miami has the best trial bar in America, and you will meet some of the best lawyers in these chapters. The defendants here are hospitals, doctors, governments and powerful business concerns.

The courtroom is one of the last competitive arenas on the American scene. It is not mediation or arbitration or negotiation—it is literally combat with a great deal of money and ego at stake. Medical malpractice cases, in particular, constitute a head-to-head confrontation between the nation's two most controversial professions. The animosity of doctors for plaintiffs' lawyers who dare sue them is legendary.

Four chapters here are devoted to the subject of *medical* malpractice. But malpractice is just another term for negligence and can refer to an improper practice in *any* field of endeavor. Other chapters deal with malpractice by the police, jail personnel, a city, a county, an adoption agency, a law firm, and the deliverer of a potentially explosive jet fuel.

I have been privileged to represent individuals in some memorable and historic cases. Several of the verdicts were record breakers, but I have not selected cases merely for the results achieved. I have been more interested in a cross-section of trials to illustrate the varied challenges faced by the advocate in civil practice.

I wrote this book partly to dispel the "media myth" that the greatest courtroom collisions take place in criminal cases. The great majority of trials occur on the civil side of the court, but it is the criminals who get most of the attention. I hope that after you read the cases which follow, you will agree with my contention that "malpractice" is where the action really is.

Malpractice and Other Malfeasances

I

Linda Powell
VS.
Dr. Lewis Fagan
Malpractice and Perjury

Every morning hundreds of Miami women arise, look admiringly in the mirror and are grateful for the surgical skill of Dr. Lewis Fagan. They were grateful, too, back in 1966 when Linda Powell, a twenty-one-year-old clerk-typist for the Miami Police Department, went to see him. Her treatment led to the legal fight of my life, of Linda Powell's life and Dr. Lewis Fagan's life.

Dr. Fagan was a specialist in ear, nose and throat, and facial plastic surgery. He graduated from Chicago Medical School in 1953. After specialty training, he had practiced in Miami ever since. His surgical skill was such that, among both patients and hospital personnel, he was widely believed to do the "best nose job in town."

Linda Powell was the only child of a Cuban mother and an American father. She was born in Schenectady, New York, and came to Miami in 1959. Her parents were divorced when she was a youngster. Linda lived with her mother, who worked in a bank in downtown Miami, and

13

her maternal grandmother. She spoke both English and Spanish fluently; a great advantage in south Florida, where about a third of the population is Cuban. Since her graduation from high school, Linda had worked at the Miami Police Department—a job she found interesting and glamorous. She was attractive, healthy, and active. She loved dealing with people, had a very even temperament, and was a warm and sought-after friend.

Before she ever went to Dr. Fagan, Linda was already known to Jerry Burke, my close friend and investigator. Jerry would drop by the police station once or twice a month to pick up accident reports on various office cases. Because both he and Linda were friendly, outgoing people, they got to know one another.

In May 1966, Linda had been to Dr. Fagan to get a "prettier nose" although, as Jerry told me, there was absolutely nothing wrong with the old one. Dr. Fagan operated on her at South Miami Hospital on June 23, 1966.

One day in October 1967, sixteen months after this operation, Jerry received a very strange call from Linda. She was a patient at St. Francis Hospital in Miami Beach. Her doctors there were frightening her about a "blood problem." Jerry and I went to see her at the hospital. This was the first time I ever met her.

Linda was as Jerry had described her. She appeared pale but calm. She told us that Dr. Eduardo Anderson and some consultants he had called in had been asking a lot of questions about doctors she had seen and drugs she had taken in the last year or so. In particular they seemed to attach significance to a drug called Chloromycetin, which she had taken in 1966 and 1967, while under Dr. Fagan's care. Linda had called me in because she had been told she had some type of blood condition caused by Chloromycetin, and although none of the doctors had directly said so, it was her distinct impression that Dr. Fagan had been wrong to give her that drug. She was confused and frightened. Would we please look into the situation? Our "look into the situation" was to involve years of work and thousands of hours of time—both Jerry's and mine.

All professionals owe a duty to clients and patients to keep up the state of their skill and knowledge. One real problem of modern medical practice is that many doctors do not keep up-to-date on the potential dangers of the drugs they prescribe. Every day millions of patients take various medications and suffer no adverse side effects, but there are some very powerful drugs which doctors simply should not prescribe unless it is absolutely necessary. (This is not "Stanley M. Rosenblatt on Medicine," but is the opinion of the vast body of medical experts who have studied the subject.)

In recent decades, one of the most dangerous drugs to find its way on the market was Chloromycetin. This drug is an extremely powerful antibiotic—but it has one very deadly possible side effect. It can cause aplastic anemia, a killer disease of the bone marrow and blood. Linda Powell went to Dr. Fagan for a cosmetic procedure—a "nose job." Dr. Fagan prescribed Chloromycetin. Linda contracted aplastic anemia and received a death sentence.

Was this malpractice? Yes. But who says so? I can say so and I may be able to get an expert to say so, too, but there is only one group of people who matter when it comes to deciding the question. A jury. If we left it to the doctors (uncontrolled by the ordinary processes of law), they would almost always exonerate their colleagues. I could give hundreds of examples of doctors doing just that. If we left it to six or twelve lay people to decide on their own, there would be no serious way of testing the truth, as no layman really has the ability, without help, to wade through all the legal and medical complexities of: "What is malpractice?"

That is where the malpractice specialist comes in. The

Court informs the jury of the law that applies—(simply negligence judged by the accepted standards of the profession of which the defendant doctor is a member). The lawyer's job is to present the medical facts as clearly as possible to the jury, using expert witnesses he has retained. In addition, he must use his own acquired medical knowledge to cross-examine the defendant and the defendant's expert witnesses, in turn.

Because of the expense and difficulty involved, malpractice cases should never be taken without serious thought. After my first review of potential malpractice cases, I turn down at least four out of every five. I spend many unpaid hours each week reviewing and rejecting possible malpractice cases. Next I try to obtain consultations from the few doctors who are not so paranoid about medical malpractice that they are willing to be associated with me, a lawyer who sues doctors. Finally, if their opinions are favorable, I have to prove a case against the extremely vigorous and well-organized defense of doctors, insurance personnel, and defense attorneys.

After meeting Linda, I did some preliminary reading on Chloromycetin. It can be very effective against certain bacterial infections, but is highly dangerous. It was to be used only for life-threatening infections.

This was strange. Linda had not been ill when her cosmetic surgery was performed, nor had she had any severe illnesses in the meantime. So why Chloromycetin?

Jerry and I made an appointment to see Dr. Eduardo Anderson. He told us that Linda had aplastic anemia, a condition which involves a severe deficiency of blood-cell formation. It is usually fatal, and is almost always so when caused by a drug. Of all drugs, Chloromycetin is the drug most frequently associated with aplastic anemia.

The word "Chloromycetin" had meant nothing to Linda, but in describing her various medications, she mentioned a white capsule with a gray band around the middle. Dr. Anderson had shown her photographs of several capsules and pills, and she had positively identified Chloromycetin as one of the drugs prescribed by Dr. Fagan. Dr. Anderson had phoned Dr. Fagan to get details of the amount of the drug administered and the reasons why it was given. To Anderson's surprise, Dr. Fagan denied ever prescribing Chloromycetin for her.

Linda Powell became a client. Jerry started canvassing various drugstores that Linda and her family used for prescriptions, and I started research in earnest about Chloromycetin and aplastic anemia. I learned in short order that even if we could establish that Linda had received "Chloro" from Dr. Fagan, it would still be very difficult to prove that this *caused* her disease.

Chloromycetin—or its generic or chemical name (chloramphenicol)—had been on the market for only fifteen years or so. Aplastic anemia was a recognized disease one hundred years ago. Many people become victims of aplastic anemia who have never had any contact with Chloromycetin. Statistically speaking, the relationship between Chloromycetin intake and aplastic anemia was only about one in every 40,500 persons. Moreover, there is no test known to medical science to determine beforehand whether a particular person will be susceptible to the disease.

Jerry located one "Chloro" prescription from Dr. Fagan dated June 25, 1966. It was for twelve capsules, 250 mg. each, to be taken every six hours. Although Linda told us Dr. Fagan had prescribed Chloro on at least three separate occasions, this single prescription was the only one we ever found. This was a significant hurdle, but one which we would just have to overcome.

From my review of the pharmaceutical literature, I found that if aplastic anemia is caused by Chloro, the disease will develop within two weeks to seven months after the drug is taken. This was the time frame, according to all available medical evidence. We could not find the other two prescriptions Linda told us she had had from Dr. Fagan in 1967. Since her condition was not diagnosed until October 1967, the defense attorneys would no doubt argue that Chloro taken in June of 1966 could not have caused Linda's aplastic anemia. We sued Dr. Fagan for malpractice in prescribing a dangerous drug for a trivial infection.

The suit enabled us to obtain copies of Dr. Fagan's office records concerning Linda. Only on one occasion—Linda's very last visit to him on June 29, 1967—did his records indicate that he had prescribed Chloromycetin.

This illustrates one very substantial problem of medical malpractice cases. One of the most vital pieces of evidence in a suit is likely to be a physician's office records, which contain a summary of a patient's complaints, treatments, and progress. In order to see these, however, a patient's attorney usually has to file suit. It is almost useless to ask a doctor for a copy of his records. Moreover, the incidence of changes in doctors' and hospital records in cases of professional negligence is greater than you would think. Indeed, I have some "doctored" records in several cases in my office right now.

The medical profession in the United States has its share of Marcus Welbys, no doubt, but basically medicine has become a business, and its practitioners, generally successful businessmen. They have two great advantages over other professionals and businessmen, though; the title "doctor" and the trust of the public. A good proportion of the doctors I have met seem to have developed an unreal idea of their importance and an attitude that whatever they do, as a professional, is above criticism. On the occasions when it appears that an attorney is investigating and is likely to be able to prove malpractice, the temptation to "doctor" the vital office records and hospital charts is sometimes too great to resist.

A doctor sued for malpractice has the right, of course, to hire his own lawyer to defend him, but realistically, he does not need to. His insurance company will be the one to pay up if he loses, and the insurance companies hire the best defense lawyers of all. Dr. Fagan had as skilled defense counsel as existed in the state of Florida—John R. Hoehl and Francis Sevier of the law firm of Blackwell, Walker & Gray, and L. Norton Preddy, of Preddy, Haddad, Kutner & Hardy.

Under the Florida Rules of Civil Procedure, either side can take the detailed testimony of the other by way of deposition. A court reporter is present to transcribe all questions and answers, as are all attorneys. I spent several hours taking the deposition of Dr. Fagan over a three-day period. It became obvious very quickly that either Linda Powell was mistaken or Dr. Fagan was a liar. There were just too many conflicts between them for the differences to be honest.

Jerry Burke was with me throughout all the depositions. Jerry and I became convinced that Dr. Lewis Fagan was a liar, and a clever one. To get a jury to believe that there was malpractice would be hard enough with the correct records. In addition, now we had to prove that his records were phony; that Dr. Fagan, a respected professional, was lying under oath.

We had taken the depositions of Dr. Fagan's office personnel and his medical experts. The defense had deposed Linda Powell, her friends, and our medical witnesses. The trial began on Tuesday, March 18, 1969, before Dade County Circuit Judge Raymond G. Nathan. In the year and a half since I first met Linda in St. Francis Hospital, both sides had put hundreds of hours into the preparation of the case. Each of us knew what to expect from each other's witnesses. The only exception was that Dr. Fagan did not know that we had been unable to locate the prescription which would prove that Linda had taken the Chloro he prescribed in June 1967.

This was not merely a malpractice trial. It was to develop

into a detective story involving crime and punishment. No
lawyer ever had a more interesting or heartbreaking case.

I called Dr. Anderson early to establish the fact that Dr.
Fagan could not be believed.

Q. When was the very first time that you saw Linda Powell?
A. October 9, 1967 (sixteen months after the nose surgery).
Q. What were the results of your examination?
A. Well, physically she looked pretty healthy, but the main thing
was the blemishes or black and blue marks all over the body,
and tiredness. That is why I put her into St. Francis Hospital
where blood tests confirmed that she was suffering from
aplastic anemia.
Q. Dr. Anderson, did you ever have a conversation with Dr.
Lewis Fagan concerning Linda Powell?
A. Yes sir.
Q. Tell us what was said by you and what was said by him.
A. I asked him if he had given her Chloromycetin and he said
"no." He said he gave polycillin, and he mentioned three or
four other antibiotics. Linda told me he did give her Chloromycetin, so I was confused. (Fagan's own records showed he
had prescribed Chloro on June 29, 1967).

Linda had seen Dr. Fagan first in 1966 and had returned
to see him in June 1967. In between these visits, she had
been seen by Dr. Ernest Pierleoni, who had hospitalized her
for abdominal complaints which turned out to be minor.
During this hospitalization, Dr. Pierleoni prescribed Madribon, one of the sulfa derivatives, for a mild infection. The
defense would argue that Madribon was just as likely a
cause of Linda's aplastic anemia as was the Chloromycetin.
The dates of Linda's treatment by Dr. Fagan explained why
the defense had two separate "heavyweight" law firms. Norton Preddy represented Aetna Casualty & Surety Co., which
provided Dr. Fagan with $100,000 in insurance coverage for
1966. Any malpractice which may have occurred in 1967
was of no concern to Preddy or Aetna.

Jack Hoehl and Frank Sevier represented The Employer's Group of Insurance Companies, which provided Fagan with the same amount of coverage for 1967. The doctor also had "an umbrella policy" with Insurance Company of North America, which covered him up to $1,000,000 for both years. The lawyers for INA did not participate in the trial, as it was the responsibility of the "primary" carriers to provide legal representation.

The defense made two points through Dr. Pierleoni: that as of ten months following Linda Powell's nose operation, there was no evidence of aplastic anemia; and that they had introduced Madribon, a "red herring" drug.

On the other hand, the cross-examination was costly for them. Dr. Pierleoni readily admitted that if he had been looking for aplastic anemia, there were ways of finding it. He also indirectly showed what a physician should do, both in recording and in selecting the medications given.

Dr. Anderson had referred Linda to an eminent specialist, Dr. John B. Miale. He was my expert witness. Dr. Miale was a graduate of the University of Rochester in 1940, with postgraduate training at Cornell and at the University of North Carolina in Chapel Hill.

Q. In what fields of medicine are you board certified?
A. I am certified in Pathologic Anatomy, and I have a second certificate in Clinical Pathology and a third certificate in Hematology.
Q. What is your title at Jackson Memorial Hospital and the University of Miami Medical School?
A. I am Professor of Pathology and Chairman of the Department and Director of the Clinical Pathology Laboratories.
Q. Have you written any books?
A. Yes, I have written a book on Hematology that is in its third edition: *Laboratory Medicine, Hematology.*
Q. Have you written any articles that have appeared in medical journals?

A. Yes. I think I have 67 or 68 published articles.

The jury could have no doubt that he was a solid expert. I continued:

Q. When did you first see Linda Powell?
A. I saw Linda on November 8, 1967.
Q. What did your blood studies reveal?
A. When I first saw her she had a very low platelet count. They were practically nonexistent. She had a moderately low red blood cell count and a moderately low white blood cell count.
Q. What is the function of platelets in the blood?
A. Well, there are three blood cells in the blood—the red cells and the white cells, and then these cells called platelets. These have to do with the prevention of bleeding. In the absence of platelets, a patient begins to bleed under the skin, and this is the bruising that she showed. They also may have various internal hemorrhages—intestinal, brain, or lung. So the absence of platelets is the most serious complication in this case.
Q. What is the most likely complication from lack of platelets?
A. She is a prime candidate for a brain hemorrhage or an intestinal hemorrhage, which are the chief causes of death in these cases.
Q. Were you able to make a diagnosis on that visit?
A. Yes, I was. I felt that she had aplastic anemia, which is a lowering of all the blood cells; and with a history of Chloromycetin, my diagnosis was Chloromycetin toxicity.

This was important! Dr. Miale, an unquestioned expert in the field of blood diseases, had tied the aplastic anemia of November, 1967 to Chloromycetin, *whenever* it was administered. In legal terms he had testified to one essential element I had to prove: "proximate or legal cause."

Q. In other words, Chloro *caused her* lowered blood coun
A. Yes.

Dr. Miale would help me show the jury the extent of Linda's physical suffering, too.
A. Halotestin.
Q. What course of treatment did you undertake?
A. Well, I saw her weekly or every two weeks until February, 1968. I prescribed Corticosteroids and a male sex hormone and continued to follow her blood counts to see whether she was responding to treatment.
Q. What was the male sex hormone you prescribed?
Q. Did the sex hormone have any adverse side effects?
A. Yes. Both of these drugs have severe side effects.
Q. What were they?
A. Well, the administration of the Corticosteroids produces what is called the Cushingoid Syndrome—a great increase in weight, a round face, quite different from the normal appearance of the patient, and retention of water. The male hormone changes the characteristics of a woman to more masculine characteristics such as heavy black hair on the face, and while she was under my care she was beginning to show these signs.
Q. How frequently was she required to take these medications?
A. Well, she was taking four tablets of the steroids and three tablets of the male hormone every day.
Q. What did your later blood studies reveal?
A. They were the same or worse. The red blood cell count and the white blood count both dropped further than when I had first seen her. She was requiring blood transfusions.
Q. Doctor, is Linda's condition of aplastic anemia permanent?
A. I think that all the evidence is that this is an irreversible process when caused by Chloromycetin. She will continue to have this and will probably die from it.

Linda Powell was sitting next to me at the counsel table, fully aware of the meaning of her death sentence—composed, courageous, and tragic.

Q. What is her prognosis?
A. Very grave. It is impossible to be absolutely sure what will

happen in any given case, but all of the cases on record that
have this aplastic anemia with bone marrow depression had
died within eighteen months of the onset of the disease.

Q. Is Chloromycetin considered to be a dangerous drug?

A. Yes. All anyone needs to do is read the warning box in the
Physician's Desk Reference, which lists information on
approximately 2500 drug products.

This answer permitted me to offer in evidence the product
description of the manufacturer, Parke-Davis, contained in
the book *Physician's Desk Reference.* It read as follows:

WARNING

SERIOUS AND EVEN FATAL BLOOD DYSCRASIAS
(aplastic anemia, hypoplastic anemia, thrombocytopenia, granulocytopenia) are known to occur after the administration of
Chloramphenicol. Blood dyscrasias have occurred after both
short term and prolonged therapy with this drug. Bearing in
mind the possibility that such reactions may occur, Chloramphenicol should be used only for serious infections caused by
organisms which are susceptible to its anti-bacterial effects.
Chloramphenicol should not be used when other less potentially
dangerous agents will be effective, or in the treatment of trivial
infections such as colds, influenza, or viral infections of the
throat, or as a prophylactic agent.

While blood studies may detect early peripheral blood changes,
such as leukopenia or granulocytopenia, before they become
irreversible, such studies cannot be relied on to detect bone
marrow depression prior to development of aplastic anemia.

I was getting ready to ask Dr. Miale if he thought Dr.
Fagan had been negligent. For legal reasons, however, I could
not ask this question so simply. Prior to asking the key question, I had to meet certain legal criteria, which required me
to read Dr. Fagan's office records. The question therefore
had to assume that what those records said was true.

Q. Doctor, I am going to ask you a lengthy question, and in this
question I want you to assume certain facts. I am going to give

you Linda Powell's past medical history, and at the conclusion of those facts I will ask you a question. I want to assume that Linda Powell went to Dr. Fagan for the first time on May 20, 1966, and that his office records reflect the following:

"May 20, 1966:

"Difficulty breathing, both nares. Interested in having straightened on outside. S-shaped deviation, nasal septum; slight thickening of mucous membranes, bilateral. Right nasal bone deviated medially. Hospitalization and fee and surgery discussed with patient. She will think it over.

"June 20, 1966 visit: Patient states she ran into door during night, June 18, 1966. Experienced pain, swelling and deformity of nose. Profuse bleeding at that time. Congestion afterward and persisting. Marked swelling and some ecchymosis over dorsum. Nasal bones markedly deviated to right, freely movable and crepitant. Nasal septum markedly buckled and causing obstruction of both nares. Long, large laceration involving mucous membranes and vestibule of right nostril. Surgical correction advised."

Linda denied that she ever ran into a door or suffered any injury to her nose. Pure and simple, she went to Fagan for cosmetic surgery. This was to be but one of many total conflicts between Plaintiff and Defendant.

Q. Dr. Fagan put Miss Powell in South Miami Hospital from June 22, through June 27, 1966, with an admitting diagnosis of "deviated nasal septum." On June 23 the doctor performed an open reduction of compound nasal fracture and submucous resection. On June 25, 1966, while Miss Powell was still in the hospital, the defendant gave her *a prescription for Chloromycetin,* 250 milligrams, a three-day supply at four capsules per day. Now, doctor, before I continue, have you had the opportunity to review the records of South Miami Hospital?

A. Yes, I have.

Q. After Linda was discharged from South Miami Hospital on

June 27, she returned to Dr. Fagan's office the very next day,
June 28. His note is as follows:

"Five days postoperative. Afebrile. Packing out. Slight
congestion of mucous membranes of nostrils, bilateral. No
complaints. Laceration sutures removed. Healing okay. On
Ornade."

What does afebrile mean?

A. It means no fever.

Q. On July 1, 1966, Dr. Fagan's note is as follows:

"Afebrile. Eight days postoperative. Nares sprayed and
suctioned. Moderate congestion bilateral. Laceration healing okay. No pain over dorsum.

"July 5, 1966: Twelve days postoperative. Afebrile. Nose
sprayed and suctioned. Cortisporin ointment applied to
vestibules. Moderate edema bilaterally. Stay on Ornade.

"July 12: Patient didn't show.

"July 15: 22 days postoperative. Afebrile. Mucous membranes healing slowly. Continue Ornade. Cortisporin ointment applied to both nostrils.

"August 12, 1966: One and a half months postoperative.
Afebrile. Slight congestion comes and goes. Healing satisfactory. Continue ointment and Ornade."

Dr. Fagan did not see Miss Powell from August 12, 1966,
according to his records, until the following year, on June 6,
1967. Between those visits Miss Powell saw a Dr. Pierleoni,
who hospitalized her at Hialeah Hospital from April 22, 1967,
through April 25, 1967, with a diagnosis of acute gastritis and
a history of abdominal pain and indigestion and heartburn.
Doctor, in our conference, did you completely review the
records of Hialeah Hospital?

A. Yes.

Q. "June 6, 1967: Eleven and three-quarter months postoperative. Complaining of frontal and ethmoid pain, bilateral, for past few weeks. Congestion of nose. Suppurative
rhinosinusitis, bilateral. Purulent exudate on inferior turbi-
nates bilaterial. Polycillin capsules, 250 milligrams. Ornade
spansules. Nose sprayed and suctioned.

"June 13, 1967: Some improvement. Still has moderate amount of edema both nostrils. Suppurative exudate still present bilaterally. Sprayed and suctioned. Continue Ornade. Combiotic, half-strength. Patient to return for Combiotic injection."

Doctor, what is Combiotic?

A. It is an antibiotic, as is Polycillin.

Q. "June 14, 1967: Combiotic, half-strength."

"June 15: Combiotic, half-strength."

"June 23, 1967: Temperature 99 degrees. Still experiencing frontal and ethmoid headaches bilateral. Nasal congestion comes and goes, worse on right. Still has suppurative exudate. Patient advised to get culture and sensitivity tests. Very reluctant to do so because of time and money. Patient told that if new antibiotic ordered today does not result in improvement, she will have to get tests. Tetrex capsules, three days."

"June 29, 1967: (*The last time that Dr. Fagan ever saw Linda Powell as a patient. Linda said this vital note was a total fabrication*). Temperature 100 degrees. Same complaints. No improvement. Patient requests Chloromycetin because girlfriend given this medication by doctor for sinusitis and responded immediately. Patient advised of dangers of Chloromycetin, blood dyscrasias, and told cases have been fatal. Patient states that she was on Chloro in the past before coming to me and responded well. Patient given slip to take to South Miami Hospital for culture and sensitivity tests. Given prescription for Chloro, three days, but promises not to fill it until tests have been taken and reviewed by me to see if less dangerous antibiotic could be used. Patient also told that Chloro may not even be effective against her particular infection. Patient says she will have tests tomorrow.

"July 3, 1967: Called South Miami Hospital lab. Patient has not made appointment. Linda [Stone] to call patient." (*I was now ready for the trial's most important single question.*)

Now, Dr. Miale, after that very long-winded predicate, my question to you is this: based on Dr. Fagan's office records and the records of South Miami and Hialeah Hospitals, do you have an opinion based on reasonable medical certainty, whether or not the defendant departed from the accepted and reasonable standard of care and treatment used by physicians in Miami and other metropolitan areas, in his treatment of Linda Powell in 1966 and 1967?

A. Yes, I believe he departed from accepted medical care. The toxicity of this drug has been known for about fifteen years. It has been emphasized in many, many medical journals and in many conferences and symposia throughout the United States. All who deal with antibiotics have agreed that it should be used only in a lifesaving situation. There is no indication from the records that Linda had a really serious infection either in 1966 or in 1967.

He had said Dr. Fagan had committed malpractice. Dr. Miale reached this conclusion based on the defendant's records—his version of the facts. I still had to do more. I had to convince the jury that Dr. Miale was correct.

Linda had been referred to the Mayo Clinic in Rochester, Minnesota, in late March 1968. Her condition had deteriorated, and she was prohibited from traveling back to Miami. Her family had relatives in Grand Rapids, Michigan, so Linda, her mother, her grandmother, her uncle, and his wife all moved there. They were a very closely knit and devoted family.

Prior to trial I had flown to Grand Rapids with Jerry to take the deposition of Linda's main treating physician—Dr. Jerry Anderson, a hematologist (blood-disease specialist), no relation to the Miami Dr. Eduardo Anderson. We used the transcript of the deposition at the trial. Naturally, Jack Hoehl and Norton Preddy participated in questioning Dr. Anderson. Jerry Burke read the questions and I portrayed Dr. Jerry Anderson on the witness stand.

Q. When was the very first time you saw Linda Powell?

A. April 9, 1968.

Q. Please tell us about your physical examination.

A. She was markedly cushingoid. She had acne on her back, which is a complication of cortisone and male hormones. She had many small black and blue spots all over her body.

Q. Did you hospitalize her on April 9, 1968?

A. Yes, at Butterworth Hospital.

Q. What was done for her?

A. The treatment was devoted to giving her blood transfusions of four units of packed red blood cells. She was continued on Prednisone and Halotestin medications which she had been taking earlier. She was discharged from the hospital on April 12, and the next time I saw her in the office was on April 15, 1968. At that time she was complaining of bleeding from her gums, bleeding from her tongue, and hemorrhaging into her soft palate. I readmitted her to the hospital immediately.

Q. What do you mean when you say she was hemorrhaging?

A. She was bleeding under her skin, in the linings of her mouth and in her intestinal tract. She was hemorrhaging into the white part of her right eye, and she was bleeding from her vagina, which was very difficult to control. She received blood just about every day in the form of either fresh, whole blood or platelet packs.

Q. Please read your hospital progress note of April 22.

A. "Much blood in urine. Many small ecchymoses, arms and legs. Transfused fresh, whole blood and platelets. Things look bad."

Q. What did you mean by that?

A. I was afraid that she might bleed into a vital organ and die, or have some permanent side effects. However, the bleeding was brought under control and she was discharged on April 30.

Q. When was the next time you hospitalized Linda?

A. May 5, 1968.

Q. For what reason?

A. She was admitted with severe headache and she had fainted, and the family wondered if she had had a seizure. She had also vomited on two occasions and when seen in the emergency room was pale and had numerous ecchymoses and petechiae, which are small hemorrhages. This hospitalization was also complicated by bleeding.

Q. What was her course?

A. She again had bleeding from the gums intermittently, bleeding from the urinary tract, bleeding from the vagina, bleeding into the skin. She was swallowing blood from nose bleeds and was vomiting blood. During this hospitalization, she was very ill, and I had serious doubts whether she would recover. One of my notes says "outlook desperate and family so notified." She was treated again with fresh whole blood transfusions and platelet concentrates. The cortisone and the male hormones were markedly increased in dosage. She finally did improve and was discharged on May 28 on large doses of cortisone, male hormones, vitamins, and medications to protect her stomach from the side effects of the cortisone.

One of the items of damage for which you ask a jury to return a money verdict is "pain and suffering, past (to the date of trial), and future." Dr. Anderson was documenting Linda's suffering.

Another item of damage was loss of Linda's working ability.

Q. Do you feel that Linda is capable of being gainfully employed?

A. No.

Q. Why not?

A. Because of lack of endurance, she could not do anything which would involve bumping or possible injury, because of the danger of bleeding. Also, I don't think she should be exposed to crowds of people because her resistance to infection has been greatly reduced. Her bone marrow is incapable of producing the blood cells which a person must have to fight off infections.

Q. Do you have an opinion, based upon reasonable medical certainty, as to what the future holds for Linda?

A. Yes. I think that most likely she will die from this condition. The biggest danger to her is the low blood platelet count, and she is in constant danger of having a serious uncontrolled hemorrhage. Because of the disease, her body is incapable of responding properly to a hemorrhage.

Q. What is your experience with Chloromycetin?

A. The times I have prescribed it have been in hospitalized patients with bloodstream infections so severe that the drug had to be administered intravenously. It is proper to use the drug also against typhoid fever.

I asked Dr. Anderson the same lengthy questions I had asked Dr. Miale, which incorporated all the medical records.

A. I feel Dr. Fragan departed from accepted medical standards in prescribing Chloromycetin to Linda Powell in both years. Chloromycetin is the most common drug associated with aplastic anemia, and therefore it should not be given except in very serious or life-threatening situations. If Chloromycetin is to be given, it should only be given after culture and sensitivity results have proven that it will destroy the particular infection.

Dr. Anderson made a critical point. As Dr. Fagan said in his own note of June 29, 1967, "patient given slip to take to South Miami Hospital for culture and sensitivity tests . . . patient also told that Chloromycetin may not even be effective against her particular infection."

I was convinced that Dr. Fagan mentioned these tests only because he realized that they were one of the keys to the case. If he had known that we never located this particular prescription, I am sure he would have denied ever giving it.

The lawyer handling malpractice cases develops a feel for medical records. Dr. Fagan's office note of June 29, 1967,

was simply too self-serving to be true. I knew this, but
would the jury?

I had to learn a lot about infections and antibiotics in this
case. It is extremely reckless to prescribe a dangerous drug
like Chloromycetin for a patient—even one who is seriously
ill—when you don't even know that it will destroy the germ
involved. Of course, in extreme cases or in emergencies, the
risk may have to be taken, but otherwise a culture and sensitivity test should be done first.

The overuse and misuse of all kinds of antibiotics is one
of the scars on the face of the medical profession today.
Many doctors just "shotgun" antibiotics hoping that they
will work against whatever infection may be involved, without regard to or knowledge of the side effects.

Many strains of infection have become resistant to certain
antibiotics because of their overutilization. Antibiotics have
no effect on viral infections, as opposed to bacterial infections. This is why there is no wonder drug for the "common
cold" or viral pneumonia.

A cotton swab of discharge or mucous congestion can be
used as a culture to grow the bacteria causing the infection.
In the laboratory the bacteria are subjected to testing against
a variety of antibiotics. This "sensitivity" test tells the physician whether the particular organism will be killed by a
particular antibiotic. In this way, a culture from Linda
Powell could have been tested for sensitivity not only to
Chloromycetin but also to penicillin, Tetracycline, and any
number of far safer antibiotics.

A major tactic of the defense in a malpractice case is
"muddying the waters." Jack Hoehl tried to show that the
mere sinus infections Linda had had in 1966 and 1967 could
have killed her (thereby justifying the use of a dangerous
drug like Chloro). To do this, he put Dr. Fagan himself on
the stand. He asked:

Q. Tell us about the consequences you had to consider in her case.

A. Well, there are direct channels that lead from the nose and the sinuses directly to the brain, and a resistant infection can cause meningitis, encephalitis, brain abscess, mastoiditis. It can lead to blindness. Bacteria can get into the bloodstream and go not only to the brain but to the heart, lungs and the kidneys and cause severe damage.

Q. What are some other complications?

A. Well, I haven't even included the cosmetic deformities that can result with saddle noses and severely twisted noses. A saddle nose is where the nose becomes completely collapsed. It looks horrible.

Q. Doctor, in your opinion and in your belief and in your knowledge are you stating today that your care and treatment of the overall problems of Linda Powell, in 1966 and 1967, conformed to good acceptable medical practice in this community?

A. I definitely do.

Linda's medical insurance was obtained through the Miami Police Department where she worked. Before paying, an insurance company will want a doctor's records or a report. I cross-examined:

Q. Does Metropolitan Life Insurance Company, the company that had the group policy with the Miami Police Department, pay for purely cosmetic nose surgery?

A. I do not know.

Like the great majority of health and accident policies, it did not pay for cosmetic surgery, and Dr. Fagan knew it. Collecting from an insurance company was far easier than awaiting payment from individual patients.

Q. Isn't it a fact, doctor, that on nearly all your "nose surgeries," the patients have "injured their noses" one way or the other?

Hoehl jumped up: "Now just a minute, your Honor, this is absolutely improper. Could we have the jury excused for a minute? This line of questioning is unfair in the utmost. I think we ought to try the issues in this case."

The Court: Excuse the jury, Mr. Bailiff.

Mr. Hoehl: Now, your Honor, I don't think counsel is willing to try this case on the issues. It is absolutely immaterial what Dr. Fagan does with other patients. The issue in this case is what he did with Linda Powell and no others.

Rosenblatt: Mr. Hoehl is taking the position that where there is an absolute conflict in the testimony given between Miss Powell and Dr. Fagan that I cannot introduce other evidence to show that my client is the one who is telling the truth. Is it just a coincidence that all his patients "break" their noses? I want to bring in records of South Miami and other hospitals on other patients to show that he is lying, and that's it in a nutshell. His credibility and his records are vital issues in this case.

Fagan admitted that only about 10 per cent of his patients have pure "nose jobs." I was convinced that less than 10 per cent of his operations involved legitimate injuries.

The judge limited me in my exploration of other patients and their supposed injuries. It is true that this had nothing to do with the pure issue of medical malpractice, yet it went to the underlying test of veracity. I felt that if the jury believed Linda, we could win, and if they believed Fagan, we would lose. To me, this was every bit as important as the medical testimony from the experts.

I questioned Fagan at length about why he was so concerned with culture and sensitivity tests on June 29, 1967, when a year earlier he had prescribed Chloromycetin without considering such tests. He replied that a culture *had* been taken prior to Linda's admission to South Miami Hospital in June 1966! This was a complete surprise to me:

Q. How come you didn't know that when I took your deposition for at least eight hours on three separate days?

A. I didn't know it because the paper was not present in my office chart.

Q. And all the questions I had asked about Chloromycetin did not jog your memory about this test in 1966?

A. No.

Q. It wasn't present in the office chart and it wasn't present in the hospital record. Well, where did it turn up a week ago?

A. It turned up—my bookkeeper—we were going from a regular bookkeeping system to a pegboard, and she was going through the lists of lab reports and she came up with this.

He handed me a crumpled piece of paper with several notes on it. The note in the handwriting of his bookkeeper, Barbara Jo Willis, said: "Tell Dr. F. lab called—Linda P. staph aureus sens. only to Chloro."

"Staph aureus" referred to the bacterial organism causing the infection and "sensitive only to Chloro" meant that Chloromycetin was the only drug which would kill it. According to Fagan, Barbara Willis happened to find this message, written on June 23, 1966, just four days before the trial began—almost three years later. The man didn't specialize in noses, he specialized in coincidences!

Q. Well, this is not the laboratory report. It is only a telephone message which was apparently taken down by one of your girls.

A. We are still looking for the official report.

Q. What is the name of this so-called laboratory?

A. I don't know, but my girls are still looking and calling labs.

Q. Prior to Linda's admission to the hospital, you saw her on May 20, 1966?

A. Yes. That is correct.

Q. Do you have on that date a single word about culture or sensitivity tests?

A. I do not, but I must have taken the tests.

Q. When did that realization hit you?

A. How would I have a slip written by my bookkeeper on a specific date, stating what the organism was and what it was sensitive to, if the test wasn't taken?

Q. Isn't it a fact that the realization came to you because you knew this case was coming to trial; and you realized that on June 29, 1967, you had a note about such tests? You realized how inconsistent that was, compared to giving her a Chloromycetin prescription in 1966 without any tests? And you knew you had to come up with something?

A. Absolutely not.

Dr. Fagan could not identify the lab which allegedly called with that message. Neither could Barbara Jo Willis. Nor could anyone else. The self-serving office record of June 29, 1967, had been suspicious, but this was incredible. Jerry and I were overjoyed that Dr. Fagan had pulled this stunt. The six men on the jury would have to be absolute fools, we thought, to believe that that message was authentic.

Dr. Miale testified that in twenty-five years of studying bacteria and laboratory reports, he had never heard of a staph aureus organism which was "sensitive only to Chloromycetin." The imaginary lab slip was as counterfeit as the rest of Fagan's records.

I continued with Dr. Fagan:

Q. Is it fair to say that you had completely forgotten about your 1966 prescription for Chloro until after this lawsuit was filed?

A. That is true.

Q. Now let us look at your note of June 29, 1967. Even though your note says that Miss Powell told you that a girlfriend of hers had used Chloro and that she herself had been given this drug by some other doctor, you still did not remember that you had given her a Chloromycetin prescription one year earlier?

A. I believe that is true.

Q. Isn't it true that you cannot recall ever giving a patient a prescription to have filled only after they had arranged for culture and sensitivity tests?

A. Well, let's say it is highly unusual. (*It is so unusual as to be preposterous. Obviously you should let the patient have the tests first and then, on the basis of what the tests show, decide upon the appropriate drug.*

Q. Doctor, shortly before this lawsuit was filed, did you find out that Miss Powell had been hospitalized at St. Francis Hospital?

A. I believe so.

My first witness, the "Miami" Dr. Anderson, had testified that Dr. Fagan had denied giving Linda Chloromycetin. I asked Dr. Fagan:

Q. Can you recall, sir, ever having a conversation with Dr. Eduardo Anderson?

A. I don't recall any specific conversation.

Q. Can you recall a general conversation?

A. I don't recall.

Q. He was the doctor who hospitalized Miss Powell at St. Francis Hospital and made the diagnosis of aplastic anemia. Does that refresh your recollection at all concerning any conversation you may have had with him?

A. No.

This was Dr. Fagan at his most evasive. He was fully aware of what Dr. Anderson said about their conversation relating to Chloromycetin. Since he was directly contradicting Linda Powell on many points, he preferred to be in a position of saying "I don't remember. I can't recall." These were Dr. Fagan's favorite expressions throughout the trial.

I called Linda Powell to the witness stand.

Q. What was your reason for going to see Dr. Fagan?

A. I wanted to get plastic surgery.

Q. What was it about your nose that bothered you?

A. Well, it had a bump on it. It was a rather rounded nose on top.

Q. How long had you had the bump?
A. Since I was born.

My questions at this point were directed not to damages, to Linda's tragedy, but to liability. I asked short questions which evoked answers squarely contradicting Dr. Fagan.

Q. Linda, did you work the day you went into South Miami Hospital for this surgery?
A. Yes, all day.

She certainly could not have worked all day if she had had the terribly broken nose as described in the defendant's records.

Q. Did you ever tell Dr. Fagan that you walked into a door at night?
A. No.
Q. Did you ever tell him anything remotely similar to that?
A. No.
Q. Did anyone ever tell you that you had a serious infection while you were in South Miami Hospital?
A. No one ever did. No.
Q. Why did you go to see Dr. Fagan after your discharge from Hialeah Hospital in 1967?
A. I had a very annoying postnasal drip, and it seemed like I kept swallowing something from my nose.
Q. While you were seeing Dr. Fagan in June of 1967, were you very sick?
A. No. I just thought he was giving me all those medications to dry up my sinuses.
Q. Were you working at the police station during June 1967?
A. Yes, I was.
Q. Linda, before Dr. Fagan gave you Chloro either in 1966 or 1967, did he tell you that it was a dangerous drug?
A. No. Never, or I would never have taken it.
Q. In June of 1967, or at any other time, did you tell Dr. Fagan that you had taken Chloro from some other physician before you came to see him?

A. No, never.

Q. Did he ever tell you to have culture and sensitivity tests taken?

A. No.

Q. Are you sure?

A. Yes.

The defense in this case was nothing if not resourceful. They called Mrs. Carolyn Greaves, the vice-president of the First National Bank of South Miami, who was also a patient of Dr. Fagan. She was put on to corroborate the alleged conversation between the doctor and Linda on June 29, 1967. She said, "I overheard him say she was to have some examinations made, some tests made, before she took a certain medication; and she promised him she would."

A loyal employee, Linda Proffitt Stone, said she was present, too, and overheard the same conversation. So it was Greaves, Stone, Willis, Fagan, and his office records against the unsupported word of my client. If the jury believed them, we were done for.

I brought out the fact that the defendant banked at Mrs. Greaves's bank and that she and her husband socialized with the Fagans. Mr. Greaves had "broken his nose" several times, and would you believe that the prim and proper lady banker had "broken her nose" twice—once when the lid of her washing machine fell on her, the second time during a bank softball game! Naturally, Dr. Fagan was there—both times—to repair the disasters and to collect from the insurance companies.

This type of disgusting testimony is not as rare as you might think. We were suing for a lot of money, and the one thing insurance companies hate, above all, is paying out a lot of money.

Jerry and I listened, sick. "Could anyone believe this garbage?" he whispered. "She hears part of a conversation, which means nothing to her, and then a year later Fagan walks into the bank, after being sued, and asks her if she remembers the time he warned a patient about tests and the dangers of Chloromycetin. Even if she did hear it, why would she remember it? It's not even a good lie, it's a dumb lie!"

I disagreed. Fagan was a shrewd liar. Not only did he have an attractive patient, but a solid citizen, a banker, yet, to corroborate his fantasy. This woman, with her elegant Fagan-built nose, would say anything to help him.

Most lawyers like to work in teams on important and complex cases. Jerry, a nonlawyer, and I were a cohesive unit on this case. I valued his interpretation of what the effect of various witnesses would be on the jury. We could see by their expressions that the bailiff, the court reporter, and even the judge thought that Fagan was lying—but would the jury?

The defense put on some very impressive medical testimony on behalf of Dr. Fagan. The Blackwell firm has defended more doctors in malpractice cases than any other law firm in the southern United States. Consequently, through their own contacts and through the insurance companies, they have their choice of experts.

My witnesses on the question of malpractice were "treating physicians"—Dr. Jerry Anderson and Dr. John Miale. I didn't have to shop around for experts. Both men were eminently qualified. Any jury would have to be impressed with their sincerity. They were not Linda's friends and they were not my friends. I had never met either doctor before my involvement in this lawsuit.

It is the rare doctor who is willing to testify against a colleague, but the error of prescribing Chloromycetin was so flagrant that they were willing to do so. The error was flagrant even if they assumed that Dr. Fagan's records were 100 per cent accurate. Both doctors felt that by speaking out they could prevent similar tragedies in the future.

Senator Gaylord Nelson of Wisconsin had recently held extensive hearings in the United States Senate on the misuse of Chloromycetin and other drugs and the pathetic consequences which frequently resulted. The enormous nationwide sales of Chloromycetin demonstrated clearly that the Parke-Davis salesmen were infinitely better at their jobs than the doctors were at theirs.

The fact that Chloromycetin was so widely prescribed became a problem in Linda's case, because it is a defense to malpractice to say, in effect, "I may have been wrong, but the majority of doctors do the same thing." The defendant is not held to an outstanding standard. He need only conform to generally acceptable and reasonable standards of care and treatment.

Dr. Fagan's position was somewhat different. He admitted that Chloro was a very dangerous drug which could cause blood disorders, but he said that the seriousness of Linda's infections in both 1966 and 1967 justified its use. If he said, as other doctors in other cases had said, that the manufacturer misled him, then Linda would have had a good lawsuit against Parke-Davis as well. I believe that Fagan was ignorant of the dangers of Chloro in 1966 and 1967, but he was too much of an egomaniac to admit it.

Hoehl brought in three Miami ear, nose, and throat specialists, who all said that it was proper for Fagan to prescribe Chloromycetin in both years. They accepted his explanation that the infections were serious and very resistant to less dangerous antibiotics.

One thing you must prove in all malpractice cases is that the negligent action or omission on the part of the doctor actually caused your client's damages. In a drug case, this can be very difficult. The insurance companies with their batteries of lawyers and home office doctors can spend a fortune defending a big case. Despite recent misleading publicity and the crocodile tears of the medical profession, most malpractice cases that are tried are still won by the defense.

Proving that Chloromycetin actually caused Linda's aplastic anemia was troublesome. The two Dr. Andersons and Dr. Miale all said that Chloromycetin was responsible for the condition. In cross-examination of my medical witnesses, and through their own specialists, Hoehl and Sevier hammered away at their defense theory that aplastic anemia can be caused by all kinds of things.

Sevier brought in Kenneth Lampe, a University of Miami professor with a Ph.D. in pharmacology. Lampe said that eighty separate drugs had been associated with aplastic anemia. Among them were Madribon, Tetrex, Polycillin, and even aspirin! He testified that gasoline, pesticides, hair dyes and rinses had likewise been indicted by some scholars as being related to the development of the disease.

Linda, as the plaintiff, had the burden of proof. Through Dr. Fagan himself, through Dr. Lampe and through three local ear, nose and throat specialists, the defense had built up a wall of obstacles.

The whole lawsuit had been tried on the basis of what was in Dr. Fagan's records. I had had to attack him and to cross-examine all the defense experts who had testified, on the basis that those records were correct. I now had to use precious time in bearing down on these records in my summation:

Ladies and gentlemen . . . if we just look at these hospital records, without anyone interpreting them for us, we know that Linda Powell did not have any life-threatening infection. But Dr. Fagan says she did because that is the only way he can attempt to justify the use of Chloromycetin. Let me quote from these South Miami Hospital records:

Physical findings by the resident physician: "General appearance, good, skin, normal." Operative report by Dr. Fagan: "The patient tolerated these procedures well and left the operating room in good condition."

A sample of nurses' notes on various days: "Appears comfortable at present. Sleeping quietly. Comfortable. No oozing noted. No apparent complaints."

Discharge Summary by Dr. Fagan. "The postoperative course has been essentially uneventful."

I continued:

Dr. Fagan doesn't even mention the word "pus" or the word "infection" or the words "suppurative exudate." He had time to write all about "suppurative exudate" in his office notes, but when he is dictating his Discharge Summary on a machine, he doesn't say a word about it. The serious "life-threatening organism" is never identified in the hospital records.

What does Dr. Fagan's note say on her first office visit to him—the day after she was discharged from the hospital? "Afebrile, no complaints, healing okay." So obviously she did not need Chloromycetin at that time. He didn't even remember that three days earlier he had given her the prescription.

There is not a single word of warning about Chloromycetin in June of 1966. Review these office records carefully. There is not a single word of warning about any other drug either—no, not until June 29, 1967. And then there is a full page of warning, a long, involved warning.

In the hospital he gave her at least ten different drugs and in the office he gave her all these antibiotics and not one word saying this drug has this side effect, or that drug has that side effect. The June 29, 1967, note is unique, and the reason it's unique is because it is contrived and it is manufactured.

And isn't it interesting that both prescriptions for Chloromycetin were completely unprecedented in Dr. Fagan's experience. He had never before given a patient a Chloromycetin prescription and failed to make a note of it as he did in 1966. The 1967 prescription was unique in that he never gave any of his thousands of patients a Chloro prescription on the basis that they would have laboratory tests done later.

Look at this June 29, 1967, note. According to him, Linda Powell was the one who requested Chloro. He doesn't check with the mythical prior doctor to find out how much Chloro she had taken, or why it had been prescribed. He tells her that Chloro may not even be effective for her particular infection. Then why, oh why, oh why, take the risk? What is the emergency on June 29, 1967?

We proved by the Miami Police Department records that Linda worked that day, so she couldn't have been all that sick. We proved that she worked the day that she went into South Miami Hospital a year earlier, so how could her nose have been broken?

What do you think would have happened if we had been unable to find the 1966 prescription? Dr. Fagan would have said that since it wasn't in his notes he didn't write it. You heard him say time after time how busy he is, how he can't recollect specific dealings with his thousands of patients, how he "can only go by notes."

I went to the question of Linda's damages.

What has Linda Powell's life been since Dr. Eduardo Anderson put her in St. Francis Hospital? Go through these many hospital records, gentlemen. Count the blood transfusions, and think of what it means to live through the blood of others. Blood transfusions can be dangerous just as the steroids and hormones have their side effects. These records reflect an endurance of pain that grown, tough men couldn't take. Linda Powell is a courageous young woman who is still fighting for her life.

Here is a girl who watched her body deteriorate, watched herself get more unappealing and unattractive every day. And the hideous irony is that she takes pills and capsules every day to stay alive, yet it was a drug that made her ill in the first place. For months she was taking sixteen Prednisone and six capsules of Halotestin every day. They made her fat; they made her hairy and mannish; they hardened up her muscles. She weighed 117 pounds when Dr. Eduardo Anderson hospitalized her. She ballooned to 182 pounds less than one year later.

She sits around the house and watches television. She was an active, busy, vibrant girl who had loads of friends. [I showed them the pre-Fagan photographs of Linda which had been introduced in evidence. She was slim with a marvelous figure, delicate skin, shining eyes and striking black hair. She had been the essence of femininity and now she was fat and ugly].

How does someone maintain their sanity in going from this to what she is now? As she walks along the street now, what kind of glances does she get? And even when she is with her friends, she knows that they remember what she was and although they may smile and be sympathetic, it's not the same. Everything is different.

Hoehl's summary was next.

I would just like to say at the outset that this is a very important day for Dr. Fagan also, and I feel an extremely heavy burden being the spokesman for a fellow man, a doctor in this community who has spent his life preparing to practice medicine and who in the practice of medicine, is being charged with what Dr. Fagan is being charged with in this case.

[This was not a *criminal* case. Nobody was being "charged" with anything—yet—but Hoehl did not miss a chance to let the jury infer that the "good doctor" might even get into criminal troubles too.]

Counsel has very strongly implied throughout this trial that Dr. Fagan is not to be believed, that he is the kind of man who would falsify records. I think the facts in this case speak so loudly for the truthfulness of this doctor and the truthfulness of his employees that it just beggars any question at all in anyone's mind.

[Dr. Fagan's self-serving note of June 29, 1967, was first seen by me at his deposition after the lawsuit had been filed—but before Fagan became aware that we were unable to locate that prescription. He had therefore been forced to concede that he gave Linda the Chloromycetin in 1967. But Hoehl did not fail to notice that I had not put into evidence a receipt showing that Linda had actually purchased the medication.]

Gentlemen, I don't think you are going to believe from the evidence in this case that in the year 1966 or 1967 Linda Powell ever filled any prescription other than the one I am holding in my hand now. There is not one iota of proof in this case that the 1967 prescription was ever filled. When she was discovered to be seriously ill in October of 1967, she would have had a lot easier time in finding that prescription then she did in finding the 1966 prescription. But it wasn't found, and I don't believe for a minute that Miss Powell really took any Chloromycetin in the year of 1967.

The burden of proof is on the plaintiff to establish that Chloromycetin caused her aplastic anemia, and I ask that you gentlemen consider that carefully when you go into the jury room. Have they proved that to your satisfaction? We do not have to prove that some other specific thing caused her problem. Have they ruled out of your mind the likelihood that she came down with this condition from other known or unknown causes?

We have a motto hanging up in these courtrooms. It says, "We who labor here seek only truth." That's a very high purposeful motto. This is what jurors go for and I think you are going to shoot for it and reach it in this case. I respectfully ask that you consider this evidence and that you return a verdict in favor of the defendant, because I believe that's what justice calls for and that's what the truth in this case calls for.

Judge Nathan gave the jury an explanation of the applicable Florida law. At 12:03 P.M., the jury retired to consider their verdict. At 3:52 P.M. came the sound that can make any trial lawyer jump right out of his skin—the knock on the jury-room door which means they have a verdict.

The Court: Gentlemen, have you arrived at a verdict?

The Foreman: We have, your honor.

The Court: Hand your verdict to the clerk. All right, Mr. Clerk, publish the verdict.

The Clerk: In Circuit Court, Dade County, Florida, Case No. 68-3781. Linda Powell, plaintiff v. Dr. Lewis Fagan, defendant.

We, the jury, find for the defendant, so say we all. Everett L. Martin, foreman. Dated March 22, 1969.

It was the saddest moment of my life as a lawyer. I had so much admiration for Linda and so much contempt for Fagan. How could it have happened? How did he get away with it? Linda took the verdict calmly.

I had to control myself. Fagan and his wife were overjoyed. He was receiving congratulations from all his "girls" —employees and patients. I could not look at him. I looked at the six male jurors; not one could look me in the eye.

I looked at the foreman. A cold shudder went through me. He was actually happy. He was smiling at Fagan and Hoehl. Even if he believed he had done the right thing, there was no reason to be happy. He never once looked at Linda. Why was he so pleased?

We left the building with Linda and her family. Jerry and I said our good-byes to them on Flagler Street, which was deserted on this hot Saturday afternoon. They thanked us genuinely and profusely for all that we had done. I made the parting quick because I just had to get out of there.

Jerry and I walked to our cars across the railroad tracks. I glanced back at the Dade County Courthouse which was built in 1925 and which for nearly fifty years had been the loftiest structure in Miami. Years ago flocks of vultures began spending their days from October through April perched atop the skyscraper. They were hovering overhead and their presence seemed all too appropriate.

After eighteen months of intensive and expensive work on behalf of our client—a warm, uncomplaining young woman who had become a dear friend—we were desolate. With tears streaming down his face, Jerry gave me a bear hug. We got into our cars. We had not said one word to each other after the verdict. What was there to say?

We talked on Monday. Jerry had seen the smiling visage of the foreman, Martin. What had his attitude meant? I discussed the case with Alan Schwartz, a brilliant appellate lawyer whom I often used in cases when his special talents were useful. He said, "Forget about appealing the verdict. There were factual disputes to be resolved by a jury, and they resolved them in favor of Fagan." He did not think that Judge Nathan had committed reversible error.

Jerry and I had to know why the jury found in favor of Fagan. On March 28, 1968, therefore, I filed a Notice of Intention to Interview Jurors.

Jerry talked to them all, except Martin. We learned that when they went back to the jury room, three of the men leaned toward Linda, two leaned toward Fagan, and Everett Martin was 100 percent for the defendant. Martin went back there and fought for this man. The others were impressed with his strong feelings and his reasons. He convinced them that the proper verdict was one in favor of Dr. Fagan.

I moved for a new trial, filing this affidavit:

Everett L. Martin, Foreman of the Jury, was asked the following questions during jury selection:

Q. Are you conscious of any reason why you can't sit on this jury as a fair and impartial juror?

A. No, sir.

Q. Will you be able to treat a doctor just like any other citizen and let the chips fall where they may, depending upon the evidence and the court's instructions, at the conclusion of the case?

A. Yes. I think so.

Q. And once again Mr. Martin, do you know of any reason at all, based on what you have heard, why you could not be completely fair and impartial to both sides and decide this case strictly on the evidence and the law?

A. No.

My affidavit went on:

Mr. Martin is and was a close personal friend of Dr. George Wessel. Dr. Wessel has been Mr. Martin's family physician for many years. Mr. Martin and Dr. Wessel have served together as members of the Hialeah YMCA and as members of the Hialeah-Miami Springs Chamber of Commerce.

On April 25, 1962, a jury verdict was returned against Dr. George Wessel in a malpractice case in an amount in excess of One hundred ninety thousand dollars ($190,000.00). During said trial, Dr. Wessel was represented by attorney John R. Hoehl.

Jerry Burke, my investigator, interviewed Mr. Martin's former wife, Mrs. Regina M. McCoslin. Mrs. McCoslin had in her possession the 1966 edition of *Physician's Desk Reference,* with the pages folded back under the Parke-Davis section."

Parke-Davis is the manufacturer of Chloromycetin. The *PDR* is updated every year, and the 1966 edition was the one which applied to the Powell case—quite a coincidence.

The affidavit continued:

Mrs. McCoslin said that Dr. Wessel had earlier told them the malpractice verdict against him was "phony" and that he did "nothing wrong" in that case.

We ascertained that foreman Martin constantly talked about Dr. Wessel in the jury room. Mr. Martin knew of the malpractice verdict against his family physician and close personal friend and believed it to be a verdict based upon a "phony case."

The situation with the *Physician's Desk Reference* could not have been a coincidence. Fagan and Wessel must have talked. Wessel must then have talked to Martin. This had to be the answer, but proving it was something else.

Not surprisingly, Judge Nathan denied our Motion for a New Trial. We relayed the news to Linda in Grand Rapids. She responded in her typical, non-complaining, good-humored way:

Dear Jerry & Stanley:
Maybe it's just as well because the whole thing was an ordeal

for all of us, especially for you who worked so hard. As I said before, I leave everything to your better judgment . . .

A little about how things are progressing with us. I went to the doctor last week and he said I was in good shape. (Not literally, naturally, just a form of speech). . . . Lost a little weight too, down to 165, realizing that ain't too down but it is a helluva lot better than 185. At least, though I am still a big girl, I don't look quite so rotund as before.

Welfare has reviewed my case and since I get social security they have dropped payment of doctor and medication costs, so only hospitalization is now covered. You can imagine I am even more anxious to return to Miami, being I am going to have to pay doctors here or there, it might as well be where I like it best.

Here's wishing you both good health and success. Kisses for you both.

LINDA

We had lost the trial, and our appellate expert said we had no real grounds for appeal. It looked almost hopeless, but we refused to give up. I am and always have been a very bad loser!

Jerry's persistence again paid off. He started searching the Dade County court records and discovered a remarkable lawsuit filed by Dr. Fagan against Drs. Thomas J. Baker and George Paxton. The suit had been filed by William Frates, who was later to become nationally known as John Ehrlichman's attorney in the Watergate trials.

Fagan's complaint against the doctors alleged in part:

Prior to the defamatory and malicious conspiracy hereinabove alleged, the plaintiff had an excellent reputation in his profession, and more particularly in his specialty of otolaryngology; he had obtained respect from other members of the medical profession, his patients, his associates and from the community at large, and the plaintiff has built a substantial and profitable medical practice.

The conduct of the defendants included false and slanderous statements that the plaintiff was not qualified to practice his

profession and specialty; that he was an incompetent and unfit
medical practitioner and had engaged in dishonest and fradulent
practices with his patients and the insurance companies. *(Where
the hell were Baker and Paxton when I needed them?)*

Dr. Fagan had filed his slander suit too soon, and he
would live to regret it. Dr. Baker was represented by attorney Bill Hicks. I asked Hicks if he had come up with anything which could assist me in obtaining a new trial. He
said no, but he did have an appointment to get statements
from Barbara Jo Willis and Linda Stone, who, he advised
me, were no longer working for Dr. Fagan. Sworn statements to be followed, no doubt, by depositions concerning
Dr. Fagan's office procedures and professional practice.

Jerry contacted both these ladies to see if they would help
us. They refused. I kept after Bill Hicks, who gave me the
good news. Barbara Jo Willis admitted that she had lied
during our trial. Would she repeat the admission before
Judge Nathan, who had the power to set aside a jury verdict
for "fraud, misrepresentation or other misconduct of an
adverse party"?

I asked Hicks why Willis made that damaging admission
to him. "Well," he answered, "Fagan promised her money
for her testimony, but he never came through. She wanted
me to sue him to collect. Can you imagine that?"

"I can imagine anything from her," I replied. "Why are
they willing to help your client in the slander case? These
lovelies don't do anything simply because it is right or just."

"Stan, these girls now hate Fagan and they are worried.
The IRS is investigating Fagan for evasion of thousands of
dollars in taxes. Willis and Stone helped him rewrite the
books, and they are both bargaining for immunity from
prosecution."

I had known that Fagan was a liar all along, but I had my
doubts that I would ever be able to prove it in time to do

Linda any good. Jerry and I were overjoyed at this incredible turn of events.

Our celebration was premature. Willis and Linda Stone would not make any admission of complicity to Judge Nathan. They were interested only in not being indicted on federal tax charges. Bill Hicks had been very helpful, but his primary responsibility was to his own client, Dr. Baker.

Jerry and I talked to Dr. Baker, who had been present when Barbara Jo Willis confessed. He was reluctant to get her into any trouble since she had helped him to expose Fagan as a liar and a cheat.

Howard Gordon, Dr. Baker's partner, entered the office during our discussion. Dr. Gordon had overheard Willis as well, but to my disgust said that he would deny it under oath! He was interested only in implicating Fagan criminally, and would not help the terminally ill Linda Powell obtain the justice she deserved.

After all we had been through, we were not to quit now. I could see that we were going to get nowhere with these pillars of the community. I therefore went to see attorney Alfonso C. Sepe in the office of State Attorney Richard E. Gerstein. I had no subpoena power in criminal affairs. But Sepe did! He began a vigorous investigation, subpoenaed Willis, and soon had what I needed; corroboration of my contention that perjury had been committed before Judge Nathan.

On January 21, 1970, Mr. Sepe wrote Judge Nathan the following letter:

On January 16, 1970, Barbara Willis and Linda Proffitt Stone having been immunized from prosecution and punishment by the State of Florida, testified under oath that they committed perjury in the trial of *Powell* v. *Fagan.*

Briefly, these witnesses testified that Dr. Fagan induced them under promises of payments of money and threats of exposure to the Internal Revenue Service for falsifying records, to make a false note in an old record stating—"tell Dr. Fagan lab called. Linda Powell staph aureus sensitive only to Chloro."

The jury in our trial had chose to believe four witnesses against Linda's word. Now two of the four were admitting that they were perjurers, and they were accusing a third, Dr. Fagan.

Sepe's letter continued:

A date of June 23, 1966 was falsely placed on the note in the upper left-hand corner. Further, Linda Proffitt Stone testified that records, purporting to be original records of Dr. Fagan, that were introduced in the trial were falsified as to dates by Dr. Fagan, and were in fact not accurate records.

I regret that such perjury had been committed before you during this trial, but felt it my duty to report this to you as soon as possible for whatever action you feel appropriate and fitting.

The information Sepe had obtained against Fagan was not absolute proof, though. Fagan could still be believed. In order to overturn the jury verdict which Fagan had won against Linda, we had to have a nonjury trial before Judge Nathan on the question of whether there really had been perjury. If we could prevail now and get a new trial. I would be able to cross-examine Dr. Fagan ruthlessly, using his own prior lies to convict him. Anticipating that there would be numerous purely legal battles, I called in my technical expert and friend, Alan Schwartz, to assist me.

At this trial, I called as my first witness, Barbara Jo Willis. Dr. Fagan was again represented by Jack Hoehl.

Mr. Hoehl: I wish at this time to renew our motion to suppress the testimony of this witness on the ground that she has confessed to committing perjury and that under the Statute this is equivalent to a conviction of perjury; and she, therefore, is barred as a perjurer from giving testimony in this cause.

The Court: Your motion to suppress is denied. (*A nice technical objection, but Judge Nathan was getting very interested.*)

Q. How did you happen to write that note about staph aureus?

A. Dr. Fagan asked me to.

Q. When did you write it?

A. I believe it was a week or so before the trial was to go on.

Q. There is a date in the upper left-hand corner—June 23, 1966. Is that date in your handwriting?

A. Yes, sir.

Q. How did you happen to write that date?

A. That was the date Dr. Fagan gave me.

Q. And the date that the notation was actually made would have been sometime in March of 1969?

A. Yes, sir.

Q. Mechanically, how did you happen to use these precise words? Did he dictate the note to you?

A. No. He made a rough draft showing me what it should say.

Q. Yet during the trial you told the jury that the note was legitimate and you just happened to find it?

A. Yes.

Q. And that was a lie?

A. Yes.

Q. Why did you write this phony note for him?

A. We were in the process of buying a new home and the extra little fees were piling up, and we were about $1,000 short. Dr. Fagan knew this. I asked him one day if he would loan us the money. He remark was, "I will loan it to you if you will help me," and that is when he told me that he needed something backing up that tests were done.

Q. Other than his promise to help you and your husband on the purchase of the home, did he make any other threat or promise?

A. Yes, sir. We were setting up a double set of books in his office all the way through, and every time he wanted us to do something, his remark was we could get "two to five years" with him for doing his second set of books.

Q. How did the books work?

A. When a patient came in and paid cash, the patient's name would be taken off the office books. This way it seemed his income was less.

Q. Who else participated in the creation of the second set of books?

A. Linda Stone.

Q. Did you and Miss Stone create the false set of books before the Linda Powell trial?

A. Yes.

Q. The thing that made you eventually come forward and tell the truth was the action taken by Mr. Sepe, is that correct?

A. It was fear, yes, sir.

Q. Fear of punishment to you?

A. Fear that it was me they had found out about.

Q. You would not have confessed otherwise, would you?

A. If I had known that I had to go through the hell that I have gone through, I would never have confessed, no, sir. Maybe it is mean and cruel to say this, but I think it would have been better for me to live with my conscience than to go through what I have gone through.

Q. And by the hell that you have gone through you are referring specifically to things like today—lawyers and questions?

A. That is correct. Having to take off from work, answering questions which have been answered before.

She was alive. Her blood was normal. Barbara Jo Willis was healthy. She had testified on behalf of a man people looked up to, a medical doctor whom she knew to be a crook, against Linda Powell, whose life had been devastated —and Barbara Jo Willis thought that she was going through hell!

I called Linda Stone, the second half of this twosome:

Q. Did Dr. Fagan ever ask you to give him Linda Powell's records when she was not in the office?

A. Yes, sir.

Q. When was that in relation to the day when Dr. Fagan was served with a copy of this lawsuit?

A. Well, to the best of my recollection, it was on the same day.

Q. Did he ask you for anything else?

A. Yes, sir.

Q. What?

A. Some blank green sheets.

Q. In looking through these green sheets on Miss Powell, can you see the handwriting of any person other than Dr. Fagan?

A. No, sir.

Q. When Linda Powell was a patient in 1966 and 1967, wasn't it always customary for one of the girls to write a date of a particular visit?

A. Yes, sir.

Q. In these records, who has written every single date?

A. All the dates appear to be in Dr. Lewis Fagan's handwriting.

Q. Do you have any explanation as to why Linda Powell's chart is singular in this respect?

A. No, sir.

Q. With respect to the phony set of books, how did all that come about?

A. Well, I was working for Dr. Fagan, and in the latter part of 1966 and in the early part of 1967, I started making a second set of books.

Q. How did he get you to do that?

A. Dr. Fagan told me that the patient logs for 1964 and 1965 were lost and that they needed another set made. Later on he told me I would have to continue making a second set of books, that he already had some in my handwriting which he could use against me.

Q. And these threats were made before the *Powell* v. *Fagan* case began, is that correct?

A. Yes, sir.

Jack Hoehl called William H. Appleby as his first defense witness. Mr. Appleby, a self-described "religious healer" and an ordained minister in the Episcopal Church, was also Dr. Fagan's father-in-law. He was hired one week after the Powell trial ended, to "straighten out" Dr. Fagan's books.

Q. Did Barbara Willis at any time say anything to you in the nature of a threat?

A. She certainly did, very definitely.

Q. Would you tell the Court the circumstances, the entire conversation, as best you can recall it?

A. Well, I told her that her work was very unsatisfactory and I didn't like the way the office was being handled. She said, "Well, it is going to be either you or me in this office and if I go, I am going to get you and I am going to get Dr. Fagan." I said, "Woman you are out of your mind."

Q. And what did she say to that?

A. I walked out of the office then because I was too emotional having a woman talk to me that way. I had never met such a malicious and vicious woman in all my days, and I am seventy-five years old.

Q. How soon thereafter did she leave the office as an employee?

A. Four days later. I think this conversation took place on Wednesday. She did not come in the following Monday morning.

Jack Hoehl is the classic insurance company lawyer. In the first trial he had sung the praises of Willis and Stone, as well as of the doctor who "had spent his life preparing to practice medicine in the service of his fellow man." Now, in order to defend Fagan, he was attacking Barbara Jo Willis and Linda Stone.

Dr. Fagan's lawyers continued their attack on their former star witnesses. Hoehl's partner, Frank Sevier, called Cordelia Herman, another loyal employee of Dr. Fagan. She said that Linda Stone tried to induce her to go to the state attorney's office to help slander Fagan's name.

Sevier questioned her.

Q. Now in this telephone conversation were both Stone and Willis involved?

A. Well, Linda called first and then about fifteen minutes later Barbara called and they were both on the same extension.

They were at Barbara's house and both talked to me at the same time.

Q. Did they say they had discussed this business of perjury with anybody else?

A. Yes, definitely. They said they had gone to Dr. Baker's office and there was a lawyer named Mr. Hicks that was involved in the whole thing, and this is who they had been talking to.

Plastic surgeons routinely take "before" and "after" pictures of their patients. Fagan had none of Linda, so we could not use them to disprove his contention that Linda had had a broken nose. Herman conveniently explained this away. She had them in her car and they were stolen.

In my cross-examination of Herman, I wanted to continue to show a pattern of how Fagan purchased loyalty.

Q. Has Dr. Fagan ever treated you or any member of your family?

A. He did a tonsillectomy on my daughter and he did a nose operation on me.

Q. You were satisfied with the nose operation, weren't you?

A. Yes sir, very much.

Q. You think he does the best nose in town, don't you?

A. Yes.

Q. Did he charge you for the operation or did he do it free?

A. Courtesy.

Q. Did he also show you courtesy on your daughter's operation?

A. Yes.

Q. Has Dr. Fagan ever loaned you any money?

A. When my grandmother died, he loaned me some money to go home which I paid back.

Q. How much was that?

A. I think it was $350, because I had to fly up to New Hampshire and back.

Q. Has he ever done you any other favors?

A. He cosigned for us once when our car was repossessed so the bank would let us keep it.

A good cross-examiner's best weapon is thorough preparation and advance knowledge of what answers to expect.
Jerry had been working feverishly. Through him I knew
exactly what Cordelia Herman's answers would be. Just as
an outstanding director can make an actor look good, so a
great trial preparation man can make an attorney look
good. Fagan did people favors, got them beholden to him,
and was not at all reluctant to collect when he needed
some friendly testimony.

I continued:

Q. You have quite a bit of knowledge concerning Dr. Fagan's
lawsuit against Dr. Baker and Dr. Paxton, don't you?

A. Yes.

Q. You basically substantiate his charge against them?

A. Yes.

Q. I guess you just happened to overhear a conversation between
Dr. Baker and Dr. Paxton when they said terrible things about
Dr. Fagan. (*My voice was dripping with venom and sarcasm.*)

A. I sat in a nurse's lounge and overheard their conversation.
(*What colossal gall. I wondered what Judge Nathan thought
about that.*)

Q. What did they say?

A. That they wanted to get Dr. Fagan out of South Miami Hospital because he used too many beds and too much space in
the operating room. They didn't like his type of surgery. It
sounded like jealousy, more or less, because he does more
nasal surgery than they do.

Q. So Drs. Baker and Paxton were attempting to slander him
just like Linda Stone and Barbara Willis are doing in this
case?

A. Yes.

Q. Did you have anything to do with Linda Powell?

A. Well, I was his office assistant, so when he would look at her
and examine her, I would be in the room.

Q. You, not Linda Stone?

A. No, me. That is what my job was in the office.

Q. All right. So if she would have been there, let's say on June 13, June 23, and June 29, 1967, you would have been assisting Dr. Fagan?

A. Yes.

Q. Not Linda Stone? (*I am a great believer in repetition*).

A. Right.

Q. You are sure of that? (*I pinned this down again because it was critical*).

A. Yes.

Q. Do you recall any conversation between Dr. Fagan and Linda Powell in June of 1967 when they discussed the drug Chloromycetin?

A. No.

This is what cross-examination is all about. It searches the prior testimony and exposes the fallibility of liars. Herman had been "prepped" on Linda Stone and Barbara Jo Willis, but Fagan had not expected me to ask her about the June 29, 1967, conversation. That is why she told the truth. This was dynamite testimony.

Herman testified over and over again that she was the only girl in the office after 5:00 P.M. All the witnesses had said that Linda Powell always came after 5:30 P.M.—after work—so Linda Stone could not have overheard the critical conversation. Fagan obviously preferred to use Linda Stone for corroboration because he had more on her.

Q. Did Dr. Fagan at any time ask you to testify in the case of *Powell* v. *Fagan*?

A. No.

Q. You said Linda Stone's reputation for truth and veracity is pretty bad?

A. Yes.

Q. In other words, she is a liar?

A. Yes.

I finished with this witness by establishing that she did

not work for Dr. Fagan back on June 23, 1966, the date of the note on the imaginary lab report. I was to come back to this later in my summation.

Frank Sevier called Mrs. Ruth Davidson, yet another convenient eavesdropper.

He asked:

Q. Tell me what you heard and what took place in April of 1969.
A. The door was opened, presumably by someone who started to leave Dr. Fagan's private office. It was ajar a couple of inches, and I heard Linda Stone saying, "We will fix you, Dr. Fagan. We are going to hang you. We know how to get even with you by fixing the logs." Dr. Fagan replied, "Linda, I am sorry you are taking this attitude but in view of this, I would like the keys to the office and to my house."
Q. Was anyone else present?
A. Yes, Barbara Willis.

Judge Nathan had to be seeing through this despicable charade. Some of my cross-examination, as always, had to be extemporaneous. I took a chance. Had Mrs. Davidson also been under the Fagan knife? She had! Fagan had done a nose job on her and also an ear operation on her mother.

The defense put two more witnesses on. Shirley Mahler and Carol Winn had both observed "suspicious" cash transactions between Linda Stone and Barbara Willis. Winn had given a written statement to Dr. Fagan. So favorably impressed was he with it that he hired her as his assistant. She, her husband, son, and daughter were patients of the defendant, and he had performed numerous operative procedures on them. Mrs. Mahler had been seeing Dr. Fagan once a week for years. As expected, he had performed ear and nose surgery on her as well.

I wanted to see Winn's statement. Hoehl objected that

this was "work product," privileged material prepared in anticipation of litigation.

The Court: They prepared statements and have told us what the contents of the statement were. I think the best evidence, of course, is the statement itself, and it ought to be produced.

The statements were not important, really, but *Powell v. Fagan* was already a part of my life and Jack Hoehl's life. His client was in trouble, and he continued to argue.

Rosenblatt: The judge has ruled. I don't know what it is about the law firm of Blackwell, Walker & Gray [Hoehl's "establishment" firm] that makes them think they can ignore the Court's ruling. They continue to argue as though a ruling had not been made. They did that for five days last year and I am sick of it.

Mr. Hoehl: If you want to attack me personally, why don't you do it outside the court. Go down some alley where you are used to being, apparently.

The polished, unflappable defense lawyer had finally lost his cool—and it was a joy to behold.

I had three opponents: Hoehl, Sevier and Preddy—all hotshot insurance lawyers. Hoehl's outburst indicated to me that the pressure I was applying was beginning to tell.

Hoehl put his client on the stand.

Q. Please state your name for the record.
A. Lewis Fagan, M.D.

By now Dr. Fagan had worries over and above Linda's lawsuit for damages. He faced criminal charges and had wisely retained Max Kogen, one of Florida's finest criminal lawyers. Kogen is regularly called in when politicians, judges, or public figures are indicted in South Florida. It was interesting to see Dr. Fagan's personal counsel objecting to questions propounded to him by his insurance company lawyers.

Attorney Kogen: Just a minute, before you proceed. At this
point, your Honor, I am going to advise my client not to testify
on the grounds that anything he says may incriminate him,
based on the Fifth and Fourteenth Amendments to the United
States Constitution, and the Twelfth Amendment of the
Florida Declaration of Rights. The Court is well aware that
Dr. Fagan will be charged with perjury and/or suborning
perjury by the state attorney's office.

The three-day hearing before Judge Nathan was starting
to look like a lawyers' convention. Hoehl, Sevier, and Preddy
were there, along with several assistants. My colleague,
Alan R. Schwartz, was backing me up. Two lawyers were
there on behalf of the Insurance Company of North America as observers, the same role they played throughout the
first trial. Attorney Robert Josefberg was present, representing Willis and Stone. Kogen and a representative from
Bill Frates's office were also in the lineup, although Hoehl
and Sevier were carrying the ball in terms of active partici-
pation. I was to learn later that Fagan had four more
lawyers advising him behind the scenes. If Fagan had paid
Willis her $1,000, he could have saved thousands in legal
fees. But I will be everlastingly grateful for his cheapness.

Dr. Fagan did not testify. After a recess I began my summation. I had to get Judge Nathan to overturn the heartbreaking defeat we had suffered at the hands of a jury who
had been told à pack of lies:

Your Honor, let me remind you that there were many direct
conflicts between the testimony of Dr. Fagan and of Linda
Powell. It is very hard to prove who is telling the truth particularly when a jury is able to look at a doctor's office records which
substantiate his version.

Look at the note of June 29, 1967—the last time that Linda
Powell ever saw Dr. Fagan. Miss Powell took the witness stand
and said under oath that that note was a complete fabrication.
These records permeated every phase of the trial. These records

hovered over your court room for five days one year ago. Poison has permeated the fountain of justice.

Every question I asked my experts about whether or not Dr. Fagan had committed malpractice was based on his own records. And certainly every question defense counsel asked their experts was based on his records and his account of what transpired. If Fagan lied, the conclusions of his experts were worthless.

It was Linda Powell's naked word against his official records. Even if the jury was skeptical of Dr. Fagan, they understandably failed to reach the conclusion that the records were false. Unfortunately, we did not have the evidence before them that we have before your honor. That jury heard lovely, sweet, all-American-type ladies corroborate what was in the office records. It was this prominent medical doctor, and it was Linda Stone and Barbara Willis and Carolyn Greaves and those manufactured records against the word of Linda Powell. The jury was reluctant to conclude that the doctor was a liar. But if they knew then what we know now, there could only have been one verdict.

Did Linda Powell have a broken nose? Conveniently, the before and after photographs were "stolen" from Cordelia Herman's automobile according to her testimony. Linda Powell worked the day his records say she broke her nose and she worked the day she was admitted to South Miami Hospital. Look at his very first note on May 20, 1966—he made the decision to do surgery at that time before any alleged injury.

She had this terrible infection in South Miami Hospital, yet her white blood cell count was 9,900, which is normal. It is medically impossible to have a normal white count and a serious infection. And if Linda Powell had the kind of injury Dr. Fagan described, her white count could not have been normal.

Even if we were to disregard Linda Stone's testimony, common sense tells us that these records are a fraud upon this court. Dr. Eduardo Anderson came into your courtroom and said that he had a telephone conversation with Dr. Fagan, who was obviously looking at his office records, since he itemized several antibiotics. But Fagan denied that he ever gave Linda Powell Chloromycetin. Is Dr. Anderson lying or is Dr. Fagan lying?

And this defendant sits here and listens to these charges and doesn't have the manhood to take the stand and deny them. Sure, he has a constitutional right to take the Fifth Amendment and I have a constitutional right to infer his reason for doing so. What about Linda Powell's constitutional rights? What about her right to a fair trial?

These girls falsified his entire books, so what's a little perjury between friends? "I've got you in my hip pocket and you have to do anything I tell you to do. Otherwise, you can get two to five years."

This very busy doctor has time to write "telephoned, unable to reach," a strictly ministerial, secretarial function—but in Linda Powell's unique case Dr. Fagan, because of his great interest in the welfare of this girl, telephoned her himself. And then he wrote the notes himself. It is an affront to credulity.

Look again at common sense. On June 25, 1966 he gives her a prescription for Chloro and doesn't say a single word about it in any record. Then look at June 29, 1967—in total contrast to the prescription a year earlier. See this detailed precise note. It is not consistent with any other note the man made or any other office visit of Linda Powell.

In June 1967 he says, "Go to the hospital for tests." But in June 1966, when Linda is already a patient in the hospital where she remains for six days, he does no tests at all.

Then look at that lab slip which has to be a lie. And it's not even a *smart* lie because Dr. Miale said that in twenty-five years of experience with bacteria he has never seen a staph aureus that was sensitive only to Chloro. The handwriting above Barbara Willis's on this slip of paper belongs to Cordelia Herman. Oh, how very clever he was. He took a piece of paper with other messages on it so it would look more authentic. "Oh, what a tangled web we weave when first we practice to deceive." But they have a big problem which proves the message was dreamed up. Barbara Willis's date is June 23, 1966—but Cordelia Herman wasn't even employed by Dr. Fagan at that time.

That sign which Mr. Hoehl brought to the jury's attention during last year's trial—"We who labor here seek only truth"—and your robes, and the flags of the United States and the state of Florida which are in all our courtrooms are a mockery if people can get on the witness stand and lie and get away with it. Perjury constitutes the strongest reason in the world for vacating a judgment and granting a new trial.

They have dared to put on in defense of this motion the same kind of contrived road show they put on last year—only the cast of characters is different. I would submit that the testimony you have heard from patients as to what they allegedly overheard is not to be believed. It is preposterous on its face. Do they think we're idiots? Just as in the first trial they want to sell the idea that women friendly to Dr. Fagan just happened to see and over-hear critically important conversations and transactions.

Willis and Stone certainly have not changed their testimony because they want to do Stan Rosenblatt or Jerry Burke or Linda Powell and her family any favors. They cooperated with the Federal Government to get immunity and they cooperated with the State of Florida to get immunity. They told the truth because they were scared, not because they suddenly found Jesus.

I remember Mr. Hoehl's argument last year and that sancti-monious approach he has developed into a science. He said—"Barbara Willis, wife of a serviceman, a mother with a little child, gentlemen, would she lie"? Would Linda Stone, daughter of a serviceman, polite and pretty as she could be, lie?" He said that Dr. Fagan was to be believed and that Linda Powell was not to be believed. That is a travesty—no one has ever provided any reason for us to disbelieve Linda Powell.

Justice and truth and our whole system cry out for a reversal of this stained verdict.

On March 20, 1970, two days short of one year from the jury verdict, Judge Nathan issued the following Order:

The Court finds, by and on the basis of clear and convincing evidence that, in the jury trial of this cause, the defendant, Dr. Lewis Fagan, was guilty of fraud on the Court and other misconduct, in committing perjury, suborning perjury, and engaging in a fraudulent scheme for the production of fraudulent testimony and documents.

Judge Nathan vacated the jury verdict and ordered a new trial to "be held at the earliest possible time because of the condition of the Plaintiff."

Round two to us. Needless to say, Jerry and I took great satisfaction from this victory. The investigation he had done to prepare for this second trial had been magnificent. For me the triumph was super sweet because even if the jury had not seen it, even if the insurance lawyers would not admit it, I knew that my client was right.

Both Aetna and Employers appealed Judge Nathan's decision. The Third District Court of Appeal decided the matter swiftly in an opinion dated July 14, 1970.

We have examined the record in the light of argument of counsel, and we find that the evidence amply supports the Order appealed from. We hold that the testimony concerning the fraudulent conduct is sufficient to support the trial court's ruling.

Fagan's lawyers sought a delay of the retrial until after his criminal problems had been resolved. The district court had mercy for Linda. "We find no basis in justice," it said, "for Dr. Fagan's request."

Judge Nathan had been affirmed in all respects. Linda was to get another chance. Judge Nathan rightfully recused himself from the case since, after his findings of fraud and perjury, he could no longer be considered impartial. The case was transferred to the Division of Circuit Judge James W. Kehoe.

Now came another bombshell. All the insurance companies refused to defend Dr. Fagan any further! They had found an "out." These insurance giants had spent a fortune in attorneys' fees and costs, but not a dime for Linda Powell.

This was the most outrageous example of insurance company hypocrisy that I had ever seen. They were dumping Dr. Fagan because he had breached his contract of insurance by "failure to cooperate." Actually, he over-cooperated, and even lined up the witnesses to testify at the second trial before Judge Nathan. As long as he was getting away with his perjury, they all loved him. They didn't mind the crime, only the sin of getting caught.

The cynical bastards were hoping Linda would die during these drawn-out legal proceedings. If she did, the case would have no value, according to the law, since she was unmarried. A malpractice policy says, in effect, "If the insured commits malpractice, the company will pay." Obviously, if Fagan had told the truth, that he prescribed Chloromycetin for a trivial infection, it would have been clear malpractice. We finally convinced them that he was a liar and they abandoned ship.

The next time you see a television advertisement telling you that "you are in good hands" with one insurance company, or that you are safe and sound if you buy a "piece of the rock," or that the representatives of another insurance company consider it the main part of their job to be sure that people who are supposed to be protected by insurance are paid promptly, efficiently, and with a minimum of questions asked—you would do well to think about *Powell v. Fagan.*

The purpose of malpractice insurance, as far as the doctor is concerned, is to protect himself from personal liabiltiy if because of his negligence somebody is injured. The public has a right to have such protection, and, of course, it pays for it through medical expenses. As far as the insurance companies are concerned, however, their purpose is not primarily to fully and fairly compensate people because of the negligence of the insured doctor, but to *avoid* paying if at all possible.

One step at a time. The next thing we had to do was win the case before Judge Kehoe. If we did, then we would go to trial against the insurance companies, contending that they had to pay the amount of any verdict we might obtain.

The insurance attorneys I had battled with were out of the case now. Max Kogen and a new attorney, James Henderson, were retained by Dr. Fagan.

On March 2, 1971, Lewis Fagan was found "Not Guilty" by a criminal court jury, of perjury and subornation of perjury. His charm was still working. Max Kogen had done his job well. Our trial before Judge Kehoe was set to begin Monday, May 17, 1971.

I had tried many cases before James Kehoe, a forceful and decisive judge. Once he ruled, that was it! He tolerated no further argument by the attorneys. As he often said, "Let there be no mistake about who is rowing the boat here." Judge Kehoe was not at all reluctant to jail an attorney for contempt. He knew the law of evidence, and unlike many other judges, he would not sit and listen to an invalid exposition of the law just to be polite.

Judge Kehoe laid down his ground rules:

No one is at any time, under any condition, to mention the fact that there has been a prior trial. No one is to mention that this Defendant was ever charged with any offense involving perjury or anything else, nor is anyone to mention that he was found Not Guilty.

This jury was to learn nothing about allegations of perjury or the phony lab slip. Kehoe felt that if I could put on testimony about lying, Fagan could then bring in the same road show that he had put on at the nonjury trial before Judge Nathan. The judge wanted this case tried only on the question of whether or not malpractice had been committed.

We still had problems. We still could not locate other
Chloromycetin prescriptions. I felt positive that there had
been collusion between Fagan and a certain druggist, but
I could not prove it.

The defense was just as vigorous as in the first case
in showing all the possible causes for Linda's condition.
They brought in the same experts who were still willing to
testify for their buddy in spite of what they had learned
about him since the first trial.

Despite Judge Kehoe's ruling, I had some questions for
Dr. Fagan about his office records.

Q. In 1966 and 1967, if you were examining a patient and
   wanted to make a note, would you make that note with a
   pen that was in your pocket or did you use a particular pen
   in the office?
A. I don't remember. (*Here we go again.*)
Q. Did you make all your notes on the same days you saw the
   patient?
A. I could not positively say that. I see perhaps thirty or forty
   patients a day. Sometimes I make notations at home.
Q. When you took the charts home, what did you use to write
   with? Did you use a particular pen at home?
A. I don't remember.
Q. Was the note of June 29, 1967, made on that date?
A. I can't answer the question accurately today.

For this trial, I had retained Robert Vollmer, a distin-
guished Police Department handwriting expert. He was
ready to testify that all of Fagan's notes on Linda Powell
were written with the same ballpoint pen. Preparing this
case for trial, Jerry and I thought Vollmer might be our
most important witness. If we could convince the jury that
Fagan rewrote his records after he was sued, they wouldn't
believe anything he had to say.

As much as I had learned to despise Fagan, I had to
admire his fertile imagination. He advanced a totally

new theory in this case because he knew I could prove that all the notes were made at the same time with the same pen. He said that one of his personal attorneys, Ray Dwyer, "asked me to rewrite the records because he had so much difficulty reading my originals. I don't know if these records [*set before the jury*] are the originals or the ones I wrote up for Mr. Dwyer."

This was, of course, asinine. It would be simple for the very person who rewrote the records to identify the set which he did in one sitting for purposes of neatness. But Fagan had been successful with many transparent ploys during the first jury trial. I doubted that Dwyer ever asked him to rewrite the records because it would have been much more logical to have Fagan dictate them to Dwyer's secretary, so he could have them in perfectly understandable typed form.

I called Ray Dwyer, an insurance defense lawyer, to the witness stand. He invoked the lawyer-client privilege, which prevents a lawyer from disclosing confidential transactions with his client. That was that. Or was it? I had an ace or two up my sleeve.

I called Vollmer to the witness stand and had him recite his impressive qualifications. He was a veteran of the Miami Police Department, a former supervisor in the Identification Bureau and Crime Laboratory. He was skilled in handwriting analysis, including analysis of the types of writing implements used and of the timing and sequence of writings. Kogen objected. The jury was excused for legal argument on this important point.

Fagan's evasiveness paid off again. Judge Kehoe refused to let Vollmer testify because Dr. Fagan "could not state whether these were his original records or the ones he wrote for his personal attorney. Since the doctor has not said these are his original records, you would not be impeaching anything." When the jury returned, Vollmer had been excused, but I was pretty sure they had the message. That is precisely why I put him on the stand even though I anticipated the judge's ruling. Certainly they understood that I called him to say that there was something wrong with the records. They could only surmise that he was prevented from testifying on a "technicality." As far as I was concerned, this supposition was correct, and the judge was wrong in refusing to allow in Vollmer's opinion.

Jerry and I had been busy, and had obtained a sworn statement from Mrs. Greaves, the bank vice-president friend of Fagan. In it she completely contradicted her testimony in the first trial:

Q. Did you ever hear Dr. Lewis Fagan tell Miss Powell to have examinations made or tests made before she took any medication?

A. No.

Q. Did you ever hear Dr. Fagan give Linda Powell any warning of any kind concerning any medication?

A. No.

Q. Did you ever hear any conversation between Dr. Fagan and Linda Powell at all?

A. No.

Q. Well, what you have just said completely refutes the testimony you gave before Judge Nathan in March of 1969. Why did you give that testimony if it was untrue?

A. Dr. Fagan asked me to.

Q. And you did it as a favor to him?

A. Yes.

Dr. Fagan did not know that I had this statement. I asked him:

Q. This conversation that you had with my client on June 29, 1967—did anyone overhear that conversation?

A. I believe so.

Q. What do you mean when you say—you believe so?

A. Someone was present. Yes.

Q. Who?

A. In that particular year it would be Linda Stone, and subsequently we found out that Carolyn Greaves was present.

I was not worried about Mrs. Greaves or Linda Stone corroborating that lie! I continued with Dr. Fagan.

Q. Are you calling them as witnesses to verify that fact?

Henderson jumped up to object. The Court sustained the objection and excused the jury.

Henderson: We move for a mistrial.
The Court: Denied.
Kogen: This was done in bad faith, with due respect to his ability as a lawyer. We could not possibly call them as witnesses because of what transpired previously; so the mere sustaining of the objection is insufficient. We are in a position now where Dr. Fagan has made a positive statement about people overhearing it; then counsel asks whether they are going to appear, and he knows darn well that unless he calls them, they are not going to appear.
The Court: The Motion for a mistrial is denied. (*Judge Kehoe was not the type of judge who felt any need to explain his rulings*).

Max Kogen was so right. What had "transpired previously" was that in the first trial Fagan put on perjured corroboration. Now I would be able to demand in summation, "Where are the ladies who allegedly overheard this very important conversation? Why was Dr. Fagan afraid to call them as witnesses?"

Dr. Fagan was in no position to deny, now, that they had overheard the discussion, since I could pull out his earlier testimony and pummel him with it. I could slither, too, when dealing with a snake, and I continued:

Q. Do you still have an appointment book covering June 1967?
A. I don't know where the appointment book is.

Q. So the appointment book which verified the fact that Mrs.
Greaves was a patient on June 29 has disappeared?
A. I no longer have possession of it, Mr. Rosenblatt, but I be-
lieve you have seen it.
Q. No, I have not, but I would like to see it. Is there any way
that you have to produce that appointment book?

Kogen and Henderson were on their feet objecting to
my tactics. The expression on my face said to the jury,
"Gee whiz! This guy sure loses things, doesn't he?" Internal
Revenue had the appointment book, as well as a truckload
of other records from his office, but Dr. Fagan could hardly
admit that. Having scored again, I dropped the subject.

Although Fagan could not use the contrived lab
message, his inventive and devious mind did not fail him.
His explanation now was that when Linda was hospitalized
in 1966, he knew the type of organism that was involved
without the benefit of culture and sensitivity tests.

A. When I prescribed Chloromycetin, it was absolutely necessary
to save this girl's life and I didn't have time to wait for test
results. In June of 1967, I was 95 percent certain that it was
the drug of choice when I prescribed it. (*"Absolutely necessary" to save her life during recuperation from a "nose job"!*)

Henderson went on:

Q. Did you reach a conclusion as to the nature of the organism
that was causing the infection in 1966?
A. Yes, I felt the organism was definitely a proteus, and I
especially felt this way after removing some of the packing
from the nose and seeing that we had a muddy yellow type
of pus with a foul odor. There have been deaths following
nasal surgery in this town.
Q. How many different drugs have been linked to aplastic
anemia in one way or the other?
A. A minimum, I would say of five hundred, beginning with

aspirin and going through cleaning fluids and ending with arsenic.

Q. All of these various things cause blood dyscrasias?

A. Cause dyscrasias and most of them can be proven by the medical research people to be directly causative of aplastic anemia. Unlike Chloro, which is by association or guesswork.

I cross-examined him on this subject:

Q. Doctor, you said that you have hospitalized thousands of patients since the last time you saw Miss Powell in 1967. Is that correct?

A. Yes.

Q. You have done thousands of noses in the last ten years?

A. That is correct.

Q. How did you happen to remember the color and consistency of the pus when you do not have a note saying one word about it?

A. I remember it because I was so worried about Miss Powell.

Q. It is not in the record, but you remember from 1966, five years ago, that her pus was muddy, thick, and yellow?

Henderson jumped up: "Objection your honor. This is repetitive and argumentative."

The Court: Sustained.

It did not matter. I had made my point.

Q. Where do the records of South Miami Hospital or your office records mention anything about a proteus bacteria?

A. It is not in the record. It is from experience. (*The old Fagan shuffle.*)

Q. The only way you can identify a proteus or other specific organism is by way of a culture. That is the whole purpose of these tests, isn't it?

A. I think I can do it clinically based on my experience.

There has probably never been a malpractice case where the defendant has not tried to excuse his negligent lapses by referring to "clinical judgment." "Clinical judgment" is often used as a kind of code phrase which means "I goofed, but in my opinion my goof was within an allowable range of goofing."

This ridiculous statement was accompanied by a look of injured innocence. Fagan was treacherous because he had the ability to invoke sympathy for himself and play the role of the underdog. I had to be very careful not to push too hard because it could boomerang. His expression seemed to say, "Why is that bad man asking me all these terrible questions?"

To prepare for this trial, I had lined up two more experts, in addition to Dr. Jerry Anderson and Dr. Miale. We had written to Dr. John R. Blinks, head of the Department of Pharmacology at Mayo Clinic. He was unavailable, but gave me the name of Dr. Richard Burack, who had written a book about drugs.

Dr. Burack was a find. He was a former faculty member at the Harvard Medical School Pharmacology Department, and was a specialist in internal medicine. He was also a virgin in that he had never before testified in a malpractice case.

Henderson searched very hard for a chink in his armor.

Q. Why did you agree to testify in this case?
A. My response to Mr. Rosenblatt was, "Before I would be interested in coming down here as a witness, I would certainly want to know much more about the case, and I would need to review the medical records. Those were sent to me and having read them, I came to the conclusion that I had a duty to come here and speak out."

Beautiful answer. This man, who practiced medicine at a small town hospital in North Conway, New Hampshire, became angry when he saw such a low level of medical practice.

Henderson dug himself a deeper hole.

Q. You had a duty to come here and speak out.

A. Well, some of us, you know, are idealistic in the medical profession.

Q. How many times in your practice have you prescribed Chloromycetin?

A. Inasmuch as it is only indicated for typhoid fever and hemophilus influenza meningitis, I can't imagine more than about 400 or 500 of those cases in the entire country per year. The answer to your question is that I have never prescribed Chloromycetin. (*And Fagan prescribed it like cotton candy!*)

Q. It's obvious from Dr. Fagan's records in June of 1967 that she was getting different medications and there was no improvement. Don't you consider that a serious, resistant infection?

A. No, I do not. I think the answer is that not enough time was given on any one medication for it to do its job properly.

Q. Would you have any way of knowing what type of organism you were fighting on the basis of his records?

A. No, sir. That is why I said that I would wait for the culture reports to come back from the laboratory before I made any bold moves. I do not think that anybody is going to die from a trivial purulent, pussy infection of the nose.

I had acquired the services of a local ear, nose, and throat specialist who believed that Dr. Fagan was giving the medical profession a bad name. He was on the ethics committee of the American Academy of Facial Plastic and Reconstructive Surgery and took his duties seriously. Dr. Fredric W. Pullen, II, a University of Michigan Medical School graduate, had served his residency at the Massachusetts Eye & Ear Infirmary, and had been chief of the department of otolaryngology at the Veterans Administration Hospital in Miami. At the time he gave testimony, he was Director of the Neuro-Otology Laboratory at the University of Miami School of Medicine. His testimony, like Dr. Burack's, was devastating.

In addition to the defense experts from the first trial, Kogen called Dr. Ben L. Harrison, a Miami ear, nose, and throat specialist. Of course, Dr. Harrison said that everything Fagan did was within the reasonable and accepted standards of care in the community. He testified that the seriousness of the infection justified the use of Chloromycetin both in 1966 and 1967.

As I watched Dr. Harrison, I got the idea that he wished he were somewhere else, and that he had not reviewed the records very carefully. I began:

Q. Dr. Harrison, when a person has what is known as the "common cold," if you were to look down his throat you would see an infection—is that correct?

A. Yes.

Q. They say if you have a cold and go to see a doctor and he gives you all kinds of medications and you do everything he says, you will be cured in one week; if you do nothing you will be cured in seven days.

A. Exactly.

Q. Of course, people got colds and pus and infection before penicillin or any of the antibiotics were discovered.

A. Yes.

Q. And most of them recovered?

A. Yes.

Q. In answer to counsel's questions, you said that prescribing Chloromycetin on June 25, 1966, constituted acceptable medical practice. Dr. Fagan's note in the hospital record on the very same day says "no fever, no complaints, swelling subsided." Why in the world would she have needed Chloro on that date?

A. I can't answer that. I am not competent to answer that. (*It was obvious I had told Harrison something he had not known. His assured presence became confused and stumbling.*)

Q. Well, then, I don't understand your answer on direct examination.

A. I understood the question to be "where several antibiotics had been used and had failed, is it within the scope of good medicine to prescribe another antibiotic, one which may carry a risk?" That is what I answered.

Q. Yes, sir. You apparently understood the question in a very general sense. Now, I want to ask you a very specific question. Is there any indication to you in that record that giving Miss Powell a prescription for Chloro on June 25, 1966, was good medical practice?

Dr. Harrison sat there, studying the records, for two or three minutes and he literally began to twitch. I walked right up to the witness chair and folded my arms. My eyes were fixed on his head. Very quietly, I said, "Well, doctor?"

A. I think it behooves the doctor to answer that question himself. It is self-evident. I would not have given it. Unless this is a mistake or something, it doesn't make sense. If she is afebrile and everything is going well, I would keep her on the antibiotic which she had for a few days. I certainly wouldn't change horses in midstream if everything was going well.

Q. On June 26 and 27, there is no evidence in that record of any infection, is there?

A. No infection. No evidence. No, there is none.

I sat down delighted. A defense star had become a superlative witness for the plaintiff. Henderson tried to rescue the situation, but it was too late.

Q. If there was marked edema still present at the time of discharge or the problem was not moving along in a manner which that particular doctor felt was correct, would it then be unacceptable practice to change antibiotics?

A. That is a terrible question. The answer is yes. You don't give any other antibiotics or change horses in midstream because of swelling. I'm sorry.

Yeah, baby, but not half as sorry as Lew Fagan.

Jerry, Alan Schwartz and I were quite concerned that even if we won, we might not "win big." This jury, unlike the jury in 1969, saw an attractive Linda Powell. She was no longer taking large doses of steroids and male hormones, and so her weight was nearly back to normal. She looked fine and did not seem to be in pain. Her only medical treatment now consisted of periodic blood transfusions. Without question, she still had aplastic anemia, but her condition had apparently stabilized.

"Winning big" from my point of view was anything over $200,000. While the jury was deliberating, my thoughts kept returning to the verdict which had been returned before Judge Nathan. I had been retained in October 1967, and it was now May 1971. I had thousands of hours and thousands of dollars in the case.

On Thursday afternoon, May 20, 1971, the four woman– two man jury returned its verdict. They awarded Linda $500,000. Linda exhibited pure, unrestrained, quiet joy. Jerry and I shook hands for a long time. Words were again unnecessary.

We let everyone, including ourselves, savor the triumph. Jerry and I knew that, great as it was, it was still only a paper victory. We now had to collect from the insurance companies which had denied coverage to Dr. Fagan.

Because this was now a "coverage question," I had the rare opportunity to take the depositions of Hoehl, Sevier, and Preddy, to find out what had been going on behind the scenes. Aetna and Employers were now represented by still different law firms, since the trial counsel they originally had would have to be witnesses at the insurance trial scheduled before Judge Kehoe in November 1971.

The history of astonishing events connected with this
case had by no means ended. I learned that Dr. Fagan
and his personal counsel had been pushing the insurance
companies to settle with me before and during the 1969
trial. INA, which had the $1,000,000 umbrella policy, was
pushing the "primary" carriers to settle, too, at that time.
Fagan had written Hoehl and Preddy a letter which said:

I demand that each of you offer the full limits of my liability
insurance coverage in order that I may not be held liable for an
amount in excess of my coverage with you.

On March 20, 1969, during the third day of the first
trial, attorney David S. Batcheller of the law firm of
Smathers and Thompson, hand-delivered the following
letter to Hoehl and Preddy:

Demand has been made by Mr. William Frates, counsel for Dr.
Fagan, that this case be settled within the policy limits. It is the
considered judgment of the Insurance Company of North America that this lawsuit has an exposure in excess of $200,000, and in
properly protecting the interests of Dr. Lewis Fagan, every effort
should be made to settle this lawsuit to avoid the exposure of
a substantial judgment. The Insurance Company of North
America does hereby reaffirm the demands which have been
made upon each of you as attorneys for Aetna and Employers
Insurance Company that the $100,000 limit of each of these companies, or a total of $200,000 be made available for the purposes
of settlement negotiations. As you both know, it is altogether
probable that a settlement could be negotiated for a sum less
than $200,000, thereby resulting in a saving to each of the primary carriers on their limits."

The most extraordinary testimony was yet to come.
Thomas R. Herbig, head claims manager of INA in Miami,
said:

That on March 21, 1969, the settlement demands made by the
plaintiff, Linda Powell, through her attorneys, were reduced to

$275,000. That Employers Insurance Company agreed to make its primary limits available to the settlement fund and that the Insurance Company of North America would have settled the lawsuit up to the plaintiff's demand of $275,000, subject to the primary limits of $200,000 of Aetna and Employers being made available to contribute toward such settlement fund.

That we were advised by Mr. Batcheller that late in the afternoon of March 21, 1969, Dr. Lewis Fagan had withdrawn his consent to settle the lawsuit, which consent was required under the terms of the malpractice contracts of insurance of the primary carriers. The case would have been settled if Dr. Fagan had not withdrawn his authorization to settle.

So Aetna was prepared to pay its $100,000 and Employers was ready to pay its $100,000. INA would have added the difference to settle the case. But I never knew any of this!

Now I knew the "fix" had to be in. This was the only thing which could have caused Fagan to change his mind so totally regarding settlement. I knew in my heart and bones that Foreman Everett Martin was the key.

Fagan and his personal counsel had demanded that the insurance companies settle. Suddenly, without warning, without explanation they did a total about-face. This happened after the completion of the next to last day of the trial. Fagan had to know, by then, that he would win or, at least, that he would have a hung jury.

Why didn't all this high-class legal talent find out the reason for Fagan's sudden reversal! How could they be so lacking in curiosity? Or were they afraid to know? Since Fagan was so anxious to have his companies settle for a substantial amount of money, it had to be because he knew he was responsible for Linda's condition.

Although they had been willing to pay all that money before Fagan withdrew his authorization, these multi-million-dollar corporate titans had tried to get home free.

Now they said that even if we won in November they would appeal it all the way to the United States Supreme Court, which could take years. Nice fellows!

Linda had outlived her life expectancy already. I wanted to see her enjoy the fruits of victory. This rare girl—who never once expressed hatred for Fagan, who never once complained about her plight, who never once said, "Why me?"—was entitled to some sunshine.

After the summer of 1971, we all began to negotiate in earnest. I rejected $100,000, and then $200,000. Linda and her mother left it completely in our hands. Jerry and I figured that they would come up with more money as the trial date drew near. On the very morning the insurance trial was to begin, the case was settled in Judge Kehoe's chambers for the total sum of $338,000. It was divided as follows:

Aetna Casualty and Surety Company	75,000
The Employers Group of Insurance companies	75,000
Insurance Company of North America	128,000
Dr. Lewis Fagan (personally)	60,000

At last it was over. However, the United States government still had some unfinished business with Dr. Fagan. E. David Rosen, Meyer Lansky's attorney, defended Fagan, who was found guilty of income tax evasion on February 22, 1972, by a twelve-member Federal District Court jury in Miami.

Because of appeals and other delays, Fagan did not report to a federal marshal to begin serving his time until March 11, 1974. Although he faced a maximum penalty of fifteen years and a $30,000 fine, he was sentenced to a mere ninety days plus a $10,000 fine, and probation for a period of five years.

His formal commitment required the following:

Immediately upon discharge from incarceration, the defendant shall obtain weekly outpatient psychiatric care with monthly reports of the attending psychiatrist to be furnished to the U.S. Probation Office.

He had already been diagnosed as having a "severe personality disorder" by a psychiatrist at the Menninger Clinic in Topeka, Kansas. Jerry and I could have told them that.

If Lewis Fagan had not sued Drs. Baker and Paxton, the Linda Powell case would undoubtedly have ended when the first jury returned its verdict before Judge Nathan. The seeds of his own destruction were within him. We owe a special debt of thanks to Bill Hicks, Al Sepe, and Dade County State's attorney, Richard Gerstein.

Against all medical odds, Linda Powell became the wife of City of Miami Police officer John E. O'Brien on July 28, 1973. She still has aplastic anemia but looks beautiful and functions almost normally. No one is more deserving of a medical miracle, and here's hoping.

II

Gus Burgel
——VS.——
Red Wing Carriers
Explosion and
Paralysis

Gus Burgel was a welder at Aerodex when he was nearly killed by an explosion on August 25, 1966. Aerodex is located at Miami International Airport and had a military contract with the United States government to overhaul and maintain various types of aircraft. The trial began on Monday, July 15, 1968, at 9:30 A.M. before Dade County Circuit Judge Gene Williams. I was opposed by one of the most prestigious and largest law firms in the state of Florida—Dixon, DeJarnette, Bradford, Williams, McKay, Kimbrell & Hamann.

It was finally beginning; a case that Jerry and I had worked on relentlessly for the past two years. The first time we saw Gus, several weeks after his accident in the hospital, he had not been able to talk and had motioned us out of the room. His wife Helen had retained me while

85

he was unconscious. Through his union, another firm of attorneys had been retained on his behalf, and Gus was not interested in my services. The law firm representing Gus was concerned only with the workmen's compensation claim against Aerodex. After investigating the case, they were so convinced that Gus did not have a valid action against Red Wing that they agreed to forgo any portion of the fee if by some wild miracle we were successful in our lawsuit.

Gus, Jerry, and I became the best of friends once he was out of intensive care and transferred to a nursing home, and he was able to appreciate what we were doing in his behalf. By the time the trial began, there was a bond of real trust between us.

This case had the largest potential of any lawsuit I had ever been involved in to that time. Up until then, I had never tried a case where I had any possibility of getting a verdict as high as $100,000. I had built a reputation by consistently getting $20,000 and $30,000 jury verdicts in cases which were evaluted by the insurance companies as being in the $5,000 to 10,000 range. However, you don't build up a solid reputation until you achieve some large verdicts.

I always felt that I could obtain substantial verdicts if I ever had cases with enough potential. The woods are full of lawyers who can try little auto accident cases very completely but just don't have the extra ingredient to get huge awards in big injury cases. Gus's case presented a real opportunity.

Gus had been welding a 55-gallon drum at Aerodex with an acetylene torch when it exploded. He suffered massive injuries, foremost of which was a permanent paralysis of the right side of his body.

Of course, Gus had a clear-cut workmen's compensation claim. In workmen's compensation, all you have to prove is that you were injured on the job and the insurance company for your employer must pay certain benefits irrespective of how the accident happened. In return for this, however, the employer (in this case, Aerodex) and its insurance company are immune from a lawsuit.

We filed suit on the unique theory that the drum or barrel Gus had been working on exploded because of a residue of JP4 jet propulsion fuel which remained in the drum following a delivery to Aerodex by a Red Wing truck driver over two months earlier, on June 14, 1966. The biggest problem would be relating the alleged negligence of Red Wing to the explosion seventy-two days later. This was the all-important issue of proximate or legal cause.

In picking the jury, I exercised all three of my peremptory challenges. Warren Hamann exercised two of his three. We ended up with a jury consisting of five men and one woman, including a realtor, two salesman, a customer-service representative for National Airlines, a diesel mechanic, and a professional musician. As is common in Florida, five of the six were from out of the state.

During my opening statement, I had to explain the relationship between two important dates—June 14 and August 25, 1966. When the delivery was made on June 14, the Red Wing truck driver had loaded his fuel into the single 10,000-gallon outdoor storage tank for JP4 fuel on the premises of Aerodex. The tank was filled up, and there were still approximately 800 gallons remaining in the truck. After consultation with Aerodex personnel, it was decided that the balance would be put into empty 55-gallon barrels.

We contended that when the Red Wing driver did this he was negligent. The defense of Red Wing was along several lines. Basically, they would argue that even if the truck driver had been negligent on June 14, 1966, in unloading the fuel—and they vigorously denied that—there was no way that we could prove that the empty drum which exploded weeks later was one of the fifteen which had been filled with JP4. Hamann was absolutely correct that I could not prove it by direct evidence, but I intended to prove our case with circumstantial or inferential evidence.

At the time of the explosion, Gus had been working in a "test cell" at the Aerodex plant. My first witness was Douglas E. Phillips, Jr., an Aerodex test-cell inspector.

Q. Do you have anything to do with receiving fuel delivered by outside carriers to the premises of Aerodex?

A. Yes, sir.

Q. In June of 1966, who was your immediate superior?

A. Henry Holland. *(This man was to be an important witness.)*

Q. When you receive fuel, what is your function?

A. They bring the truck over to us and we take a stick which has a water-detecting paste on it. We go to the tanker and break the seals and poke the stick into the tank of the truck to check for water.

Q. All right. And if you check for water and find none, what do you do then?

A. Well, the driver then unloads the fuel and I go back to my designated work area.

Q. Do you have anything to do with assisting or instructing any driver concerning where to put the fuel?

A. No, I don't.

Q. What was your first contact with Red Wing's driver, Hugh DeBrocque, on June 14, 1966?

A. I received a phone call that a load of JP4 was being delivered, and naturally it was my responsibility to check the truck, which I did.

Q. What did you do after checking for water?

A. I went back into the test cell.

Q. What was the next contact that you had with DeBrocque on that day?

A. He came into the test cell and told me that his tanker truck was not empty, and he wanted to know what to do with the fuel. I told him he would have to call another office and find out.

Q. Did you personally give him any instructions at all about where to put the excess fuel?

A. No, I didn't.

I was laying the groundwork for some very significant conflicts between DeBrocque's testimony and that of certain key Aerodex employees. Red Wing took the position that their driver had to be guided by Aerodex personnel, that he had a duty to follow their instructions about where to put the fuel, and that in fact, he was not able to leave the premises without authorization by Aerodex and without an empty fuel tank. I continued:

Q. Did you on June 14, 1966, have anything at all to do with bringing over any drums or barrels in which he could place the excess?

A. No, sir.

Red Wing said it was simply delivering fuel to a customer. It was certainly not their fault that the outdoor storage tank was full, and they followed Aerodex's instructions in placing the excess fuel in drums belonging to Aerodex. If there was any negligence at all, it was on the part of Aerodex. This would relegate Gus to his remedies under the workmen's compensation laws of the state of Florida. Under that law, it is not necessary to prove negligence on the part of anyone in order to recover benefits. All you need to do is prove that the employee was injured while in the course and scope of his employment. Everyone admitted that Gus was working at the time of his injury. The problem with compensation benefits is that they are limited. We felt that Gus's injuries would be worth ten times as much if we could prove fault on the part of Red Wing. The larger problem was proving that the negligence also caused the explosion ten weeks later.

Hamann stressed that a truck driver could not leave the premises of Aerodex if he still had some fuel left in his tanker truck. He emphasized the point that DeBrocque had to do whatever he was told by Aerodex employees. He asked Phillips:

Q. Can a man leave the premises without your signature?
A. No, sir.
Q. What is required before you will sign him out?
A. That his truck be empty.
Q. You do not sign the voucher or the delivery receipt until the truck is empty?
A. No, sir, I don't.

I called Henry Holland, who was the supervisor of quality control in the test cells. Holland's answers would help me.

Q. Is it part of the test-cell inspector's job to tell a truck driver delivering fuel where to place that fuel?
A. No, sir.
Q. Would a test cell inspector be wrong to tell a truck driver where to put the JP4?
A. He certainly would be.

In other words, Aerodex had no real control over Red Wing's drivers—the old pass-the-buck situation which prevails in any huge organization. I had to make the confusion work to our benefit.

Q. Referring to June 14, 1966, specifically—did Mr. DeBrocque talk to you or ask you if it was all right for him to place excess JP4 into 55-gallon drums?
A. No, sir.
Q. Are you absolutely certain of that?
A. I am positive.

I stressed this since I had already taken DeBrocque's deposition and knew that he told a completely different story.

Q. What is your personal knowledge, if any, of 55-gallon drums being brought over to the outdoor storage tank?

A. I hadn't anything to do with calling for drums. I remember the incident because I drove by when they were putting the fuel in the drums, and that's all I know about it.

Q. Did you stop and talk to the truck drivers?

A. I stopped but I don't remember having any conversation with them.

Q. And approximately how long did you remain there?

A. Oh, I wasn't there for a minute. I didn't even get out of my car.

Mr. Hamann cross-examined:

Q. Can a driver make that decision, or does somebody at Aerodex make the decision as to where the excess fuel is delivered?

A. I would say that would have to be somebody at Aerodex. (*But Holland really didn't know who, specifically*).

Q. Can the test-cell inspector release the truck if it still has some fuel in it?

A. No, sir.

Q. What has happened on other occasions when aviation gas or other types of fuel wouldn't all go in a tank, when somebody in another department at Aerodex had made a mistake?

A. On occasion, the trailer has been left on Aerodex's property overnight and sometimes over a weekend.

Q. Whose responsibility would it have been to see that JP4 was taken out of the drums and put into the main outdoor storage tank when space became available?

A. Material Control.

Hamann was getting the witness to say that whatever occurred between the date of delivery and the date of injury was solely the responsibility of Aerodex. This was valid, since Red Wing had no further contact with this load of JP4 or the drums after DeBrocque left the premises in his empty truck. My theory was that there was negligence

by Red Wing in the beginning, and the intervening time
period couldn't change that fact. Red Wing's neligence set
everything in motion.

My next witness was Edward B. Gregory.

Q. What kind of work do you do for Aerodex?

A. I am a Material Control Coordinator.

Q. Now what does that mean in English?

A. Well, I handle all the gasoline, the oil, the jet fuel, or any
kind of combustible fuel that might be used in the testing of
our engines and the running of the engines.

Q. Mr. Gregory, let me direct your attention to June 14, 1966,
when, as I understand it, some drums were brought over to
the outdoor storage JP4 tank. Do you recall that?

A. Yes, sir.

Q. On that date, who told you that a truck driver needed empty
drums?

A. Mr. Philip Supinger. He told me that he wanted fifteen clean
Trichlorethylene drums picked up. We have what we call a
scrap drum area or "graveyard." All drums from the whole
plant are gathered there. For a purpose like this we need a
perfectly clean, dry drum.

We agreed with that. If they had had one, Gus would
not have been injured. We contended that the "empty"
drum which exploded still had a residue of JP4 fuel in it.

Q. After you had this conversation with Mr. Supinger, what did
you do?

A. Well, I went to the drum stockyard and picked out the drums
myself.

Q. Do you see the same type drums in the courtroom?

A. Yes, sir. That is the type they were.

I had a very specific reason for having two empty 55-
gallon "Tri" drums in the courtroom. Jerry and I had busted
our humps getting them there. After the trial, they remained
in Jerry's garage for years.

Q. Why did you get Trichlorethylene drums?

A. Whenever you pour Tri out, it evaporates and there is no residue left. It is a perfectly dry drum. I put masking tape on the side of each of the fifteen drums.

Q. Did you put any tape on the top of the drums?

A. No. After I put the tape on the sides of all the drums, Phil Supinger wrote the words "JP4 Jet Fuel."

The question of labeling was one of the critical issues in the lawsuit. There was no JP4 label of any kind on the drum which exploded on August 25, 1966. Hamann thought that this greatly favored him.

Q. When you were marking these drums, was any truck driver for Red Wing Carriers present?

A. No, sir.

This is what is known in the "trade" as a "setup" question. I knew DeBrocque would give a totally different account—the more witnesses who contradicted him, the better for us.

Q. Did you do anything to cross out or paint over the "Tri" labels on these drums?

A. No, sir.

Q. What is "Tri"?

A. It is a cleaning solvent manufactured by DuPont.

Q. The drums still said "Tri" even though you had added the masking tape?

A. Yes, sir.

The Tri label was permanent, whereas the tape could easily come off or be removed. I was to contend that De-Brocque was negligent in placing a dangerous fuel into an innocently labeled drum. If Aerodex employees were stupid, too, this did not get Red Wing off the hook.

My next witness was Walter A. Rosenkranz, who was Gus's boss as test-cell maintenance foreman. Through him

I wished to establish something about Gus: that he was a very careful worker.

Q. How would you describe Mr. Burgel as a worker?
A. Very conscientious. Anything he did was done real well.
Q. Were there ever any complaints about the way he worked?
A. Well, the only thing was that he was too particular, as a rule, and he was slow because of that.
Q. You mean he was so careful that he was slow?
A. Yes.

Mr. Hamann: Your Honor. Mr. Rosenblatt continually leads the witness and suggests answers.
The Court: Sustained.

Hamann was right and the judge was right, but I had made my point.

Q. At the time of Gus's accident on August 25, 1966, was there any testing of engines going on in that cell?
A. No. We had stripped the cell down and were preparing to put a T–56 or turbine engine cell in. The cell had been steam-cleaned and we were using it as a temporary workshop.
Q. Did you actually see the explosion?
A. No. I came back from Eastern Airlines about a half hour or so later. Gus had already been removed by ambulance.
Q. Did you see the words "JP4" anywhere on the barrels?
A. No, I did not.

Hamann would use this testimony to argue that the drum which exploded was not one of the drums which had been filled with JP4 on June 14. No one ever saw any JP4 label on either drum that Gus was working on at the time of the explosion.

Q. Mr. Rosenkranz, have you ever had occasion to burn off either the top or bottom of a Tri drum?
A. Yes.

Q. Would you use an acetylene torch? (*That's what Gus had been using.*)
A. Yes.
Q. On any of those occasions did the drum explode?
A. No.
Q. When you burned Tri drums, did you always wash them out before starting the torch?
A. No.
Q. Yet the drums never burned or exploded—is that correct?
A. Yes.
Q. Does Tri have a peculiar odor?
A. Yes.
Q. What does it smell like?
A. It has a very pungent odor that hurts your lungs if you inhale it.

Hamann's cross-examination of Rosenkranz:

Q. Did you find any evidence of water in the second drum, the one which exploded?
A. No, I didn't see any.
Q. You found evidence of water in the first drum but not in the second one?
A. Yes.

This was a red herring that Hamann pushed throughout the trial. There was no reason to wash a drum which contained only Tri. If the drum had actually contained JP4, washing would not solve the problem because the leftover residue could still cause an explosion.

I put Albert M. Mooney on the stand. He had been employed by Aerodex for eleven and a half years.

Q. During August of 1966, was Gus Burgel a member of your crew?
A. Yes, sir.
Q. How would you describe Gus's work?
A. He was a very good worker. He was dependable. He was

slow. He took his time to get things done right. Once he
done it, you forgot it. It was done.

Q. Were you inside the test cell at the time of the explosion?
A. Yes, sir.
Q. Was anyone else present?
A. No, sir.

Mooney admitted, as did Rosenkranz, that there was
no evidence of water in the exploded drum. If Hamann
could convince the jury that Gus was negligent in any
way, this would bar recovery. The same disastrous result
would prevail even if they also believed that Red Wing
had been guilty of greater negligence. This was the Florida
law on contributory negligence of a plaintiff at that time.

Q. Have you ever in your life filled a drum with water before
cutting it or using a torch in it?
A. No.
Q. Well, why not?
A. Never wanted to take the time, I guess.
Q. Did any of those empty Tri drums ever explode in your
face?
A. No, sir.

I was emphasizing the fact that washing or not washing
was a phony issue.

I then called the man who was by far the most important
witness in the case. If the jury liked him and believed him,
we would lose. It was that simple. I questioned Hugh De-
Brocque, the Red Wing driver, as an adverse witness. This
gave me the right of cross-examination.

Q. What do you do for Red Wing?
A. I am a lease operator. I own my own equipment and drive
for them.
Q. You own the tractor part of the truck and you get the trailer
from Red Wing—is that right?
A. Yes.

Q. JP4 is a jet fuel, isn't it?
A. Yes.
Q. You know that JP4 is flammable and volatile?
A. Yes.
Q. What does "flammable" mean?
A. It will ignite with a spark, a match, or any kind of combustion.
Q. What does "volatile" mean?
A. It is very dangerous.
Q. What is it that actually explodes—is it the liquid itself or is it the fumes?
A. The fumes are more dangerous than the liquid itself. We all know that. An empty container will explode faster than a full one. A full container will burn; it will not explode.

Just my point. The residue left in the drum after it had been emptied into the outdoor tank was more dangerous than a drum full of JP4.

Q. How many gallons did you have in your truck on June 14, 1966, before you began to unload?
A. Around 7,300.
Q. After you became aware of the excess situation, who was the very first person you spoke to about it?
A. Doug Phillips.
Q. As a result of your conversation with Phillips, what did he do?
A. Mr. Phillips contacted someone higher up in authority. *(Phillips had denied calling anyone).*
Q. Who did he call?
A. Henry Holland *(the Aerodex supervisor).*
Q. You knew Henry Holland pretty well, didn't you?
A. Yes.
Q. What happened as a result of the telephone conversation between Doug Phillips and Henry Holland?
A. Mr. Holland came up a few minutes later and looked the situation over, and asked me how much I thought I had left

in the truck. I told him roughly between 700 and 900 gallons
—I didn't know for sure. And from there they took it.

Holland's testimony had been completely different.

Q. Where were you when you had this conversation with
Holland?
A. At the truck.
Q. Is it your testimony, sir, that Henry Holland told you to put
the JP4 in Tri drums?
A. Yes, it is. He ordered the drums. (*Gregory had said Supinger
ordered the drums.*)
Q. Is there absolutely no doubt about that in your mind? (*It is
important to establish direct conflicts in the testimony so that
they are perfectly clear to the jury.*)
A. Holland was right there and supervising everything when the
drums came. He was right there.

I was elated that DeBrocque was so positive about this,
but that's the kind of guy he was—dogmatic and very sure
of himself. And he was going to show a smartass lawyer a
thing or two by being very certain of the role everyone
played.

Q. What happened after the drums were brought over?
A. They started stenciling them.
Q. Who was doing the stenciling?
A. An employee of Aerodex, but I did not know the man.
Q. What would be your best estimate of the amount of time it
took to fill the fifteen drums?
A. I would say roughly thirty-five to forty-five minutes.
Q. Was Max Wagner present while the drums were being filled
and while the Aerodex employee was doing the stenciling?

Wagner was another Red Wing driver who had just
made a delivery of aviation fuel to Aerodex, and upon seeing DeBrocque's predicament came over to help out. Also,
he had the special drum fitting or nozzle which could be
used to turn the fuel on and off right at the drum.

A. Yes, he was working the valve at the drums.

Q. Where was the man doing the stenciling and what was he writing?

A. I do not know. He was marking something. He was marking on the top of the drums.

Q. How about on the side of the drums?

A. I don't remember anything on the side. (*Gregory said he put tape on the sides*).

Q. Could you see what the man with the stencil was writing on the top of the drums?

A. I did not get that close to the drums. I stayed at the cab of the truck and worked the pump.

Q. You didn't even look at what the Aerodex employee was writing?

A. That's correct. I just surmised he was putting JP4 on them.

This was central to a showing of DeBrocque's attitude: get rid of the fuel, get paid, and get out.

Q. Was Max Wagner there the whole time that Henry Holland was there during this process of filling the empty drums with JP4?

A. Yes.

It would be a great boon to us when Wagner contradicted DeBrocque both as to Holland's role and the stenciling. This was yet another circumstantial conflict adding to the case I was trying to build.

I continued:

Q. During this time, did you ever call Red Wing Carriers, Inc.?

A. No, I did not.

Q. You didn't feel it was necessary?

A. They would have said, "Why are you calling us? You know to fill the drums."

Q. Are you a mind reader or a truck driver? (*I was pushing him, hoping to provoke an outburst.*)

A. When things like this happened before, that's what they always said. *(So this situation had occurred before yet, Red Wing never developed a policy to deal with it.)*

Q. Were you aware of any labels on the drums that were brought over?

A. For all I know, they could have been marked "Procter & Gamble Soap," sir.

Q. I'm sorry, I don't understand that remark. *(I understood his frustration but wanted him to reemphasize that comment.)*

A. It could be marked "Procter & Gamble Soap." The label has no bearing on it.

"Procter & Gamble" was an unexpected gift. He was annoyed with me for pursuing the matter and would show the jury how ridiculous and petty I was being. Unwittingly, he provided me with great material for my summation.

Q. I understand that is your attitude. My question is, what did the drums say? You're not really sure if they said Trichlorethylene or not, are you?

A. That's right.

Q. And that is about how much interest you had in what the stencil said? You couldn't have cared less if they did put "Procter & Gamble Soap" on the top? Is that a fact?

A. Yes.

Q. That is about it?

A. Yes.

Anger and stubbornness can be very useful at times. Juries often penalize a defendant corporation when an involved employee is uninterested; particularly when a disaster ensues.

I turned to another meaty area of cross-examination. Red Wing's own rule book said: "Maintaining customer's tank: if for any reason a customer's tank is full and the customer directs you to make the delivery *elsewhere,* you *must* call Red Wing's office for instructions and do nothing until you get them. If you cannot complete your delivery for any reason, you *must* call the dispatcher by telephone for fur-

ther instructions immediately, using the nearest telephone."
Speaking very slowly, I asked DeBrocque:

Q. What does the word "elsewhere" mean to you?
A. It means if I cannot complete the delivery and have to take
It elsewhere. That is, taking it to another location. *(This is
how he tried to justify not calling the office. "Elsewhere" was
to become the most important single word in the life of Gus
Burgel.)*

My next witness was Max Wagner. He, like DeBrocque,
was a lease operator for Red Wing who owned and drove
his own tractor in the delivery of fuels. He was quite
familiar with JP4 jet fuel since he had delivered it to the
Homestead Air Force Base, about 35 miles south of Miami
International Airport, every day for more than three years.
Wagner never had occasion to deliver JP4 to Aerodex prior
to June 14, 1966.

Q. While the excess JP4 was being put into these drums, did you
see any employee of Aerodex?
A. I believe there were two men there but they were strangers
to me.
Q. Did you have any idea whether these two men were janitors
or vice-presidents?
A. No, sir.
Q. Did you talk to them?
A. No.
Q. All the drums that you saw on that day, did they all say
"Trichlorethylene," just as these drums do?
A. Yes, sir. They all looked alike.
Q. And were they just like these drums here in that they had the
word "Tri" on top, and in two places on the sides?
A. Yes, sir.
Q. Do you remember seeing the words "JP4" on any part of any
of the fifteen drums.
A. No.

I asked him the overriding question from Red Wing's twenty-six-page booklet titled "Rules, Regulations and Delivery Instructions," 6th edition.

Q. Did you or DeBrocque violate the instruction about calling the office if a customer told you to make the delivery "elsewhere"?

A. No, sir. That rule means if the customer's tank is full and we have to take it to another address, then we are supposed to call the dispatcher. We didn't have to take it to another address.

Q. Wouldn't "elsewhere" be in 55-gallon drums when the 10,000-gallon tank became full? Isn't that "elsewhere"?

A. No.

I had no reason to push him. I had put him on as my witness for certain purposes, but on this point he was against me. The jury would either accept or reject my point of view on the meaning of this word.

Q. On the day of this incident, did you see Henry Holland around?

A. No, sir.

Q. You know who Henry Holland is, don't you?

A. I know Henry, yes, sir.

Q. You were there the entire time that the drums were being filled with JP4, weren't you?

A. Yes, sir.

I attempted to establish a novel point with my next witness—that a truck driver who had delivered fuels should be permitted to testify as an expert under the circumstance of this case.

Expert witnesses are allowed to testify in civil trials not only about facts they know or have observed, in the same way as ordinary witnesses, but also in response to hypothetical questions posed by the lawyer within the area of their expertise. They are able to render opinions about the facts in the case. Normally, the only persons who are entitled to testify as "experts" are doctors, architects, engineers, and the like. I hoped to establish that in these circumstances an experienced truck driver should be allowed to testify as an "expert."

Forrest Huett had been a client of mine a couple of years earlier when he had sustained injuries in an accident.

Q. By whom are you employed at the present time?

A. I am working for Asbury Transportation and Neptune Storage out of New York.

Q. How many years have you been a truck driver?

A. A little over twenty.

Q. Have you traveled all over the United States in making deliveries?

A. Yes. Wherever there is a missile base, and where we take liquid propellants used for rockets and missiles.

Q. When you worked for Asbury, did you get any instructions, any course of training relative to the delivery of fuels?

A. Yes. Plus we had to take a written examination every six months.

Q. Mr. Huett, are you familiar with the customary standard of care used by truck drivers when delivering volatile fuels in this community and across the United States?

A. Yes.

I felt that he had been qualified as an expert and could render an opinion concerning DeBrocque's actions.

Q. Now, Mr. Huett, I am going to ask you to assume the following facts . . .

Mr. Hamann: Just one second. Your Honor, before we get into that I would like to be heard outside the presence of the jury.

The Court: Take the jury out, Mr. Bailiff.

Thereupon the jury retired from the courtroom and we argued to the judge:

Mr. Hamann: I think it is perfectly apparent that Mr. Rosenblatt is attempting to qualify this man as an expert witness. It is respectfully submitted that this is improper. We are not dealing with a subject which can be presented in that manner. We are not suing a doctor or lawyer or architect for malpractice. This man's opinion would invade the province of the jury.

Naturally, we anticipated this legal argument. Alan Schwartz, my scholarly colleague, was with me ready with all available case citations. We knew that our authority was weak but felt that we had to take a shot, because if our truck drivers were permitted to express their expert opinions it would strengthen our case by at least 25 percent. We pointed out that the delivery of volatile fuels was certainly not a matter of common knowledge, which is one of the main reasons the courts allow "expert" testimony.

I said that most people had no idea at all of what would be invoved in the delivery of JP4 to a place like Aerodex. Of course, the jury would not be bound to accept our expert's opinion, but they did have the right to hear and evaluate it. Judge Williams pondered his decision for a few minutes and then announced, "The objection is sustained."

Mr. Huett was not to be allowed to testify as an expert, but as a practical matter, the jury had seen him. Even though he was not permitted to express his expert opinion, I believe the jury fully understood that what he had to say would be harmful to Red Wing. This was the same strategy we employed with the handwriting expert in the Powell case.

We still had another ace in the hole: Nicholas Romeo. Since he had worked for Red Wing, the judge permitted me wider latitude.

Mr. Romeo had worked all his adult life driving trucks, and had delivered freight and fuel for Standard Oil, Pure Oil, and Red Wing.

I questioned him:

Q. What type of substances did you deliver for Standard Oil?

A. All types of petroleum products including asphalt, kerosene, gasoline, diesel fuel and aviation gas.

Q. When you worked for Standard Oil, did you receive instructions concerning the delivery of flammable and volatile fuels?

A. Yes, sir. It was very thorough training. You got that before you went out on a truck.

I was interested in showing the contrast between Standard Oil and Red Wing, since Red Wing had no similar course of instruction or periodic testing. Huett had made the same point with his employer.

Q. Mr. Romeo, have you ever been employed by Red Wing Carriers, Inc.?

A. Yes, sir.

Q. When did you work for them?

A. I started February 14, 1963.

Q. And when did you stop working for them?

A. July of 1966, when I sold my truck.

Q. While working for Red Wing, were you ever faced with a situation in delivering any flammable fuel where you arrived at a location, and the container for which it was intended, either underground or aboveground, was filled and you had an excess?

A. Yes, sir.

Q. In your opinion, was the conduct of Mr. DeBrocque in emptying the excess JP4 into empty 55-gallon drums provided by Aerodex, in accordance with reasonable safety standards in the delivery of flammable and volatile fuels in this community?

Hamann objected. This opinion, he protested, was the chief issue in the case, and should be for the jury to decide; not this so-called "expert."

The judge sustained the objection, but again I felt I had made my point.

I continued with Mr. Romeo. I asked him to look into

Red Wing's rule book on page 9. It had once been his rule book as well, so he was legally entitled to interpret the language.

Q. Tell me what the word "elsewhere" means to you?

A. To me that would mean anywhere but its proper container, which in this situation would be the outdoor tank.

Q. Is a 55-gallon drum such as this a proper container for JP4?

A. No, sir.

Q. Would you place the JP4 in such drums even if the customer told you it was okay?

A. No.

Q. So, I said, *(pointing to the drum in the courtroom)*—this is "elsewhere"?

A. Yes.

Q. Did you ever have occasion while working for Red Wing to return an excess back to the terminal?

A. Yes.

Q. Would you lose any money in coming back with an excess?

A. Absolutely. *(Here I was attempting to show yet another motivation DeBrocque had for getting rid of the fuel "elsewhere" or anywhere.)*

In his cross-examination, Hamann tried to imply that Romeo was angry at Red Wing. He was not able to establish this. Romeo cheerfully admitted that while he didn't have any love for them, he didn't have any hate for them either. Hamann was also unsuccessful in establishing some kind of special relationship between my office, Forrest Huett, and Romeo.

The very favorable and crucial testimony of Nick Romeo demonstrated Jerry Burke's great ability of developing rapport with witnesses. He had that unique ability of getting a prospective witness to like him and in the frame of mind of wanting to help. This is generally a very difficult thing to accomplish because the natural reaction of most people is a desire not to get involved.

I needed testimony on what had really happened to cause the explosion. Regardless of what had happened at the time of delivery, Red Wing's position was that it could not have been the cause of the explosion, over two months later. I called as an expert witness Robert Erwin, a chemist and engineer.

Q. Mr. Erwin, at my request, did you have occasion to make some tests relative to Tri and JP4?

A. I did.

Q. Could you tell us, first of all, with respect to Tri the type of tests that you performed?

A. I was asked about the physical and chemical characteristics of Tri and JP4 jet fuel, relative to their volatility and explosive nature. I made tests on the two products by putting samples of each in containers, emptying out the containers, and then testing them with a cutting torch, an oxygen acetylene torch, to ascertain the results. I did this with Tri several times and found that nothing happened, except a very disagreeable odor.

Q. What exactly did you do with the Tri?

A. I took a new clean five-gallon steel can and put a gallon of Tri in the can, shook it around and allowed it to stand for an hour or two and then I drained it out and rinsed it twice with water. Then I applied the cutting torch to the bottom of the container. Nothing happened. I did not do the identical thing with JP4 because when it was poured into a coffee can, the material immediately would flash into flame with a minor explosion when the torch was brought near it. After dumping out the coffee can, it would still give a flash. I felt it was too dangerous to repeat this in a closed container such as a five-gallon can.

Q. If we were to put JP4 into a 55-gallon drum and a day later or a week later empty it out and wash it with a high-pressure hose, would all traces of the JP4 be removed?

A. Not with a simple washing.

Q. Why is that?

A. Because the nature of this hydrocarbon is such that it permeates the pores of the metal, and it takes considerable detergents to remove that from the surface pores of the metal.

Q. How long might JP4 remain in the pores of such metal?

A. As far as I know there is no specific time. It could remain there many months—in fact years, if it was not washed repeatedly.

Vital testimony to my case, where we had a two-month delay between delivery and the explosion. It was obvious that an empty Tri drum could not explode whereas a drum which had once contained JP4 could. And the residue of JP4 could explode even though the "empty" drum had been washed carefully.

In cross-examination of my witnesses, and later, through his own, Warren Hamann hammered away with the impressive ammunition in his arsenal. He established that many different substances were received at Aerodex in 55-gallon drums, and that some of them were dangerous and volatile. Frequently, chemicals or mineral spirits or lacquer were placed in empty drums. He said I could not pinpoint the exploded drum as one of those which was filled with JP4 two and a half months earlier—that I had therefore failed to prove causation. By the same token, he could not prove that any substance other than Tri had ever been in the drum which exploded. I certainly did not prove by direct evidence that the drum which exploded ever contained JP4.

Hamann stressed that the JP4 was the property of Aerodex, not Red Wing. They had an absolute right, he insisted, to tell the deliverer where to place the excess fuel. It was not the function of the truck driver to question the decision. Besides, it was Aerodex's duty to be sure that the outdoor storage tank would hold the amount of fuel that Aerodex had ordered. His witnesses pointed out in very convincing fashion that with thirty-five or forty forklifts on the premises, which were used for moving drums, it was extremely unlikely that these drums had remained in the same location from June 14 until Gus retrieved two on August 25, 1966, near the outdoor tank.

Lawyers differ as to how to present a case where there is very tenuous liability and impressive injuries. My preference is to intersperse the medical evidence with the testimony concerning liability.

Although this is frowned upon by the courts and objected to by defense counsel, it is generally permitted primarily to accommodate doctors who have operating schedules and office hours. I wanted to get the jury in a compassionate frame of mind so that they would concentrate on the overwhelming injuries rather than on the technical imperfections in the liability phase of the case. I had doctors physically present at the courthouse, feeling confident that Hamann would not make too big a fuss and Judge Williams would not put them to the substantial inconvenience of leaving and returning later. This gamble paid off beautifully.

To this day, Gus has no recollection of the explosion. He was knocked unconscious and was taken by ambulance to Palm Springs General Hospital in Hialeah. From there he was transferred to North Shore Hospital in Miami Shores for more extensive testing. There he was seen by a neurosurgeon and a tracheotomy was performed. At that time, very little hope was held out for his survival. His eyes were completely closed because of huge hematomas, and he had multiple fractures of his skull, jaw, face and right hand.

Gus remained unconscious for slightly over three weeks. The doctors found that he was permanently paralyzed on the right side. At the time of trial, he was able to walk with his right arm in a sling. Unfortunately, he had been right-handed. For several weeks after regaining consciousness, he was unable to speak and unable to comprehend what was being said to him. Both these conditions dramatically improved in time, although his speech was affected.

The explosion ripped out nearly all his teeth. There was such a gross distortion of his bite that months later both jaws had to be refractured by an oral surgeon. He needed six separate operative procedures on the jaws and teeth alone.

Gus came under the care of a general surgeon, a plastic surgeon, a neurosurgeon, an orthopedic specialist, an oral surgeon and an ear, nose, and throat specialist. Altogether, he underwent a total of twelve operations. Between the date of his injury and the day of trial, he spent months in various hospitals and over 400 days in a nursing home.

Intellectually, he had been impaired only slightly. His main complaint was that he could not read nearly as quickly or comprehend nearly as well as he could before. He talked slowly and with difficulty, but he was able to be understood. His sexual function had not been affected. The obvious and dramatic injury was, of course, his paralysis. In addition, the color slides kept by the oral surgeon were of great value because they allowed the jury to understand, in very graphic terms, the pain and deprivation he had been forced to bear.

I called Gus as my last witness by design. He had been in the courtroom with us the entire trial, and up until the time he testified, the jury had never heard him speak. I knew they were curious and interested and awaiting his appearance with real anticipation.

I had Gus give a brief outline of his life. He was born in Union City, New Jersey, and resided there until he came to Miami approximately fifteen years earlier. He was forty-four years old at the time of the trial. He and his wife had seven children. His formal education was limited to two years of high school. In New Jersey he had always been a long-distance truck driver, although he had never hauled fuels. In Miami he had driven trucks and had worked as a crane operator. He went to school to become a welder and had worked for Aerodex for six years prior to the date of his accident.

I called Gus to the witness stand late Tuesday afternoon. I was barely into my direct examination before Judge Williams recessed until 9:00 A.M. the following morning. This fitted into my plan perfectly because I wanted the jury to hear and evaluate Gus over a period of at least two days.

Q. At the time of this accident, what was your classification at Aerodex?

A. Class A-1 welder.

Q. In the course of working at Aerodex in the several years before this accident, had you had occasion to burn 55-gallon drums?

A. Oh, yes, that is a common occurrence.

Q. What type of drums were they that you had burned?

A. *(Pointing with his good left hand at the drums that were in the courtroom)* Right there. That kind. No other one. That kind.

Q. Why would you only have occasion to burn Tri drums and not some other type of 55-gallon drums?

A. Because when I was a welder in maintenance and they needed a trashcan or some place to put parts in, they would take Tri drums from the graveyard and bring them to the weld shop, and I would burn the tops off them.

Q. On these other occasions would you burn the drums indoors or outdoors?

A. Outdoors.

Q. And on these other occasions would you wash out the Tri drums?

A. No.

Q. Why not?

A. I never had occasion to. It is not combustible or flammable, so why go through all that work to wash out the drum that would not give me any trouble anyway?

Q. On the day of your accident, did you wash the drums?
A. Yes, sir.
Q. Why, since you hadn't done this in the past?
A. Because I was burning inside. Now maybe that didn't come out right. I know Tri will make you sick when you smell it, but if I were burning it outside, then I don't have to wash. But this is the first occasion I had to burn them inside a test cell. *(So washing or not washing was irrelevant as to any issue of Gus's own negligence.)*
Q. So you washed the drums because you were burning them indoors, is that correct?
A. The fumes when you burn them indoors will make you sick.
Q. As best you can recall what did Mr. Mooney say to you on August 25, 1966?
A. He wanted me to make a wash tank out of two drums.
Q. Did Mr. Mooney tell you where to get the drums?
A. Yes, sir. He told me to go outside by the JP tank, there is a whole bunch of drums, and use two of them.
Q. Were you going to weld the two drums together, one stacked right on the top of the other?
A. That's right.

I wanted Gus to move around so that the jury's attention would be focused on the manner in which he walked and gestured. I had him leave the witness chair and come down to where the drums were and demonstrate how he removed the plugs or bungs. The jury was obviously bothered by the smell, but I pretended not to notice.

The Court: A juror has a question.
Juror Haskins: Your Honor, that smell is awful.
Rosenblatt: Oh, I'm sorry *(Even though that is precisely what I wanted to happen)*
The Court: Put the bungs on.
Burgel: That's why I didn't stick my nose in it.

This exchange broke the back of an important portion of Hamann's cross-examination.

Q. At any time while you were working on the two drums, did you see any writing which said "JP4" on them?

A. No, sir.

Q. After you removed the large bung from both drums, how did you wash the drums?

A. In a test cell the only thing that was left after we cleaned it out, was two lines—one for air, one for water, and we had a water hose. I washed it out with a high-pressure hose.

Q. Did you thoroughly wash one drum or both of them?

A. No, both of them.

Q. After you burned the top off the first drum, what did you then do?

A. It was lunchtime.

Q. After you finished lunch and returned to the test cell to work on the second drum, what part of that drum were you going to remove?

A. The bottom.

Q. If not for the explosion, you would have removed the bottom of the second drum, and you would have then welded that bottom onto the top of the first drum?

A. That's right.

Warren Hamann cross-examined:

Q. Did you make any tests whatsoever to determine what fumes were in those barrels?

A. No, sir.

This was a theme that Hamann turned to again and again during his cross. His point was that Gus was negligent in not making sure that these drums still smelled of Tri.

Q. Now at no time did you actually smell for Tri?

A. No, sir, I did not. Why should I subject myself to smelling Tri? It will make you sick.

I had to hope the jury would understand that Gus had no reason to believe that there had ever been anything except Trichlorethylene in these drums. He knew from previous experience that Tri would not explode with him using an acetylene torch. The only reason he washed the drums on this date was to avoid the fumes since he was working indoors.

It was obvious that Hamann had done a lot of reading about welding and a lot of talking to skilled workers. He was asking detailed and technical questions, but this did not concern me at all because I had supreme confidence in Gus's ability to explain welding, cutting, and burning techniques. I knew that he was very safety conscious and that Hamann had no chance in a few months of study of developing the expertise that Gus had acquired on an everyday basis over several years.

Gus kept making remarks to Hamann such as, "We are not on the same wavelength." He would frequently say, pointing to his head, "Here I know, but it doesn't come out here"—pointing to his mouth. This was valuable because it could give the jury the impression that Hamann was trying to take advantage of Gus's inability to articulate clearly. It also helped from a damage standpoint because it was vivid demonstrative evidence of the fact that two years after the accident Gus still had difficulty expressing his thoughts.

Summation began at 9:30 A.M. Thursday, July 18, 1968. I requested two hours of final argument, and Warren Hamann told the judge that thirty minutes per side would be sufficient. This is a well-recognized defense strategy because an insufficient amount of time hurts the plaintiff considerably more than the defendant. This was a complex case which had required three full days of testimony, and I had to argue liability, causation, and damages in addition to fighting the contention that Gus Burgel was himself negligent. Judge Williams, who had been eminently fair throughout the trial, recognized the realities and allotted an hour and a half to each side.

I addressed the jury:

. . . let's consider Mr. DeBrocque's actions and his attitude. I would suggest to you that his attitude was "Let me get rid of that excess so I can get paid and leave." He knew JP4 was flammable and volatile. He knew that Tri was nonflammable, so he certainly knew that he was putting a flammable, volatile substance into an improper container.

I picked up Red Wing's booklet and brandished it:

. . . without interpretation, without being cute, just by reading English words and taking their plain meaning, you can have only one interpretation of the rule. It says that if, for any reason, "a customer's tank is full and the customer directs you to make the delivery *elsewhere,* you must call Red Wing's office for instructions and do nothing until you get them."

This is precisely what happened here since Aerodex's outdoor storage tank was full and Aerodex employees told De-Brocque to put the excess into 55-gallon drums. Yet neither De-Brocque nor Wagner called their office for instructions.

Elsewhere means somewhere else! You have a 10,000-gallon outdoor storage tank and you have a 55-gallon drum. If this drum when compared to this tank isn't elsewhere—then I don't know what is.

I have a pencil here on my desk. I am putting it elsewhere—on the chair. I don't have to take it down to the second floor of the courthouse or to my office across the street for it to be elsewhere. It was on the table and now it's on the chair. It is elsewhere!

Nick Romeo told you what the rule means. He said it applied precisely to this type of situation—and, of course, it does.

Red Wing just tells their drivers to deliver the fuel and that's it. Now that would be all right if they were delivering a sack of potatoes because if they unload them in the wrong place, they won't cripple anybody. But in delivering a highly volatile and flammable substance, for a corporate entity to tell their employees—"Well, just deliver it and do whatever anyone of those five or six thousand employees tell you to do"—that is not reasonable under the circumstances. It is not reasonable by any stretch of the imagination.

If Hugh DeBrocque had been 50 percent as careful as Gus Burgel was in doing his job, Gus wouldn't be sitting here today maimed and permanently injured. DeBrocque tells us that Henry Holland stood there and supervised the placing of the excess JP4 into the drums. Holland denies it. Max Wagner backs up Holland because he says he knows Holland and Holland wasn't there.

What does DeBrocque say about labeling? He says some kind of stencil was used which he didn't even bother to read. Wagner didn't see anybody stenciling anything, and he would have had to see it if it occurred because he was using the nozzle on the drums.

You saw DeBrocque's attitude on the witness stand. That was his same attitude on June 14, 1966. "Get rid of the excess and let me get the hell back" . . . "Well, for all I know, they were stencilling 'Procter & Gamble' on top of the drums." Yes, as far as he knew or as far as he was concerned, they could have been putting "Mickey Mouse" on with the alleged stencil.

All he had to do was the same thing that Nick Romeo did on previous occasions, and that was take the fuel back or let the truck sit there. Do what a reasonable truck driver would do in delivering a flammable and dangerous substance.

Red Wing still could have avoided the tragedy when they learned of the excess because DeBrocque's boss could have called somebody in authority at Aerodex and said—"Look, this is what was done, it doesn't sound safe. Get rid of those drums after they are emptied." But naturally, this wasn't done, and it is perfectly consistent with the way Red Wing operates.

The defendant was Red Wing, not the driver. But Red Wing was legally responsible for the negligence of its employees. I had to focus the jury on the wider issue of industrial safety, and the responsibility of Red Wing to instruct and educate its drivers when handling dangerous materials such as jet fuel.

It is all compounded by the fact that there were two truck drivers, and neither one of them saw anything wrong with placing the excess fuel into improperly labeled containers. If that doesn't say something about Red Wing's manner of training their employees, then I don't know what does. It tells you volumes about their attitude toward safety.

Was Gus a safe worker? He never had an accident or an injury of any kind while welding, while burning. His two immediate supervisors—Rosenkranz and Mooney—said he was careful to a fault, and this made him slow. "He is so careful that he aggravates me sometimes because I want it done fast, and he takes his time to make sure that it is done right." Gus had no reason to believe that these drums ever contained JP4 or any other fuel.

I turned to my client's damages.

I think it's fair to begin with this premise—no amount of money is really adequate because if Gus Burgel had the choice between fifty million dollars and being what he was before August 25, 1966, he would say, "Keep the money." But the only thing jurors have the power to do is return money damages. You do not have the power to make him whole again.

There were many doctors who saw Mr. Burgel that I didn't even bring in, and you will recall that with several of the doctors who testified I didn't go into every little detail. I didn't delve into every page of these hospital records and the X rays because you know what is involved here—you know the man suffered grievous, horrible, terrible injuries. I did not try to appeal to your sympathy by bringing in Mrs. Burgel or the children.

I told you when I was questioning you at the inception of the trial that Judge Williams is not going to say he thinks the case is worth a half million dollars or ten cents or a hundred thousand dollars. That will be your decision. The bills, including all the hospitals and all the doctors and the nursing home, come to slightly over $26,000. But these are only the tangible elements of damage and in a case of such massive injuries, the tangible damages are the least significant.

The truly meaningful elements of damage are the intangible ones. Past pain and suffering from August 25, 1966, until today is 692 days of pain and suffering, of inability to lead a normal life, of disability, of disfigurement. In cases where lawyers represent clients with whiplash or a sore back, they ask for $20 and $30 a day. I ask as a reasonable figure $100 a day for past pain and suffering. That would come to $69,200.

Then, because Gus's paralysis is permanent, I was permitted to read into evidence the mortality tables, which show that a man age forty-four had a life expectancy of over twenty-eight years.

So Gus is expected to live at least 10,403 days. At $30 a day it comes to the sum of $313,890. Yes, that sounds like a lot of money, and it's going to take a lot of money to do justice in this case.

There is no happy retirement to look forward to in his future. He can't play ball with his boys or reach out and hug his kids. What is that worth?

Gus had remained stoic and businesslike throughout the trial. Although I was completely wrapped up in my discourse, I heard a disturbance at counsel table. It was Gus, who had completely broken down. Although this was totally unplanned, it had me worried; because if jurors feel that you are tugging at their heartstrings, they may become hardened. Jerry reacted swiftly in helping Gus slowly out of the courtroom, but the pause had been a moment of supreme drama.

Prior to Mr. Hamann's summation, the court would take a ten-minute recess. By then Gus had composed himself, and he remained in the courtroom for the balance of the proceedings.

I continued:

These hospital records show a history of agony and pain and suffering and travail beyond my ability to express. And more importantly, Lady and Gentlemen, these voluminous records and these x-rays are a testament and a tribute to human courage and spirit, to a man who goes into work in the morning—a father, a husband, physically able and strong—and who wakes up weeks later as half a man.

What is the value to Mr. Burgel knowing that as he sits or as he walks with that cane and with his slow gait that people are looking. He is a proud man, and it doesn't matter that they feel pity or compassion because no reaction from his standpoint can be satisfying. They are staring.

What is manhood worth? What is an arm worth? What is a leg worth? What is it worth for Gus Burgel to know that every morning when he gets up, that's it? That is as well as he is ever going to be. That is the way he is going to remain until the day he dies.

A person can accept great pain and great reversals if he knows that in three months or six months or in two years he will recover, but the truly awful thing is to know that you have reached a plateau and will never get significant improvement.

No one can paint Gus Burgel a rosy picture of his future. This was a man who enjoyed his work and took pride in the manner in which he performed it. Even in his spare time, he would fix cars and television sets. I couldn't even fix a leaky faucet and that's one of the reasons I became a lawyer, because I know that if I had to make my living working with my hands, I would be on welfare.

I look at people who are handy and mechanical and I have a tremendous admiration for them because it is a gift. It is a gift in the same way that being a musician or an athlete is a blessing, and what is it worth to take that gift away? What is it worth for him to remember what he once was and what he could once do, and compare that to now? Gus Burgel is destined for the rest of his life to have many of his fine qualities and abilities imprisoned within a permanently damaged body.

In suggesting a figure to you as reasonable and fair compensation, I say that a jury verdict of from $1,000,000 to $2,000,000 would be it, and I can look every one of you square in the eye when I say that because I honestly believe that such an award would be justice in this case. It is only proper to balance a massive and substantial injury with a substantial monetary award. Thank you.

Warren Hamann fully realized that the jury had become emotionally involved and that they liked Gus and had compassion for him. So, as any outstanding defense lawyer would, he sought to defuse the sympathy angle. He started by saying:

Sometimes we become emotionally involved ourselves. I am sure there isn't a person in this room that does not have sympathy for Gus Burgel in his unfortunate position, but I think you will remember that this is a court of law, and his Honor will specifically instruct you that cases are not to be tried on whether we are sorry for somebody. Cases are not tried on our natural sympathy. Each of you when you took your oath as jurors promised and swore that you would not let your sympathy for this unfortunate person influence your judgment of the facts. . . .

The plaintiff has charged Red Wing with negligence, and they have to prove it. It is not up to the defendant, as it may be in some countries, to come in and prove that it didn't happen that way. Mr. Rosenblatt's argument was tremendous—really, from a lawyer's viewpoint he gave a tremendous argument. But let's return to the facts.

There isn't any question but that Aerodex through its employees made the decision to place the excess fuel into 55-gallon drums. Mr. Rosenblatt would have you believe that if Mr. DeBrocque called back to the dispatcher that some other decision would have been reached. It is Aerodex's fuel, not Red Wing's—that's all.

In addition to the plaintiff necessarily having the burden of establishing that DeBrocque did something wrong that day, he must tie that wrong into the eventual injury. It is called legal cause. The plaintiff has to establish the causation between that delivery and the accident. And when you try to develop that chain of evidence; you find it gets very tortuous. Now let's take this whole chain and like any other chain, if there is a broken link in it, the chain is broken. It means that each link in the chain has to be proved by the preponderance of the evidence to your satisfaction.

Causation had always been the weakest part of my case. Hamann zeroed in on it beautifully. I could not *prove* that JP4 was ever in the drum which exploded, although I could create such an inference. I could not *prove* where the exploded drum had been between June 14 and August 25, 1966. During this two and one-half months the drum was solely in the custody of Aerodex, and they could have used it for many purposes.

I had argued various inferences from circumstantial evidence concerning the delivery of the fuel and the explosion. So could Hamann, and he was in high gear.

He continued:

Maybe mineral spirits had been in this drum or some other type of gasoline or acetate. It might have contained any one of the hundreds of chemicals delivered or moved about the Aerodex premises in barrels. If somebody at Aerodex wanted to drain out some contaminated fuel from a particular tank, what would be the most logical thing that he would do. He would find an empty drum.

Just because somebody may do something wrong doesn't mean that someone else can sue them for it and collect. It is inconceivable that the drum that was filled with JP4 on June 14, 1966, remained by the storage tank until August 25, and that no other material or chemical or gasoline was put into it during that entire period of time. With all those forklifts around it is certainly likely that any or all of those drums would have been moved to different locations on the Aerodex property as they were needed.

His Honor will charge you that if Mr. Burgel contributed to

his own injury, then he cannot recover. You don't lay one party's negligence against the other and say one was hurt more than the other, and then decide that he is a better guy than the other. If Gus Burgel legally contributed to his own injury, then he cannot recover under our system and each of you has sworn to follow our law.

Not once in all his contact with these drums did Gus Burgel take a sniff to smell for Tri. If he had, this accident never would have happened. Not one time in that whole sequence did he smell for anything else.

He had two barrels sitting there side by side and he had been to lunch. He came back after lunch, put on his dark glasses, turned around with his lit torch, and put it to the wrong drum. You wash out that first one and you immediately cut it while there is still water inside. Then when you get around to starting on that second one, you are going to wash it. Why not? The hose is right there. The people that were there after the accident said that there were water beads in the first drum, and there was no evidence whatsoever of water in the second one. He forgot to wash the second drum after lunch.

It is negligence to put the torch to the wrong barrel. It is failure to use reasonable care for one's own safety and, therefore, contributory negligence not to ascertain what had been in these barrels before.

Hamann reemphasized all the points that he had made in cross-examination of my witnesses, particularly relating to causation, the seventy-two-day interim between the date of delivery and the date of the accident, and also the likelihood that the drum which exploded contained other substances which could have exploded.

Hamann continued:

Lady and gentlemen of the jury, I respectfully submit to you that if you lay the sympathy aside, when you look at the law and the facts in the cold dispassionate manner which we are all sworn to do when we try matters in an American courtroom, that the plaintiff has not sustained his burden of proof. There are several broken links in the chain and I further submit, although I would consider it immaterial under the circumstances, that Gus Burgel's actions on that day were not reasonable, and that he contributed legally to his own injury, and is, therefore barred from recovery.

Then came my chance for rebuttal argument:

The whole approach of Red Wing Carriers in this case is to try and take advantage of the confusion which admittedly exists at Aerodex. I don't care if you believe that Aerodex, through its employees, did something wrong. This would be of no consequence to the end result in this case, because if Red Wing's negligence contributed substantially to the injury, then Mr. Burgel is entitled to a verdict. This whole strategy is to lay it on Aerodex since Aerodex made the error in ordering too much fuel.

Did they bring you any witnesses from Red Wing to say that what DeBrocque did was right? Did they have any dispatcher say that what he did was right? No. "Let's speculate, let's guess because Aerodex is confusing—and because it is confusing out there, let's bring in a defense verdict."

Another concept that defense lawyers use constantly is that of "burden of proof" because they know that people have heard about proof "beyond a reasonable doubt." Well, that is applicable in a criminal case where you are going to deprive a person of his liberty. The burden of proof in a civil case is not beyond and to the exclusion of every reasonable doubt. The burden of proof in a negligence case is to prove your case by the greater weight of the evidence, which is likened to a scale or seesaw and if it tilts one point in favor of the plaintiff, he has met his burden. We are not talking about Ivory soap and 99 and 44/100ths percent pure—we are talking only about 51 percent. That is the plaintiff's burden of proof in this case, and we have more than met it.

Mr. Hamann has a lot to say about his theory of Gus Burgel's negligence. In that realm he has the burden of proof. Lawyers never cease to amaze me. Mr. Hamann gets up here and plays

welder, which I think is absolutely unreal. He says a reasonable
welder wouldn't do this and a reasonable welder wouldn't do
that. Mr. Hamann has been a lawyer for many years. I wouldn't
put Gus Burgel up there and ask him about what a reasonable
lawyer would do in trying a contract case because he wouldn't
know. If Mr. Hamann wants to say what this man did was
wrong, then let him bring in an experienced welder to say that.

On rebuttal, the plaintiff's lawyer usually decides whether
to emphasize his client's damages or the liability; one or
the other. The damages were so obvious as not to need
reemphasis. I had to counter Hamann's liability argument,
for if the jury bought it we would get zero.

I continued:

Why didn't Red Wing bring in the person who wrote that
rule book and tell us what he meant by the word *"elsewhere."*
No, "let's guess." Then he talks about circumstantial evidence
and implies that it's not evidence at all. Of course, the evidence
has to be circumstantial to create the very logical conclusion
that one of the drums that was filled with JP4 in June was the
same drum which exploded in August. The only way we could
have direct evidence is if we hired a watchman to keep his eye
on a particular drum twenty-four hours a day.

If a person is walking along the street and all of a sudden is
hit on the head by something and knocked unconscious, and
then he wakes up and sees a flowerpot next to him, this is circumstantial evidence. But it is pretty obvious that what knocked
him out was the flowerpot. He is not going to be penalized for
not looking up and seeing exactly what hit him.

There is no evidence other than pure speculation that at
anytime, JP4 or any other gasoline was placed in 55-gallon
drums, other than on June 14. They tell you there are drums,
there are chemicals, there are other gasolines—"maybe, might,
maybe, guess, could be." All the maybes in the world aren't
good enough to deprive Gus Burgel of the just compensation
that is his due.

Gus had worked on many empty Tri drums in the past and he

knew there was no danger of explosion. He had no reason to believe that these drums contained anything other than tri-chlorethylene at any time. Then why subject himself to the foul odor? Gus Burgel was told to get two Tri drums, the usual everyday-type drum that he had burned many, many times in the past. Why should he suspect anything? Why should he stick his nose in and smell it? He picked the safest place to burn the drums, in a clean stripped-down cell.

Gus Burgel is the way he is today because Hugh DeBrocque didn't care if the alleged stencil was a "Procter & Gamble" stencil. He is that way because Hugh DeBrocque didn't follow a rule laid down in his own rule book. Gus Burgel is the way he is because Hugh DeBrocque wanted to get rid of the excess fast, and because he could care less about the container in which it was placed.

What you do today on July 18, 1968, will govern this man's future for the rest of his life. When this case is over, when the verdict is in, Mr. Hamann and I and you and the judge will all be able to walk away. Gus Burgel will not be able to walk away. If all the law books and the law schools and the court-rooms and the judges are to have any real meaning in the final analysis, it must be to do justice. I say to you do right by Gus Burgel and bring back a just and fair verdict. Thank you.

Judge Williams, in his instructions to the jury, again emphasized the need to decide the case *only* on the evidence and the law. "In reaching your verdict, you are not to be swayed in the performance of your duty by prejudice, sympathy, or any other sentiment for or against either party."

The jury retired at 12:33 P.M. and ate their lunch while deliberating. Jerry, Alan and I walked all over the sixth floor of the Dade County Courthouse. We went up the elevator and down the elevator, getting off at one floor or another. There was no reason to remain in the courthouse since the judge also had gone to lunch. Even if the jury returned a quick verdict, it would not be announced until he returned. My office was just across the street, and the bailiff would have notified us in a moment of any decision or question by the jury. That was the situation logically, but emotionally we could not leave the building. Only Gus remained calm.

We couldn't eat. We didn't want to talk to anyone. We didn't really want to talk to each other because speculating at that point would be useless. None of us ever sat in one place for more than a minute at a time. I must have covered seven miles while the jury was deliberating.

I was getting all kinds of congratulations on a very moving summation, but it was all meaningless, because the only people I was trying to convince were the six on the jury. Several spectators and fellow lawyers told me that at least two members of the jury had tears rolling down their cheeks during my summation. I had no awareness of it at the time. The court reporter had been sobbing, too. I was totally unaware of that as well.

The jury had been out exactly three hours.

There was a knock on the jury door which adjoined Judge Williams's courtroom. The foreman told the bailiff the jury had a verdict. The judge put on his robe and we all went into the courtroom. I was afraid to look at the jury as they marched in and I was afraid not to. I just didn't know what I was going to do if it was a defense verdict.

Judge Williams: Members of the jury, have you reached a verdict?

Juror Meyrick: We have, your Honor.

We, the jury, find for the plaintiff, Gus Burgel, and assess his damages in the sum of $702,000.

So say we all. Lee J. Meyrick, Foreman.

Red Wing and its insurance carrier had never offered us ten cents in way of settlement.

When we got this case, Jerry and I knew nothing about

JP4, Tri, welding or Aerodex for that matter. We were to spend days on the premises of Aerodex in the test cells, at the outdoor storage tank, studying the drums, interviewing witnesses and becoming familiar with the entire operation. Gus went there with us on several occasions to answer our many questions. We took photographs of Red Wing trucks and studied their methods of fuel delivery.

We had detailed conferences with everyone who testified. Thorough preparation does not guarantee success, but a trial lawyer will seldom succeed without it.

There were some startling factual conflicts in this case. Even as between Red Wing's own employees—DeBrocque and Wagner.

DeBrocque said the Aerodex supervisor, Mr. Holland, was present and supervising the procedures whereby the fuel was transferred from the truck to the 15 drums.

Wagner said Holland had nothing to do with the entire operation.

Holland, of course, agreed with Wagner and further contradicted DeBrocque when he denied ordering the drums or telling DeBrocque where to place the excess fuel.

DeBrocque said Aerodex employees used a stencil to label the drums.

Wagner, who was present and using his nozzle the entire time the drums were being filled, knew nothing about any stencil.

Creating more confusion yet (and confusion generally works in favor of the plaintiff in a case of serious injuries) was the testimony of Aerodex employee Gregory. Gregory said he used masking tape (not a stencil) on the sides (not on tops as DeBrocque said) on all 15 drums. Gregory further said that no truck driver was present when he and Mr. Supinger labelled the drums. No one ever explained exactly why Supinger ordered the drums or whether he had any contact with DeBrocque.

According to Gregory, Supinger wrote the words "JP4
Jet Fuel" on all the drums. To my surprise, the defense
never called Supinger to testify. There was no evidence
concerning what happened to the "masking tape" or the
"stencils" between June 14 and August 25, 1966.

The lack of communication between Red Wing and
Aerodex worked to our advantage as did the lack of communication between the various departments within the
Aerodex complex. There must be a system of communication when the product is as potentially dangerous as jet
fuel, and I feel the jury resented a haphazard arrangement.
The defense did not call a single superior from Red Wing
to testify. Perhaps they felt they would be too vulnerable
on cross-examination.

If some witnesses had said other things, the result could
have been just the opposite. If the Judge had not permitted
the jury to see and hear our truck drivers we could have
lost; if the makeup of the jury had been different we could
have lost; if Gus Burgel had not been so precise and like-
able we could have lost. We were humble in the knowledge
that any change in one of a hundred variables could have
altered the result. We had succeeded beyond our wildest
expectations in our first "big case."

Naturally, Red Wing filed extensive motions supported
by impressive legal memoranda for a new trial. Judge Williams retained the power to take the verdict away from us.
He had reserved ruling on the various motions made during
the trial. Their chief emphasis, of course, was that we simply
had not presented enough evidence to show that Red Wing
had breached a duty owed to Gus, or that what their
driver did actually caused Gus's injuries.

Judge Williams heard the posttrial motions on September 13, 1968, and again reserved ruling. Waiting for his
decision was almost as trying as waiting for the jury's verdict. Finally, on October 14, 1968, he denied Red Wing's

motions. Alan Schwartz, who is almost always right, was firmly of the opinion that if Judge Williams granted a new trial, we could not have reversed him on appeal. I will always be grateful to Judge Williams for allowing the jury to decide the case.

Red Wing appealed the jury verdict to the Third District Court of Appeal of Florida. In addition to enumerating reasons for the proposition that the verdict was contrary to the evidence and the law, one of the strongest points in the brief was that the verdict was so excessive as to "shock the judicial conscience."

On September 12, 1968, Red Wing's attorney, Warren D. Hamann, offered the sum of $180,000 to settle which, on my advice, Gus rejected. On September 25, 1968, he increased the offer to $270,000 which we likewise rejected. Naturally, after Judge Williams denied Red Wing's motion for a new trial, the case became more valuable, but there was still danger in awaiting the outcome for an appeal.

Oral argument was set for March 14, 1969, before the Third District Court of Appeal. Jerry, Alan, and I had a detailed discussion with Mallory Horton, Alan's law partner and a former judge of the Court of Appeal. He and Alan recommended settlement, feeling that there was a good chance that the court might reverse the case, leaving Gus with nothing. Even if that didn't happen, there was a strong likelihood that the judges would substantially reduce the verdict as excessive. We therefore settled the case on the day before the oral argument for $475,000.

Up until this day, whenever Gus calls me or writes a letter, he identifies himself or signs his name "Elsewhere."

III

Elease Morris
VS.
St. Francis Hospital
The First of Two Unnecessary Deaths

Elease Morris and Edward Morris were married on February 3, 1968, at the New Bethel Baptist Church in Opa Locka, a small municipality about 10 miles north of Miami. Both were black, born in small rural communities in Georgia, and both came from very large families—Edward was one of seventeen children and Elease one of fourteen. Elease graduated from high school in the town where she had been born—Donalsonville, Georgia.

The Morrises were community-minded people. They always gave 10 percent of their income to the church, which was the center of their lives. Elease was very service-oriented. She had a certificate in Red Cross home nursing and had worked for a number of years at Sunland Training Center, a facility for severely retarded children and adults. It had been her custom to bring retarded residents home on weekends just to show them different and more pleasant surroundings.

Edward, a big, gentle young man, was a sanitation employee with the City of North Miami, and nearly always held down one other part-time job, usually as a mechanic.

Elease was twenty-nine years old at the time she was admitted to St. Francis Hospital on Miami Beach on October 28, 1971. She and Edward had been unable to have children. Coming from a large family, this was a source of great concern to her since she wanted more than anything else to be a mother. She had seen a gynecologist, Dr. Rupert Arnell on October 21. He had found a few small fibroid nodules on her uterus as well as some swelling in the left fallopian tube and ovary.

Dr. Arnell was confident that the problem was minor, and felt that he would be able to remedy it. He recommended a dilatation and curettage (D&C), after which he contemplated doing a pelvic laparotomy to clear up the tube and ovary. A D&C is a minor operation, taking approximately ten to fifteen minutes, whereas the pelvic laparotomy involves the opening up and exploration of the abdomen.

Elease was in excellent general health. She could have the operation under general or "regional" anesthesia, but she was not consulted about this. As is customary throughout the entire hospital system across the United States, the patient has nothing to say about choosing his or her anesthesiologist. The surgeon theoretically has the right to choose a hospital staff anesthesiologist, but in practice a particular selection by the surgeon is almost never made. Rather, the anesthesiologists simply handle surgeries on a rotation basis.

Mrs. Morris met her anethesiologist, Dr. George Small, the night before her surgery, which is usual.

There is an old cliché that there is no such thing as

"minor surgery." This really refers to anesthesia. The anesthesiologist is often much more important than the surgeon. A surgeon doing a D&C or a hemorrhoidectomy couldn't kill a patient by himself no matter how incompetent he was.

Anesthesia means "no feeling." We feel pain when the body's warning mechanisms tell us that something bad or injurious is happening to our bodies. Surgery involves cutting, of course. Although it is done for the long-term good of the patient, it is still a trauma to the body. The body, therefore, feels pain and a person will flinch and move, at the least, when being operated upon. Anesthesia has changed this.

Anesthesia nowadays also involves sedation and a lowering of the patient's consciousness. The drugs used for this purpose have very complex effects on our body chemistry. The anesthesiologist's job is to keep the patient sedated or asleep, free from pain during the procedure, and at the same time, to maintain an "airway" to keep the patient's blood rich in the oxygen which keeps the brain and all body tissue alive.

It is within the anesthesiologist's sole discretion to decide on the type of anesthesia to be administered, the number and dosages of drugs, and the method by which they are to be administered. Dr. Small did not ask Dr. Arnell for his opinion concerning anesthesia, and of course Dr. Arnell did not volunteer it.

Dr. Small decided not to give general anesthesia to Elease Morris. Instead, he gave an epidural anesthetic, which is a "regional block." Unlike general anesthesia, where an endotracheal tube is inserted down the throat and the patient is completely unconscious, when a regional block is used a patient may be at least partly aware of what is going on. A "regional block" simply means that all feeling is deadened and all movement is paralyzed below the point in the patient's body where the injection is made.

An epidural block is similar to a "spinal," but in the latter procedure the needle goes in the subarachnoid space. The needle penetrates through the bones of the spine, through a continuous tough covering called the dura, and the anesthetic comes into close contact with the big bundle of nerves making up the spinal cord.

In an epidural, the needle stops in a small area just outside the dura, which reduces slightly the possibility of nerve damage. This older method, little used for this type of procedure nowadays, is safer than a spinal in one way (less danger of damage to the spinal cord), but it is less exact. Furthermore, a far greater quantity of anesthetic agent has to be used to produce the same effect as a spinal injection, paralyzing the same nerves to the same extent. A larger needle is used in giving an epidural than a spinal. Dr. Small used about eight times as much of the anesthetic drug (Carbocaine) as he would have when giving a spinal.

On the morning of October 29, 1971, before the D&C commenced, Dr. Small turned Mrs. Morris on her left side for the epidural anesthetic with her knees drawn up to her chin, stretching the back. First, he numbed the skin and subcutaneous tissue of her back with novocaine and ephedrine. This made it possible then to puncture her back painlessly with the much larger needle containing the Carbocaine.

A sufficient amount of Carbocaine was injected to take care of the pelvic laparotomy as well. The epidural took two minutes for Dr. Small to administer. In addition, Mrs. Morris received Valium, Talwin, and atropine, other anesthetic agents.

Prior to the surgery, Dr. Arnell spoke briefly with Mrs. Morris to reassure her. The only thing she said was simply, "Please try to do something so I can have children."

After Dr. Small completed the epidural block, Mrs. Morris rolled over onto her back with the trunk of her body flat on the table. Her legs were put up in stirrups and spread—a position known as the lithotomy position. The nurse then did a "sterile prep," shaving and very thoroughly washing the operative area of the vagina. Dr. Arnell came in from "scrubbing," draped the patient, and proceeded with the D&C. Mrs. Morris remained awake throughout this minor procedure.

For the pelvic laparotomy, the patient was to be placed completely flat on the table. Her legs had to be lowered out of the stirrups and her whole body had to be moved up the table, to provide a place for her legs to rest. The bringing of the patient's legs down from the stirrups to lie flat on the operating table is a movement of critical importance. That is where things started to go wrong.

It is an accepted medical fact, as it appeared in the testimony in this case, that the ability to transfer the blood supply to a needed area quickly is diminished or may even be eliminated by the use of epidural or other regional blocks. This phenomenon can easily be illustrated by the layman. If a thin person, or a person with prominent blood vessels in his arm, holds his arms down for a time, so that the vessels are clearly visible, then raises one arm quickly above his head and again lowers that arm, he will see a very fast change. The vessel is no longer prominent. The body adjusts hemodynamically. This is normal, but an effect of regional block anesthesia is to interfere with this mechanism.

When the legs are up in stirrups, the blood drains into the general circulation and the patient has a nice, full reservoir of blood circulating so that there is an excellent supply of blood and oxygen through all the vital organs. When the patient's legs are brought down flat on the table, the blood goes into the legs and away from the brain, the heart, and other vital organs, and the patient does not have the ability to close the blood vessels and push the circulation back to those organs.

Prior to trial, during the depositions, and during the trial, there was a conflict in the testimony as to precisely how Mrs. Morris was moved, and by how many people. The surgeon, Dr. Arnell, testified that he had a distinct recollection of a nurse taking each leg out of the stirrups and slowly placing Mrs. Morris's limbs flat on the table (This would be the proper way to do it.) Nobody else in the operating room was so certain that two nurses had moved the legs. Dr. Arnell himself could not recall the names of either nurse.

The operative record in the patient's hospital chart contains an account of everything that occurs in the operating room and lists all personnel present. In Elease Morris's case, only one nurse was listed. Moreover, she was not identified as a "circulating nurse" or a "scrub nurse." If she was the scrub nurse, she would have had to be "sterile" and could not have taken part in the repositioning of Elease's body.

It was to be my contention that Mrs. Morris was moved improperly and that she was not being monitored adequately by Dr. Small during this crucial time frame. Furthermore, I intended to prove that proper procedure in this maneuver was an obligation both of the hospital employees, (the nurses in the operating room) and Dr. Small.

During the movement from the lithotomy position to the flat position Elease Morris sustained a cardiac arrest. To state it more simply, her heart stopped. What happened immediately after became very important.

Dr. Small testified that he had a stethoscope strapped to the precardial area, right over the heart, but when they were moving the patient, he removed the stethoscope because "I didn't want to hurt myself." He estimated that the stethoscope was out of his ears between one and a half and two minutes. During that time, neither Mrs. Morris's heart nor her pulse was being checked by anyone.

After the patient was flat on the table, Dr. Small returned the stethoscope to his ears. He heard no heart sounds whatever. Later, he made this note in the chart:

When placed supine and flat, blood pressure disappeared and heart sounds were not heard. Circulation was restored within two minutes.

The surgeon wrote the following in his operative report:

At surgery, an epidural anesthetic was administered. Nothing unusual was noted during the short, minor operation. After the patient was placed in position and was being prepared for the pelvic laparotomy, the anesthesiologist informed me that the heart beat was not discernible. Heartbeat, pulse, blood pressure and respiration were restored, certainly within two minutes of this notification.

As the expert testimony showed at the trial, for such a brief period of cardiac arrest, there should not be any permanent brain damage in a young, healthy individual, with normal circulation.

When a cardiac arrest occurs in an operating room, there should be a preplanned routine for resuscitation of the patient. A surgical resident had been waiting to assist Dr. Arnell in the major surgery, which never began. Dr. Arnell testified that the resident had to give only one boost or push to Mrs. Morris's chest, which revitalized her and started the heart beating again. In contrast, however, Dr. Small testified that the resident pushed on the chest between six and twelve times.

The important thing to do was to get oxygen into the patient as soon as possible. Dr. Small exposed the opening of the throat with a laryngoscope, lifting back the tongue, and inserted an endotracheal tube down Elease's throat.

After inflating a small inflatable cuff, which made sure he had a good snug seal, and that therefore there would be no air leak, he was able to inflate the lungs periodically with oxygen applied under pressure. He also administered adrenaline, sodium bicarbonate and solumedrol, agents designed to stimulate heart activity and to combat blood acidosis.

After the cardiac arrest and resuscitation, Mrs. Morris was hooked up to a cardioscope. This is an instrument for measuring electrical changes, and is the device we often see on TV shows with the constantly changing bleeps. Interestingly, Dr. Small testified that in young patients, it was not his procedure and is not the customary procedure of anesthesiologists to hook the patient up to a cardioscope. The assumption is that the patient's heart is in good condition. As Dr. Small said:

The cardioscope is a wonderful instrument for determining rhythm changes. You can have a sinus rhythm on it and have a dead patient in front of you since you are not measuring the force of the heartbeat, and electrical impulses can continue even after a patient has died.

Because the arrest in Mrs. Morris's case was so brief, and because the cardioscope showed her heart to be functioning normally, Dr. Small was convinced that she had suffered no permanent damage. The longer a cardiac arrest lasts, and the longer the brain is deprived of vital oxygen, the more likely it is that there will be permanent damage or death.

Dr. Small was so optimistic that he suggested to Dr. Arnell that they proceed with the pelvic laparotomy. Dr. Arnell wisely said no and canceled the rest of the procedure.

The surgery had started about 8:00 A.M. The cardiac arrest occurred at 8:20 A.M. Mrs. Morris had not regained consciousness by 11:30 A.M. at which time she was taken from the operating room to the recovery room.

This is the area where patients are normally taken to regain consciousness after surgery and before being returned to their rooms.

Mrs. Morris did not regain consciousness in the recovery room either. She was transferred to the intensive care unit of the hospital at 2:00 P.M. At this point, the medical niceties were breached when the medical director of St. Francis Hospital asked Dr. Morton Korn, a highly respected internist, to see the patient. Prior to this, the director had also called a neurologist, Dr. Robert Raskin. Both of these consultations were made without any discussion with Dr. Small, a fact which greatly offended him and which I believe influenced his attitude and testimony toward the hospital. Yes, psychology applies to doctors as well as to "ordinary" people. Small said about the consultants:

I practically lived with her for forty-eight hours after the arrest, even though she was taken away from me as a patient. I was essentially told I was "off the case." After all, I am not qualified as an internist. This is internal medicine we are talking about even though it happens to be in my field, but I am not looked upon as a professor. I am a nobody. I know more about it than any of those guys, but nobody asked me. They took it away from me.

The medical director and Dr. Arnell both denied that they intended in any way to have Dr. Small removed from the case; particularly since the maintenance of an airway in an unconscious patient is most clearly the responsibility of the anesthesiologist. They simply wanted additional opinions.

Amazingly, neither Dr. Korn nor Dr. Raskin had any direct contact with Dr. Small concerning Mrs. Morris. Again we see the problem of failure of communication in an age of narrower and narrower specialties. Ideally, these doctors and Dr. Arnell should have sat down together, pooled their experience and endeavored to come up with a diagnosis—and more importantly—a solution.

Lack of communication between doctors, interns, nurses and administration is endemic throughout medicine. Everyone is preoccupied with their particular niche, not the total picture or the total patient.

As to Elease Morris, there was lack of communication between doctors and nurses concerning how and when her legs should be moved. Likewise, there was confusion concerning the manner and frequency with which the patient should have been suctioned in intensive care. The defense did not call as witnesses the nurses who supposedly moved the patient, and I stressed the omission in my summation.

Dr. Raskin examined Mrs. Morris in the intensive care unit at approximately 3:00 P.M. on the day of her surgery. At that time she was unconscious and unresponsive to all forms of stimulation, including pinching, loud clapping noises, and the like. Dr. Raskin found her to have "decerebrate posturing," which is a term describing abnormal reflex movements of the arms and legs, caused by malfunctioning of the brain. At that point, however, he could not tell whether the brain damage was reversible or not. His opinion was that it was much too soon to make a prognosis, but the information given to him, that the cardiac arrest had lasted only a short time, gave some reason for optimism. He testified that he had seen patients as bad as Elease Morris get completely better without any brain damage.

Dr. Korn saw Mrs. Morris at 4:00 P.M. He felt that she had almost no chance for survival. (I was to argue that the hospital personnel had reached the same conclusion, even much earlier, and had given up on her. She did not get *intensive* care, I argued, and that was what was vital to her struggle for life.) Dr. Arnell, Dr. Small and the surgical resident had all stated that the cardiac arrest lasted two minutes or less. If so, I contended that she would have recovered if she had received aggressive and proper aftercare.

Dr. Korn's opinion was that during her cardiac arrest, Mrs. Morris must have been without effective respiration and circulation for at least three to five minutes. He based this on the amount of neurological damage he observed. He made one note which was of great importance to me during the trial. He wrote on the chart that when he saw her at 4:00 P.M., Mrs. Morris's "chest was clear."

Dr. Korn admitted that he did not know what caused the cardiac arrest. His two best guesses (and he was frank enough to admit they were only "guesses") were either a rare sensitivity to certain drugs or that Dr. Small may have mistakenly given her a total spinal anesthesia. This latter speculation was wrong, but it really upset Dr. Small.

On pretrial deposition, I asked:

Q. Dr. Small, would you have any way of knowing whether or not any of the epidural anesthetic got into the spinal cord?
A. Getting into the spinal cord would mean my needle would have to puncture the cord. That would be a fantastic catastrophe. You do that to a patient and you've really had it. God, they'd hang me by the balls if I did that.

Dr. Small was refreshingly honest, down-to-earth and undoctorlike. I became more convinced of this than ever when, although he had been on the staff of St. Francis Hospital for eighteen years, he did not hesitate to point the finger of blame at them. Of course, the hospital attorneys argued that the only reason he did this was to save his own neck.

Codefendants nearly always coordinate their defenses. They lay off each other and preserve a united front against the plaintiff. This case was an exception, though. Dr. Small and the hospital were pointing at each other.

It was my job (and one I enjoy) to exacerbate the differences between the defendants. Frequently the personalities of the defense lawyers can play into my hands. Theoretically, they are on the same side and should work together.

In practical terms, they are both primarily interested in looking good and absolving their own client. The competition among "defense" firms for insurance business is fierce so there is some incentive to see a codefendant get tagged. This makes the "winning" defense lawyer look all the better by comparison.

Hospital politics can be vicious, and the trial attorney must sensitize his antenna to be aware of every nuance. Who doesn't like whom? A fired or disgruntled employee can turn into a star witness for the other side. As a direct result of the infighting between the defendants, Dr. Small ultimately left St. Francis Hospital.

Dr. Small was on the horns of a dilemma. He had fully expected Mrs. Morris to recover from the arrest in the operating room, and yet she died in the intensive care unit without regaining consciousness. The death occurred at 5:57 P.M., October 31st, fifty-seven hours after the D&C. Since according to Dr. Small, the arrest had not been serious, it followed that the hospital follow-up care must have been deficient in some way.

At the trial, the hospital and its attorney, L. Norton Preddy, even went as far as to accuse Dr. Small of falsifying records to his advantage. He had made a highly significant note at 6:00 P.M. on the day of surgery saying that the patient's mouth was "full of secretions" or "gunk."

Before the trial, of course, the attorneys had taken the depositions of all the physicians and nursing personnel involved. I therefore had a thorough view of what the testimony at the trial would be. Dr. Small said that Elease Morris went downhill after she had been taken over by the hospital and the other consultants. Dr. Korn and others thought the damage had been done at the outset. Dr. Arnell thought that the arrest had been handled quickly and efficiently.

I did not sue Dr. Arnell because I did not regard him as a responsible party. Many plaintiff's malpractice lawyers believe you should sue everyone in sight (the shotgun approach) and let the jury decide. I feel that you offend an intelligent jury by suing someone who is not negligent, and you can thereby cloud the issues of actual malpractice and causation.

Psychologically, I had leverage over someone in Dr. Arnell's position. If he came on too strong in trying to whitewash his colleagues, I could always add him as a defendant. I did not need to use this leverage since Dr. Arnell admitted he did not know what caused the arrest or subsequent failure to respond.

The note Dr. Small had made about a mouth full of "secretions" indicated that the patient's mouth had not been suctioned out frequently enough during the afternoon to maintain an adequate airway. Preddy accused Dr. Small of inserting this note in the hospital chart two days later, after Mrs. Morris died. He asked Dr. Small:

Q. Did she get the best possible care she could get at the hospital?
A. No, specifically I think the ICU [intensive care unit] care was a little negligent in that when I came in and found her mouth full of secretions, it indicated to me that she wasn't being suctioned as frequently as was necessary.

Preddy asked this question quite innocently on Dr. Small's deposition and expected the standard answer—that everything the hospital did was fine and dandy. If Small had said the aftercare was excellent, he would be more firmly on the hook since he was in charge when the cardiac arrest occurred. This answer by Dr. Small began the battle between the defendants.

In my opinion, the two major areas of possible negligence by the hospital were the movement of the patient's legs in the operating room causing a sudden circulatory problem and precipitating the cardiac arrest, and the suctioning or lack of suctioning in the intensive care unit. Dr. Small and several other physicians testified that there is no need for specific instructions about suctioning. He added that the nursing personnel in the intensive care unit, like any qualified nurse, would know that suctioning has to be done on a regular basis. The intensive care nurses testified that suctioning was performed frequently, and that indeed there was no instance of "a mouth full of secretions."

This testimony was important, because in an unconscious patient, suctioning is performed to avoid "aspiration" or breathing in of stomach contents into the lungs. When that occurs, pneumonia and death can follow rapidly.

As in all malpractice cases, the attorneys get a cram course in a certain area of medicine. I learned that aspiration can occur even though there is an endotracheal tube in place in the throat, with a cuff around the bottom. This, however would be highly unusual. The only way to discover whether aspiration has taken place is to have a chest X ray. Dr. Korn ordered an X ray at 8:00 P.M. on the day of surgery. He made another note of enormous importance saying that the X ray showed "massive aspiration."

In deaths occurring in an unusual manner, or in unusual patients, such as a healthy twenty-nine-year-old woman, the medical examiner's office frequently performs autopsies. An autopsy was performed on Mrs. Morris by Dr. Brian D. Blackbourne, who subsequently became a medical examiner for the District of Columbia. Prior to trial, therefore, we took his deposition in Washington, D.C. This was later read to the jury in Miami. His testimony was particularly important, because not being involved in the lawsuit and being in a very precise specialty (pathology), his opinions would not be colored by self-interest.

One of the most important points the attorneys for St. Francis Hospital attempted to prove on Dr. Blackbourne's deposition, was that from his microscopic slides, he could not observe any "stomach contents" in the lungs. Their theory, of course, was that the aspiration must have taken place in the operating room while the patient was still under the care of Dr. Small and not yet under the care of hospital personnel in the recovery room or the intensive care unit. They felt that if she aspirated later, the stomach contents would have appeared on the slides—but this theory was wrong.

Dr. Blackbourne made an important distinction between the case of a person who is in an automobile accident with a partially full stomach, becomes unconscious, and subsequently breathes in meat and potatoes, and the person who has been prepared for surgery and has not eaten for some twelve hours prior to surgery. Gastric juices, he said, do not have a physical, granular, or particular structure —so there is no way of looking at the slides of a lung and identifying discernible foreign material.

The only thing that he could see on the slides was marked bronchial pneumonia. In his expert opinion, however, the cause of the pneumonia was aspiration of stomach juices. The stomach acids clogging the lungs did not produce any foreign material which could be recognized microscopically. The questions remained—when did the aspiration occur, and what caused it, and who was responsible for its occurring?

When the case was first referred to us, I had sought

the opinion of experts. Jerry and I had never been involved in an anesthesia case until this one and initially, prior to filing the lawsuit, we had had no luck in getting an anesthesiologist to criticize Mrs. Morris's treatment. This is an important point.

Unless the plaintiff has at least one doctor who will testify that the treatment afforded by another doctor fell below accepted standards, the case will never get before a jury but will be thrown out by the judge. Despite not having an expert, though, our attitude was that a young, healthy woman went into the hospital for a minor surgical procedure and came out dead. For her family and for ourselves, we had to know why.

Once the lawsuit is filed, I gain the power to subpoena records and question witnesses. It often happens that a prospective medical expert needs all this additional information before he can properly evaluate a case. So I sometimes have to sue just to find out if there is a case.

Under such circumstances I always tell my client that if we cannot discover a viable area of malpractice, I will drop the case. They are then at liberty to retain other counsel. I feel that if you have a case of serious injury or death, you owe it to the client to at least explore the matter. This attitude has been fashioned by experience since I have achieved some very large awards in cases which were turned down by other lawyers. If I'm wrong on this type of decision, I have expended time and money unnecessarily, but if I'm right the plaintiff has financial security and I have earned a substantial fee.

The anesthesiologists we spoke to initially did not think that Dr. Small overmedicated the patient, nor did they think that he used inappropriate drugs. They told us that the manner in which he had administered the epidural block was standard. We decided to file the lawsuit, take depositions, and gather together the facts. We could not dream of the incredible circumstances which would delay this trial until 1974, and make it impossible for Jerry to assist me.

By the time the trial began, I had obtained expert testimony against the hospital, but hardly any against Dr. Small. One criticism of Dr. Small's treatment related to his responsibility in directing the movement of the patient by the nurses from the stirrups to the flat-on-the-back position. If the hospital did not have sufficient personnel or sufficiently trained personnel who knew of the extreme delicacy of this maneuver, that could not be held against Dr. Small. The only other possible criticism against Dr. Small related to whether Elease Morris had been monitored properly during the time she was moved.

One of the experts whose testimony I used was Dr. Allen Shepard, the brilliant anesthesiologist from the Miami Heart Institute. Dr. Shepard, like Dr. Small, had been a general practitioner for several years before deciding to specialize in anesthesiology. Interestingly—and amazingly—Norton Preddy used Dr. Shepard's partner, Dr. Hugh Forthman, to testify in defense of the hospital. This was an unheard-of occurrence, and yet strangely, it did not cause any friction between the two doctors, even though they were taking totally different positions on the merits of the case.

Preddy, in his skillful and aggressive style, tried very hard to show that if Mrs. Morris aspirated at all, it was in the operating room. He argued that if the aspiration occurred in the operating room, that would pardon the hospital since the surgeon and the anesthesiologist were completely in charge at that juncture. Against this, I was able to argue that no chest X ray was taken throughout the whole afternoon and surely one of the physicians would have ordered an X ray if they believed aspiration had taken place so early.

None of the doctors or other personnel in the operating

room thought that aspiration had taken place there. However, there is such a thing as "silent aspiration," which can occur without anyone being aware of it. Drs. Arnell and Small agreed, but did not think this had happened.

It was Dr. Shepard's opinion that if the chest was clear at 4:00 P.M. as Dr. Korn had written, this necessarily meant that Elease aspirated after that time. The signs of aspiration, he testified, would appear within thirty to sixty minutes following ingestion of foreign contents into the lungs. There was no way the chest could have been clear at 4:00 P.M. if she had aspirated hours earlier in the operating room.

Before the case was presented to the jury, the attorney for Dr. Small and his insurance company, Employers Commercial Union, George V. Lanza, settled with my client for $90,000. Considering the vagaries of litigation, this was an offer that Edward Morris simply could not refuse. The settlement left St. Francis Hospital as the only remaining defendant.

George Lanza had been discussing settlement all along, and I was fairly certain that we would settle with his client. I had mixed emotions about this because our strongest posture would be going to the jury against both defendants. Now, if Preddy could convince the jury that the negligence (if any) had been committed only by Dr. Small, we would get nothing more. And Preddy could really tear into Small since Lanza was not there to answer him.

The law in Florida, as in most states, prevents the jury from being told of the settlement or the amount of the settlement. As far as they knew, it was the case of *Morris v. St. Francis Hospital*—period.

It is generally very difficult to fix liability on a hospital in a malpractice case because these institutions are not responsible for the negligence of physicians on their staff. Private physicians are regarded in law as independent contractors, and even when nurses do something wrong, the hospital will frequently get off on the basis that the nurses were simply following the orders of independent physicians. The general legal theory is that the doctor giving the orders is always the "captain of the ship," with overall responsibility.

We proceeded against the hospital. It was vital to my case against St. Francis Hospital to show that the aspiration occurred in the intensive care unit. Two items in the chart were critical to this: first, Dr. Small's note that the mouth was "full of secretions" at 6:00 P.M.; and second, the X ray of 8:00 P.M. which showed "massive aspiration." Since, according to Dr. Korn, the chest was clear at 4:00 P.M. and the 8:00 P.M. X ray showed massive aspiration, I argued that the aspiration necessarily had to occur between 4:00 P.M. and 8:00 P.M.

Dr. Korn spent more than an hour on the witness stand trying to explain how Elease's chest could have been clear at 4:00 P.M. even though she had aspirated hours earlier. Dr. Shepard disagreed. Just as the jury had to make a choice between Dr. Shepard and Dr. Korn on this point, they had to make a choice between Dr. Shepard and Dr. Forthman on the general issue of responsibility of the hospital personnel in the intensive care unit.

Norton Preddy, an old adversary of mine from the Linda Powell case, has had an excellent track record in defending hospitals. He was so confident that his client never offered more than $8,000 to settle the case. Even though I knew (or at least was supposed to know) that all the defense attorneys for Dr. Fagan in the Powell case had simply "been doing their job," the memories of that long-drawn-out battle still lingered.

In the Powell case, I had had quite a few altercations with Preddy, a hot-tempered redhead who used to be an amateur boxer. Back then he had taken offense at one thing

I had said and pretended to interpret it as calling him a liar. Judge Nathan had interceded that time, telling Preddy that he had misinterpreted the situation. During Elease Morris's case, a similar thing occurred.

At one recess, while we were up at the bench before Judge John Gale, arguing some point of law, and out of the presence of the jury, Preddy took a relatively innocent remark I had made out of context and threatened to "knock the goddamn hell out of me."

If he was trying to intimidate me and force me to change my tactics, it did not work. When my opponent gets rattled, I get calm. Anything I can do then to upset him will impair his judgment. And I am a pretty good upsetter of cool people, let alone hotheads.

I said, "Norton, you see my hands? Well, they're not going to move. You just take your best shot, big man. I have been hit by bigger and tougher guys than you!"

At this point, Judge Gale wisely called a recess. Preddy was seething after my comment, but did not raise his clenched fist.

It would have been worth it (looking back on it!) to take one punch just to see Preddy get stomped, and not by me. Edward Morris, who was soft-spoken and mild-mannered, was built like an ox. If Preddy had been so foolish as to strike me, I knew what my client would do to him. Besides, Judge Gale would certainly have held Preddy in contempt and then one of his partners, who would have been unprepared, would have been forced to take over the defense.

Normally, in malpractice cases, and in all serious negligence cases, the insurance company attorneys come across as "pillars of society" and respectable "middle-class types." After listening to Norton Preddy's smooth and persuasive argument, I referred to this incident, which again sent him climbing the walls. I wanted the jury to see something beneath the facade he had just shown them. (Actually, we shook hands after the trial. I respect his ability as well as his concept of the advocate's role in a courtroom. Besides, I am a very good winner.)

Edward Morris was ready to leave the courtroom after the $90,000 settlement with Dr. Small, but I had done so much work that I just had to see what this jury of three men and three women would do. We had nothing to lose by going forward.

One of the ladies on the jury who had worked for a number of years in a Catholic school worried me. I was concerned about her because Norton Preddy cleverly had the mother superior of the hospital—which is run by an order of nuns—sit with him at the counsel table for the entire five days of the trial.

On the other hand, I had a basically believable case. Edward Morris was no superstar, but was a workingman who had suffered a tragic loss. Elease, moreover, had been an unusual woman, always willing to help people and wanting nothing more than to be the mother of Edward's children.

On Friday, February 8, 1974, the jury returned a verdict in favor of Edward Morris and against St. Francis Hospital in the sum of $150,000.

In support of the adage that "life goes on," Edward Morris married Irene Larkin at the New Bethel Baptist Church on March 2, 1974, the same church where he and Elease had been married. This was just one month after the jury verdict.

Yes, it's obvious that the marriage had been in the works a long time, but my referring attorney, Irvine C. Spear, and I insisted that Edward remain single at least through the trial. In fact, evidence of his remarriage would not have been admissible at the trial, but we felt that if the jury received any hint whatever that Edward had married, the case would be worthless.

Edward and Irene had been patient. Irvine Spear and I were present at their wedding. I was happy for them, but the emotion was fused with a deep sadness for Elease Morris, whom I had never met, and for my best friend, Jerry Burke, who could never be my trial partner again.

IV

Jerry Burke
——VS.——
Dr. Marshall Kessler and Parkway General Hospital

Jerry Becomes the Biggest Case of All

In January 1972, two months after Elease Morris's death, Jerry and I had a conference about her with an anesthesiologist, Dr. Lawrence J. Saidman at the Veterans Administration Hospital in Miami. In just three weeks Jerry was scheduled to enter Parkway General Hospital for hemorrhoid surgery. While we were there, in passing, Jerry asked the doctor if "those guys at Parkway know what they are doing." Saidman laughed. He assured us that the staff anesthesiologists there were certainly competent, and that hemorrhoid surgery was very simple.

Jerry had been troubled with hemorrhoids on and off for

a number of years, but in 1971 his symptoms had become worse, with periodic bleeding and increased pain. On the recommendation of his personal physician, Dr. Harvey Fleischer, Jerry went to see a surgeon, Dr. George Segal, on June 28, 1971.

Dr. Segal examined him and recommended surgery at some time in the future. Jerry did not like the idea, but he knew that something had to be done. He timed his entry into the hospital to coincide with our trial schedule, so that he would not miss any important work.

Jerry entered Parkway General Hospital on February 6, 1972 and was scheduled for surgery on February 9. I was in the office on that day and, by prearrangement, Geraldine Burke, his wife and my friend, was to call as soon as the surgery had been completed. She called about 10:15 A.M., sounding very upset. She had not been told much, but there was a problem. The surgery had never even begun, and Jerry was being transferred to another part of the hospital. I left my office immediately.

I raced to my car in the Standard Oil garage across the tracks from the courthouse and started up the North-South Expressway. It was about a twenty-minute ride to the hospital. As I raced north, all the way I kept thinking about what had happened to Elease Morris, and repeating to myself, "Jerry—he has to be okay, he just has to be."

Jerry had become my investigator eight years before. He proved so invaluable that he developed into my trial preparation man and most valued consultant. He also became my best personal friend.

Jerry had been born in the Bronx, New York, on March 16, 1932. He came to Miami with his parents when he was seven years old, attended South Beach Elementary School and graduated from Miami Beach High School. All through my junior high and high school days I lived less than 25 yards from South Beach Elementary and likewise graduated from Miami Beach High. Jerry was four years older than me. We did not know one another as teen-agers except by sight, but our backgrounds were quite similar.

I had come to Miami Beach from Brooklyn with my parents, entering the fifth grade at Central Beach Elementary School. The one great dissimilarity between us was that Jerry's parents did not push higher education. In the milieu in which I grew up, a college education was as basic as eating.

Jerry's father had been employed by the City of Miami Beach for many years before his death. Jerry had worked at numerous jobs and, within a short time after high school, went to work as a fireman for the City of Miami Beach. When we began working together he was still a fireman. Ultimately he would put in fifteen years before quitting the department and working exclusively with me. The Fire Department work schedule of twenty-four hours on and forty-eight hours off permitted him to handle all his duties. He was able to sleep during the twenty-four hours on at the department and make all necessary phone calls in connection with the law practice.

Jerry had always worked from the time he was a kid, selling newspapers in front of the Governor Cafeteria on Washington Avenue, through his teen-age years when he hawked sodas and program at the Orange Bowl. Again there was a similarity. My own work background was quite varied. I had done time as a beachboy at several of the major oceanfront hotels, squeezed juice at Lee's Health Bar, one block north of Lincoln Road on Collins Avenue, and had delivered every newspaper in the Greater Miami area. I worked my way through college at Dubrow's Cafeteria on Lincoln Road and also as a waiter while at the University of Florida, in addition to tutoring football players there.

Jerry and Geraldine had two lovely children—Michael,

aged twelve, and Debra, aged nine. The two things that meant everything to Jerry were his family and our work. He was an incredibly hard worker and enjoyed excellent health. He looked several years younger than his age, which was thirty-nine.

Although Jerry had only a high school education, he had more insight and better judgment than 99 percent of the lawyers I have ever known. If he had had a law degree he would have been an outstanding trial lawyer. He was superb at "reading" juries, simply because he understood and liked people so much. There are many lawyers who are brilliant from an academic standpoint, and yet are inept in the courtroom. Jerry understood the minds and prejudices of the average American because of his work background, his wide reading, and a great natural curiosity.

I thought of our conversation with Dr. Saidman. I thought of what had happened to Elease Morris. All these nightmares were flashing through my consciousness as I sped to Parkway General Hospital.

I raced up to the fourth floor, the site of the Coronary Intensive Care Unit. Geraldine greeted me with a look of absolute astonishment, and utter anguish. She told me that Jerry had not yet regained consciousness. She had called her parents and brother, who were all hurrying to the hospital. She did not call Jerry's mother, Rose Spanover, because she had recently sustained a serious heart attack and did not even know Jerry was going into the hospital.

Jerry often discussed our work in detail with Geraldine. She therefore had a much better understanding than most lawyers' wives of what is involved in a lawsuit, in terms of preparation and evidence. She was all too familiar with the facts of the Elease Morris case.

I talked to Dr. Segal later that day. He said he never touched Jerry. Jerry had a cardiac arrest before the operation ever began. I then spoke to the anesthesiologist,

Dr. Marshall Kessler. He admitted that he did not know what had happened. He could not explain it. He never had a similar experience in the past, he said.

Geraldine and I noticed a commotion in the corridor outside the Coronary Intensive Care Unit. A security guard was blocking the entrance. He would not let any unauthorized person in, nor would he answer any questions. An emergency "Code Blue" had been issued over the loud speaker from the unit. I knew that this was a signal that goes to all locations of the hospital. This was about 11:00 A.M. I was to find out later that the Code Blue was for Jerry. He had sustained a second arrest.

An unbelievable sequence of events was just beginning. I was being prepared for the most harrowing month I had ever spent. Jerry never regained consciousness. After several operations and desperation measures, he died on March 7, 1972. Geraldine and I practically lived at the hospital, hoping desperately that he would show some sign of recovery. The extraordinary thing was that with Jerry's full head of black hair and his lean, athletic body, even after weeks of being in a coma, he looked so good it was difficult to accept the idea that he was doomed.

After his death, I obtained Jerry's hospital records. I took them to Dr. Saidman and to other anesthesiologists. The news of Jerry's tragedy had spread like wildfire throughout the medical community of Greater Miami. Dr. Saidman in fact, was well aware of the situation before I came to see him.

After numerous medical conferences, I was convinced that flagrant malpractice had been committed. I had to get at the bottom of it and do everything I could to provide for his family. I filed suit in the Dade County Circuit Court on June 21, 1972.

Even before I filed suit, it was obvious that I was going to have one problem. I knew Jerry's whole background, his wife, his mother, his children. I had been his friend and employer. I had been at the hospital within hours of his first cardiac arrest. I had spoken with the surgeon and the anesthesiologist, Dr. Kessler. I had seen Jerry's last tormented month of life while they operated and performed all sorts of procedures on him. Of course, I would be a major witness in the trial, and you cannot be both a lawyer and a crucial witness.

I called into the case two friends and colleagues, Richard Fuller (now a circuit judge) and Edward Moss, both excellent trial lawyers from the firm of Fuller, Brumer, Moss and Cohen. We prepared the case together. I spoke to almost every reputable anesthesiologist in town and did the most exhaustive medical research. Rick, Ed, and I attended each of the numerous depositions. We deposed every doctor, every nurse, every technician, every inhalation therapist, and anybody who had anything to do with the case.

On his deposition, Dr. Segal, the surgeon, said that he did not see Jerry at the hospital prior to his entry in the operating room on February 9, 1972. Dr. Segal went in to say hello, but by that time Jerry was on the table in the "jackknife" position and appeared to be asleep. Dr. Segal said that usually his patients are awake at this time. Seeing that Jerry was unconscious, he then proceeded to "scrub" —to make himself sterile for the operation.

Dr. Marshall Kessler administered a spinal anesthetic while Dr. Segal was scrubbing. Dr. Segal returned and looked at Jerry, who had his rump up in the air and his head and feet down on opposite sides of the table which had been "broken" in the middle. In surprise, Dr. Segal exclaimed, "It looks as though the patient is turning blue!"

When Dr. Segal made that comment, he was behind Jerry and to his rear, perhaps two to three feet away. According to Dr. Segal, when Dr. Kessler heard this exclamation, he went from his previous position at Jerry's side, where he had been administering the spinal anesthetic, to the head of the table. (If Jerry's pulse had been monitored, either by mechanical means or by a nurse taking his pulse at this time, the problem would have made itself apparent long before any change in his color occurred.)

Dr. Kessler tried to resuscitate Jerry. After Jerry was turned on his back, Dr. Segal began external cardiac massage. At the same time, he asked that the cardioscope be hooked up. The monitor showed a flat line, indicating there was no cardiac activity whatever.

Dr. Segal testified, "I think it took more than a short period of time for the heart to come back. I think we must have massaged for a minute or so before it came back."

Dr. Segal followed Jerry to the Coronary Intensive Care Unit but left him with Dr. Kessler. The surgeon returned to another operating room to perform another operation. Dr. Segal was in surgery, in fact, at the time of the Code Blue, but was able to leave everything to an assistant and go to "Coronary Care." When he arrived, Dr. Kessler was gone. Jerry was in convulsions.

No physician was present with my friend, who had suffered a second cardiac arrest! All there was was a nurse, who had several other critically ill patients to watch as well. She had observed that Jerry was not breathing, and she had issued the emergency call.

Dr. Segal and another physician attempted to place a tube down Jerry's throat to administer oxygen but could not because the throat was so swollen. They had therefore to perform a tracheotomy—a procedure where an incision is made in the throat below the Adam's apple, a hole is made into the windpipe, and a tube is pushed in. They got the heart going again.

My impression of Dr. Kessler from my limited contact with him at the hospital was that he was strange. I later learned that he had an impressive academic background and, in fact was Board Certified in the field of anesthesiology. He reminded me of some law review scholars who are knowledgeable on paper but could not handle the trial of a contested case if their lives depended on it.

My impressions were confirmed on Dr. Kessler's three depositions which extended over many, many hours. It all seemed to be a mystery to him. I didn't expect him to admit fault, but I did anticipate that he would at least express regret—something he never did. In fact, while Jerry was still deep in a coma on February 19, Dr. Kessler left on vacation, not returning till two days after Jerry's death.

Dr Kessler had held my friend's life literally in his hands. His answers to questions did not inspire much confidence in me.

Q. Please tell me your name and profession.
A. Marshall Kessler, and I am an M.D.
Q. How old are you?
A. Thirty-four, I guess.
Q. You guess? When were you born?
A. 1938.
Q. Give me your birthdate so we can work it out.
A. November 21, 1938. No—33.
Q. What condition was Jerry Burke in when you first saw him that morning?
A. He was awake and responsive.
Q. Did you chat with him when you first saw him that morning?
A. No, I didn't *chat* with him. *(This specialist was responsible for the death of my best friend, but he was playing word games with me.)*
Q. Did you talk with him then?
A. Yes, I did.

Dr. Kessler had received his M.D. degree from St. Louis University in 1965. He served his residency at Northwestern University's Department of Anesthesia, completing it in

December, 1969. He joined Dr. Miguel Figueroa, who headed a group of nine anesthesiologists, in February 1970. Dr. Figueroa's group had the anesthesia monopoly on all surgeries at Parkway General Hospital.

Q. Doctor, do you recall having a conversation with Dr. Figueroa on the morning of Jerry's Burke's surgery?

A. Yes.

Q. Was this prior to the time you saw Jerry Burke for the very first time?

A. Right.

Q. Where did that conversation take place?

A. I can't remember where we were at the time, somewhere in the operating room suite.

Q. What was the nature of the conversation that you and Dr. Figueroa had?

A. Simply that I was told by Dr. Figueroa that the patient appeared apprehensive to him, and that he had medicated him accordingly.

One of the strange things about the practice of anesthesia is that this is quite frequent; for one member of the anesthesia group to do the preoperative evaluation and see the patient prior to the operation, but for another one to do the actual procedure.

Jerry Burke would be alive today if Dr. Figueroa, in his short visit to Jerry's room the night before surgery, had not misunderstood Jerry's intellectual curiosity. Everyone who knew Jerry knew that asking questions was second nature to him. This was how he learned so much about so many different things.

It was because Dr. Figueroa thought that Jerry was unusually apprehensive that both he and Dr. Kessler overmedicated him.

Q. Was there anything that Jerry did or said during the morning of surgery that would have caused you to conclude, inde-

pendently of what Dr. Figueroa said, that he was unusually apprehensive?
A. No.

Dr. Segal did not feel that Jerry was apprehensive, either. This lack of apprehension was confirmed by a comment Jerry made to the nurses in the holding area prior to the surgery: "Everything's bottoms-up this morning."
What had happened to Jerry?
The night before the surgery, Dr. Figueroa had examined Jerry and prescribed several drugs to be administered the next day, by hospital nursing personnel and by Dr. Kessler. The first of these was Nembutal, to be administered at 10:00 P.M. on the night before surgery. The next morning, at 6:30 A.M., a nurse was to administer a shot of 100 milligrams of Nembutal I.M. (intramuscularly). Nembutal was described in his testimony by Dr. Kessler as a "rapidly acting barbiturate which causes sedation." By giving it I.M. instead of I.V. (intravenously) its effect on the body was slower and therefore longer-acting.
In addition, Dr. Figueroa ordered that two cubic centimeters of Innovar be administered at 7:40 A.M. intramuscularly, together with .4 milligrams of atropine. The atropine would decrease secretions in and relax the windpipe and bronchial tract. Innovar is an extremely potent narcotic, far more powerful than heroin. It sedates the patient, prevents pain, and induces complete oblivion so that the patient has no idea where he is.
Just before the operation was to begin, at 8:10 A.M., in the operating room itself, Dr. Kessler gave Jerry two cubic centimeters more of Innovar; this time intravenously. As soon as this had been done and Jerry was in the "desired state of oblivion," Dr. Kessler set up an intravenous drip of .04 percent Brevital, which was given between 8:10 and 8:28 A.M. Brevital is an ultra-short-acting barbiturate which

has many dangerous side effects. In fact, so dangerous is Brevital that it is one of the very few of thousands of drugs listed in the *Physician's Desk Reference* which has a warning box (such as the one for Chloromycetin in the Linda Powell case).

Jerry had arrived in the operating room before Dr. Kessler did. At that time he was able to move from the stretcher to the operating table by himself. Dr. Kessler "broke" the operating room table in the middle to set up the jackknife position, with Jerry on his stomach and each end of the table only a few inches from the floor. This meant, of course, that while Dr. Kessler was injecting the spine he could not possibly have a good view of Jerry's mouth and windpipe.

After administering the spinal anesthetic, Dr. Kessler testified that he took off his gloves and went to the head of the table. Nobody had been at the head during the three and a half minutes which Dr. Kessler estimated it took him to do everything connected with the administration of the spinal anesthetic. He was the only person "monitoring" Jerry during this period of time, and he was doing that by watching Jerry's back! I asked him:

Q. Did anything unusual happen when you returned to the head of the table after administering his spinal?
A. Yes. The patient began to hypoventilate.
Q. When did you first determine this?
A. When I reached the head of the table.

This was totally inconsistent with Dr. Segal's testimony that he was the first to notice any problem. This testimony was vital because the lapse of time during which Jerry was not breathing was critical not only legally, but also in terms of brain damage. The longer the brain is deprived of oxygen, the more likely it is that there will be irreversible damage. Most medical authorities agree that oxygen deprivation which lasts three to four minutes will result in permanent damage or death.

Q. What did you do?
A. I attempted to straighten the patient's airway and to stimulate him to take deep breaths. I did this for forty-five seconds or thereabouts. *(Kessler wasted valuable time with Jerry in an upside-down "jackknife" position, with his head below most of the rest of his body.)*
Q. Did you get Mr Burke to breathe?
A. No, I did not.
Q. Was Jerry still in the jackknife position during this time?
A. Yes.

I had, of course, obtained expert testimony in abundance before the case was ever filed, but when Dr. Kessler's account of what he did to attempt to cure the cardiac arrest problem became available to me, I obtained far more ammunition.

Q. What did you do next?
A. I attempted to ventilate him with intermittent positive pressure.
Q. By an oxygen mask?
A. I used an oxygen mask and bag, squeezing the bag.
Q. How long did you attempt this type of ventilation?
A. Probably thirty to forty-five seconds.
Q. Was Mr. Burke still in the jackknife position during that period of time?
A. Yes.

This delay in turning Jerry over onto his back was to be one of the main areas of criticism by my experts. It was readily apparent that overmedication, improper and insufficient monitoring, and leaving Jerry in the jackknife position for far too long were just the beginning steps in a unbelievable trail of neglect.

Q. Did this work?

A. No, I was not able to ventilate the patient in this position. *(Of course not—and any doctor should know that!)*

Q. What was the status of Jerry's vital signs?

A. His respiration ceased.

Q. When?

A. Some time during the course of this two-minute period of time.

Q. Isn't it true that the very first time you attempted to take Mr. Burke's pulse or blood pressure was *after* you attempted to stimulate him and after the forced oxygen procedures?

A. Yes.

Q. When Mr. Burke's pulse and blood pressure were finally taken, were you able to obtain any?

A. To my recollection, no.

Dr. Kessler had made this notation in the hospital records:

It is estimated that the patient was without adequate respiration for about 3 to 4 minutes, and without adequate circulation for about 1 minute before adequate massage was instituted. He remained unresponsive after resuscitation and was taken to Coronary Care in fair condition with stable vital signs.

At 8:20 A.M. Jerry's blood pressure was normal. The next time it was recorded in the chart was 8:35 A.M.—after Jerry had been resuscitated. According to Dr. Kessler, respiration was reestablished quickly after Jerry was put on his back. My friend would probably still be alive if he had been turned on his back immediately. This would have been done as soon as the surgeon noted that he was turning cyanotic, or blue in color.

Once Jerry's blood pressure and pulse had stabilized. Dr. Kessler became very confident that he would be "just fine." Dr. Kessler suggested that they go ahead with the surgery, but Dr. Segal wisely declined the offer.

At 9:50 A.M., Dr. Kessler left the operating room with Jerry, and went with him to the Coronary Care Unit, where the doctor remained until 10:45 A.M. At that time, he said he had every reason to believe that Jerry would return to his normal state of good health; particularly since Jerry was responding to painful stimuli such as pinching, very loud noises, and slaps.

Dr. Kessler went to another operating room and was anesthetizing another patient when Jerry's "Code Blue" was called. He did not go back to Jerry until 1:10 P.M., long after the tracheotomy had been performed and the "vital signs" again stabilized by other physicians. Prior to leaving the Coronary Care Unit at 10:45 A.M., Dr. Kessler had made no effort to insert an endotracheal tube, which is the best way of insuring that there is an adequate supply of oxygen to the patient's lungs.

In addition, where a patient has had a period of cardiac arrest and decreased circulation, there is an extreme danger of a buildup of acid, a condition called acidosis, which must be watched very closely. The way of doing this is to take samples of blood from the arteries for analysis in the laboratory. If there is acidosis, sodium bicarbonate can be administered to restore the chemical balance. Dr. Kessler had ordered no arterial blood gasses because he was confident that they were not necessary. He took no measures to guard against aspiration (the breathing in of gastric juices vomited up from the stomach), since, he testified, he was quite impressed with the quality of Jerry's reflexes. Each and every one of these failures were, in the opinion of my experts, examples of mismanagement and malpractice.

I took the deposition of Dr. Figueroa, the head of the anesthesia group. Dr. Figueroa admitted that he told Dr. Kessler that Jerry Burke was apprehensive and that he should medicate him accordingly. According to Dr. Figueroa, he did not suggest the medications to be used, or the dosages.

A substantial conflict developed in the testimony between

the two doctors as to the manner in which this conversation took place. Dr. Kessler said that they had conferred in person on the morning of surgery. Dr. Figueroa disagreed. He was doing anesthesia at another hospital during the morning of Jerry's surgery. According to Dr. Figueroa, the conversation about Jerry's apprehension took place with Dr. Kessler on the telephone on the night of February 8, and no conversation took place on the morning of the surgery.

I asked Dr. Figueroa about Jerry:

Q. Jerry appeared to be intelligent, and his questions were intelligent, weren't they?
A. Yes, sir.
Q. Did you enjoy your chat with him?
A. Yes, sir.
Q. Did you walk away liking him?
A. Yes, sir. He was quite worried about his surgery. He told me he was investigating another case that had had similar surgery done. He said, "Doctor, don't mind me. I know a little bit, and it is bad to know a little bit."

I asked Dr. Figueroa about Dr. Kessler:

Q. When Dr. Kessler came with your group, did he undergo any specific training as to what procedures he would employ during various kinds of surgeries?
A. No, sir. I relied on the training he had had.

Dr. Kessler had been asked to leave Dr. Figueroa's professional group in April 1972, shortly after Jerry's catastrophe. Another patient he had anesthetized before Jerry, and still another patient he attended to after Jerry's death, had died. I asked Dr. Kessler about this. He responded that some members of the group felt that he had a "black cloud" over his head.

While Jerry's case was pending, one of the nation's outstanding malpractice attorneys, J. B. Spence, obtained a

large damage award on behalf of a client whose child had
died under the care of yet another member of the Figueroa
group. The "black cloud" seemed to be rather diffuse.

I continued with Dr. Figueroa:

Q. What were the circumstances of Dr. Kessler's departure from
your professional association?

A. After the Burke case, he had another case where someone
died. It was a known fact that a suit would come after the
Burke case, and we were quite worried about it because of
the tremendous expense of malpractice insurance. *(But he
wasn't worried from the standpoint of finding out what went
wrong and taking affirmative measures to see that it never
happened again!)*

Q. Was your concern primarily about the expense of malpractice
insurance or were you concerned about Dr. Kessler's ability
to treat patients?

A. I don't recall being concerned about his ability to treat
patients. He came to us with the highest of credentials, and
he certainly is qualified to do anesthesia from all the papers
he's got.

After the medical depositions were transcribed, Rick, Ed,
and I sat down with other anesthesiologists. This was not a
close question as to whether or not a physician had used
poor judgment. This situation was flagrant, with one egregi-
ous error piled on top of the other.

It also was incredible because Jerry and I often joked
about the fact that our important cases, such as Burgel and
Powell, were also super-difficult from the standpoint of
proving liability. We used to ridicule other lawyers who
got big verdicts and big reputations on the easy cases, such
as a wage earner who loses a leg in a rear-end automobile
collision. We would rationalize by saying that we got much
greater satisfaction out of a case by achieving the impossible after a long and hard road had been traveled.

There are four main ingredients needed to win big for a

client. These are liability, causation, damages, and insurance coverage. Getting a case that's worth $250,000 doesn't do anyone any good if there is only $10,000 worth of insurance coverage. Ironically, in Jerry's case, all of the ingredients were present. We finally had an "easy" case.

It is difficult to imagine a malpractice case where the defendant physician and his insurance company will not be able to produce expert testimony exonerating the physician. Even here I had to assume that the insurance company would be able to get experts to come in and say that everything Dr. Kessler did was O.K. I was confident, though, that any reasonable jury would disbelieve this, and would find that massive malpractice had been committed on Jerry Burke.

Dr. Saidman had declined to testify in the Morris case, believing that Dr. Small had not committed malpractice. In Jerry's case, although Dr. Saidman had since moved to the University Hospital in San Diego, California, he agreed to testify for us. And he did this in spite of the fact that he knew Dr. Kessler quite well.

I learned of an incident which had occurred following Jerry's death. Dr. Kessler was never called before any committee at Parkway General Hospital to explain what had happened, but he did voluntarily appear at a meeting of the Anesthesia Department of the Veterans Administration Hospital. Dr. Saidman had been present, too, together with interns, residents, and nurses.

After Dr. Kessler finished explaining what had happened in the operating room on February 9, 1972, Dr. Saidman said that you could hear the proverbial pin drop. It was obvious from his own explanation that Dr. Kessler had violated several basic tenets of good anesthesia practice.

Our experts agreed that Jerry had been overmedicated. In addition to that, the various drugs had been administered to "peak" or reach their maximum effect at approximately the same time. The effect of intravenous Brevital is instantaneous. It is commonly referred to as an "induction agent," which takes a patient from a state of consciousness to an immediate state of oblivion. Jerry had received Nembutal, Innovar, atropine, and Brevital in addition to the spinal anesthetic.

The defense attorneys sent numerous detailed questions, called interrogatories, to us, feeling out the opinions of our experts. The answers left them in little doubt that we could prove our case. It was terrible anesthesia practice to put a patient to sleep before beginning the spinal anesthetic. Jerry's respiration was depressed by the medication, and by his jackknife position. It was bad practice that no one was monitoring him at the head of the table, checking his breathing and color. If an anesthesiologist leaves a sleeping patient to do a spinal under these circumstances, he has for all practical purposes abandoned the patient.

One cannot adequately monitor respiration by watching the patient's thorax. The chest may move even if no air is passing the airways down into the lungs, and with no one at the head of the table, the airway is left unguarded. Because of all the drugs he had been given, including muscle relaxants, and the position Jerry was in, it was foreseeable that his airway would become obstructed.

The jackknife position itself seriously compromises breathing because it is difficult for the diaphragm to move down (towards the feet) and go out (pushing the stomach forward), allowing the lungs to inflate. With the head down, the weight of the abdominal contents rests on the diaphragm muscle itself, making its descent even more difficult than if the patient were lying quietly on his stomach.

My experts thought Dr. Kessler was also negligent because he did not take proper remedial action once he discovered the cardiac arrest. An initial effort to restore the airway was reasonable, and should have taken about fifteen seconds. Dr. Kessler should have checked the pulse in the large artery in the neck, the carotid artery. If you obtain no carotid pulse, you should conclude that the patient's circulation is severely embarrassed, and turn him over immediately on to his back.

Nothing effective could be accomplished with the patient in the awkward jackknife position. It is even very difficult to obtain a good "fit" on the face mask to effectively push oxygen into the lungs under pressure. Since the brain is the organ of the body which is most sensitive to lack of oxygen, time was of the essence.

The catalog of errors was long. All the experts agreed that Dr. Kessler abandoned Jerry a second time when he left him in the Coronary Care Unit unconscious, unable himself to guard his airway, and without someone in the immediate vicinity who was capable of managing an obstructed airway. The tongue of a patient under anesthesia can fall back into the pharynx, or the patient can regurgitate.

The insertion of an endotracheal tube will generally prevent either of these problems but this was not done. One of these two possibilities was the most likely the cause of Jerry's second arrest, which occurred while no doctor was present.

Jerry was in a coma from February 9 through March 7, 1972. He developed serious gastrointestinal bleeding and a "stress" ulcer. He also developed severe kidney and lung problems with acute renal shut down and pneumonia.

Medical specialists of every conceivable type were called in. Three major surgical procedures were performed on him; all without anesthesia, showing how deeply he was in a coma. My friend, who had never been cut surgically in his life, was savagely mutilated on his way to the grave.

Jerry was well known among the trial lawyers in town. During his long tragic hospitalization, many of them came to see him. They knew him not merely as an excellent investigator, but also as a truly singular person whose talents and unique qualities were recognized and appreciated.

One of these lawyers, a former partner of mine, would also be a witness. David Roemer, who had been a friend of Jerry's for many years, was a frequent visitor to the hospital. In 1963 David and I were practicing law with the late Roland W. Granat, a great pioneer Miami lawyer. Back then we had been very dissatisfied with investigative services we were getting from various professional agencies.

David and I had discussed this problem in detail, and David came up with the suggestion that we take a shot with a friend of his, a fireman. It was certainly the best shot I ever took in the practice of law because within a year, Jerry proved himself to be that rarest of commodities—the indispensable man.

Jerry was earning much more money than an average investigator. He was earning more money than average lawyers as well, and I was the only one who could explain in detail why he was worth so much. Although he couldn't question witnesses or argue points of law (since he lacked a law degree) we were a "trial team" in the most meaningful sense of that phrase. Jerry was compensated according to his ability, not his "papers."

Rick and Ed would question me about what Jerry meant to my law practice. It would be simple to convey to the jury just how outstanding he was: a fireman with only a high school education who became an integral component of a team which tried important and complex cases.

I was going to be in the unique position of persuading the jury from the witness stand—and when you are telling the complete truth about someone for whom you have very deep feelings, it becomes abundantly clear to the people who must make the decision. I always tell my witnesses to play it straight and be natural, and I knew that's all I had to do.

We spent hours with our experts. I had all types available, but my preference is to get doctors with impressive academic qualifications and broad practical experience. In addition, most importantly, they must be the type of witnesses who will impress a jury. A genius who mumbles or uses excessively technical language does the plaintiff no good.

I want my expert to make it very clear as to what the defendant did wrong. If he's going to be professorial or wishy-washy, I don't need him. In this case, the experts needed little prompting, as the malpractice was so blatant.

Geraldine and I wanted Jerry's case to be tried. We, therefore, made a demand for $1,500,000 from Dr. Kessler, Parkway General Hospital, and their insurance companies. We did not expect them to come close to this figure because Jerry had died without any conscious pain or suffering. We assumed that their thinking would take into account that Geraldine was young, attractive, and would undoubtedly remarry in the not too distant future.

Our main target by far was Dr. Kessler, but we felt that the hospital certainly had a responsibility to assist in monitoring; particularly when the anesthesiologist was administering a spinal anesthetic to a fully sedated patient.

The attorney for the defendant, Dr. Kessler, was a familiar adversary: John R. Hoehl, who had defended Dr. Fagan in the Powell case. He was, of course, also representing Dr. Kessler's insurance companies, Employers Surplus Lines and Employers Commercial Union. He offered $300,000. A few weeks later the offer was increased to $400,000 and after we had completed the taking of all depositions, the offer was increased to $500,000. At this point, negotiations were joined by Hoehl's partner, Samuel J. Powers, Jr., a former president of the International Association of Insurance Counsel (who incidentally briefly represented Richard Nixon in the Watergate proceedings).

We remained firm in our demand. Rick, Ed, Geraldine, and I had discussed settlement possibilities and reached an understanding that until the defendants came to $1,000,000 there was nothing to talk about.

Parkway General Hospital was insured by the Hartford Accident & Indemnity Company, and was represented by Samuel O. (Kit) Carson, of another big firm: Walton, Lantaff, Schroeder, Carson & Wahl. Throughout the case, the hospital had always taken the position that it was not guilty of any negligence. If there was any negligence, they said it was all Dr. Kessler's.

The case was scheduled to be tried before Dade County Circuit Judge Shelby Highsmith on April 9, 1973. We thought this gave us an advantage because Judge Highsmith had been an excellent trial lawyer himself. He was bright enough to fully comprehend the issues in a case of this kind, whereas a run-of-the-mill type of judge could have been a disaster because his rulings could create error, making a successful appeal possible. Moreover, with a less competent judge, a large number of objections and legal arguments will create delays which destroy the tempo and crescendo which the plaintiff hopes to construct in the minds of the jury.

Dr. Kessler was insured through Dr. Figueroa's professional association. He had a total of $1,000,000 worth of coverage. Just a few days before trial, we settled with him for a total sum of $950,000. When an insurance company pays this kind of money, you know what their own experts have told them about whether or not there was malpractice.

The hospital and its insurance company were still adamant. They would not pay a penny. I was not about to let the hospital out of the case unless it contributed a good chunk of money. I was incensed at the hospital because its executive director never so much as reviewed Jerry's chart, and never talked to the involved doctors and nurses about what happened. How were they going to guard against a repetition to another unsuspecting soul if they didn't study what happened here?

I let the hospital know that unless it contributed a substantial payment, we would go to trial against them alone, on April 9. Just before the trial was to begin, they paid $250,000, making a total settlement of $1,200,000.

Even in death, Jerry Burke was outstanding. The settlement was a record for the death of a nonprofessional person who had no conscious pain or suffering. The defendants paid so much because any jury would have been tremendously impressed with Jerry's background. He was earning very good money, and had an expected work life of many years with an almost unlimited earning potential. Moreover, the facts of how the malpractice occurred would have made the jury angry, and our lineup of experts was unimpeachable.

Failure of communication in a recurring theme throughout the hundreds of medical malpractice cases I have handled. In Jerry's case, these failures abounded.

Kessler was doing the spinal, Segal was scrubbing for surgery, and no one was watching ("monitoring") Jerry's breathing. Were the nurses having a coffee break? Were they discussing the latest hospital romance? Who knows how long the arrest lasted before Segal or Kessler noticed any signs! Who knows how long the second arrest lasted!

Figueroa saw Jerry the night before the surgery even though Kessler was to perform the anesthesia. This type of thing is done strictly for the convenience of the doctors. They are not going to let some patient interfere with what is really important—tomorrow's golf or tennis game.

Figueroa decides that Jerry, a total stranger, is unduly apprehensive. Imagine how apprehensive Jerry would have been had he known something about Dr. Kessler. If Jerry had told Figueroa a few jokes, maybe he would have ordered half dosages. Drugs, like alcohol, affect different people in different ways. Figueroa was ordering drugs in a vacuum.

Jerry didn't seem apprehensive to Kessler or Segal. But Kessler overmedicated him because he "seemed" that way to Figueroa. Figueroa says he called Kessler on the phone the night before surgery. Kessler says he and Figueroa talked the morning of surgery at Parkway General. But this was impossible since Figueroa was at another hospital miles away. Of course, neither Figueroa nor Kessler ever asked Dr. Fleischer (Jerry's admitting doctor) anything about apprehension or the patient's reactions to various drugs.

Kessler was hired by Figueroa because his "papers" or credentials looked good. If I had looked at Jerry Burke's papers rather than at the man when he asked me for a job, I wouldn't have hired him. Kessler was put completely on his own. No one instructed him or watched him. After all who could be hurt? Only unconscious patients!

Marshall Kessler to this day thinks he did nothing wrong. It's that damn "black cloud." Right. That's why his insurance company paid $950,000! He continued to use the same methods on other unsuspecting patients. Why not?

Lawyers get disbarred or suspended from the practice of law on an almost daily basis. Equivalent sanctions are almost never taken against physicians. Crooked lawyers generally only cost people money, whereas crooked or incompetent doctors cost them their lives and health.

Even the death of a healthy young man who was hospitalized for "minor" surgery did not improve the lines of communication. The nine medical members of the Figueroa group never got together to discuss Kessler's poor technique. (Nor did any medical committee of Parkway General Hospital.) No, they got together to discuss the rise in their malpractice insurance rates.

They got rid of Kessler not because he was a bad doctor or a danger to patients, but because he was costing them money. The naïve person would think that the hospital (and anesthesiologists and surgeons in particular) would want a meeting to learn something—so that this type of abominable tragedy would not be repeated.

Lack of communication led to Jerry's second arrest in the Coronary Care Unit. Segal went to another operating room and Kessler went to put yet another patient to sleep. They didn't even order a special nurse or intern for Jerry.

In the recent publicity about malpractice, largely dominated by the medical profession and the insurance companies, very little emphasis has been placed on the positive effects of malpractice cases. Without the ultimate opportunity of the citizen, represented by a competent lawyer, to ask a jury to give compensation where negligence is proven, the individual member of the public is at the mercy of incompetent physicians.

To make it clear, many physicians do a professional job all of the time. Most of the others do a professional job most of the time, but make some mistakes. A tiny number make a lot of mistakes. I think that malpractice cases serve to encourage the medical profession, which has been very lax in this regard, to maintain and improve the standards of medical practice, and above all, weed out incompetent and sloppy work.

Jerry's case and Elease's case are but two examples demonstrating that the whole method of administration of anesthesia is in need of a rigorous overhaul. The knowledge of these cases has probably done more to stimulate an attitude of carefulness in Greater Miami hospitals than all of the meetings of the Dade County Medical Association put together in recent years.

I had to finish Jerry's case, which occupied the great majority of my time, before I could move on with the Morris case. The Morris verdict came one day short of two years after the day of Jerry's arrests. The similarity between the two cases was astounding.

Both Jerry and Elease Morris went into the hospital in excellent health. Both went in for minor surgery, and both sustained arrests on the operating room table. Jerry arrested before the surgery ever began at all, whereas Elease Morris arrested before the major surgery ever began.

Both Jerry and Elease had regional blocks, with sedation —Jerry had a spinal and Elease had an epidural. None of my experts in either case felt that the administration of a regional rather than a general anesthetic, in and of itself, had anything to do with the arrest. Dr. Kessler was preoccupied with doing the spinal anesthetic when Jerry arrested, whereas Dr. Small was preoccupied with moving Mrs. Morris when she arrested. In neither case, moreover, was a hospital employee—a nurse or an assistant physician —monitoring the patient while the epidural and the spinal anesthetic were being administered.

In neither case did the surgeon ever discuss the anesthesia, or who would do the anesthesia, with their patients prior to the operation. Neither surgeon ever discussed the method of anesthesia with the anesthesiologist either. Neither Jerry nor Elease met their anesthesiologist before entering the hospital, and neither of them had anything to do with selecting that most important member of the team. The surgeon in both cases let the choice of anesthesiologist rest completely upon the rotation system used by the hospital. I didn't sue the surgeon in either case.

Both Jerry and Mrs. Morris were first hooked up to a

cardioscope *after* they had had a cardiac arrest. They both were given closed chest massage. Both of the anesthesiologists had been so confident that no permanent damage resulted from the "brief" arrests in the operating rooms that they told their respective surgeons to go ahead with their contemplated surgery. Both surgeons refused, and both anesthesiologists were dead wrong.

The similarities continued. Neither patient regained consciousness after the arrest. In each case, the anesthesiologist left the patient, to anesthetize other patients in other operating rooms. Following Jerry Burke's death, Dr. Marshall Kessler left the anesthesia group at Parkway General Hospital. Following Mrs. Morris's death, Dr. Small severed his relationship with St. Francis Hospital.

In each case the defense experts tried to theorize that each patient had an idiosyncratic reaction to certain drugs, or perhaps had had a stroke or a heart attack. In each case we had to prove that no such thing as stroke or heart attack or rare sensitivity to drugs had occurred.

A supreme irony to me is that I have now become an expert in anesthesia cases, although the Morris case had been my first. Nowadays, every time I question an anesthesiologist, or look at a hospital chart, Jerry's face is before me. His presence is always there in his former office, and it hovers at the courthouse. I am saddened every time I review files containing his written notes and dictated memoranda.

Jerry died nine days before his fortieth birthday—a milestone he always used to kid about. It was my sad task to deliver the eulogy at his funeral which was attended by hundreds of people from every walk of life. There were many lawyers, doctors and judges in the audience.

Just a few months later, Alan Schwartz and I had the privilege of participating in Michael's bar mitzvah, an occasion which was acutely solemnized by his father's absence. For Geraldine and Jerry's mother, it was a day of very mixed emotions.

About a year later, Jerry missed another event which would have given him great pleasure—the installation of Alan Schwartz as a Dade County Circuit Court judge. Alan, who had been at the hospital nearly every day of that awful month, regarded Jerry as a close friend.

Whenever he wanted to put "Burkie" in his proper place, Alan would do his famous imitation of a fire siren. It was fascinating to observe the Harvard Phi Beta Kappa arguing with the former Miami Beach fireman about points of law and tactics. In the majority of practical situations, Jerry would convince Alan to come around to his viewpoint.

My friend was in the prime of his life, and in the prime of a career he truly loved. He was a perfect blend of toughness and compassion and knew when each was appropriate. His word was his bond with everyone, and he brightened the lives of many people with his humor, understanding, and perceptiveness.

This book is dedicated to Jerry Burke. I do not expect to look upon his like again.

V

Antoinette Boatman
──VS.──
Osteopathic General Hospital

Malpractice and the Duty to Make a Decision

Antoinette Giambalvo, an Italian Catholic, married James Boatman in St. Louis, Missouri, in 1964. Her first husband had been killed in an automobile accident, leaving her with two daughters. Jim Boatman's first wife had also died, leaving him a daughter. Antoinette and Jim had no children from their own marriage. In 1968, they came from St. Louis to Miami, where Jim worked as a mechanic for Eastern Airlines.

Antoinette became a Jehovah's Witness some time after her marriage to Jim. The conversion began with that famous (or infamous) weekend knock on the door which is characteristic of that sect. Their religion became the dominant factor in her case.

Antoinette died in Osteopathic General Hospital on March 27, 1971. The cause of death was a "ruptured ectopic pregnancy with massive internal bleeding."

Several basic principles came into conflict in this case. One of those is written into the United States Constitution; that the free exercise of religion shall not be impaired. Another, built into the ethics of the medical profession for many centuries, is that doctors should always strive to preserve life. A third is that when a person is not in full control of his mental faculties he is presumed to be incapable of deciding what is best. In such circumstances, the spouse (as in this case), a parent or a legal guardian has the right and even the duty to make decisions for him.

One of the freedoms we cherish is the freedom to follow our consciences. An important tenet of the Jehovah's Witness religion is that a person is damned to hell and worse if he receives the blood of another. This is a well-known problem to medical doctors, some of whom have refused to treat Jehovah's Witnesses. There have been cases where courts have issued orders authorizing doctors to give transfusions to children over the strenuous religious objections of their parents. In the case of children, of course, one reason for such orders was that, although the parents had the right to follow their own conscience, where the effect of their decision was to endanger the lives of others, the children had a paramount right which the courts would protect. In the case of a fully competent adult, however, it is different.

Some time before the crisis which occurred in Antoinette's medical treatment, she had discussed her religious belief with Dr. Victor Glazer, who extracted from her an agreement that if and *only* if it became absolutely necessary for her to receive blood, she would accept it. During the last day of her life, however, while her body was going into shock and while she was bleeding to death, the other physicians who examined and treated her testified that she refused a life-saving blood transfusion.

Most of my cases are referred by other attorneys. Normally I prefer to investigate and develop the case from the beginning, but sometimes, as in this situation, the referral will take place after much of the work has been done. Mrs. Boatman's case came to me in a rather unusual way, in that her original attorney, Jay Swidler, had been the victim of a still-unsolved murder, subsequent to filing the Boatman case.

Swidler had filed suit against Osteopathic General Hospital and numerous defendants, including Drs. Newman, Yeamans, Shore, and Glazer. His theory of the case was that a medical doctor, Dr. Glazer, had initially misdiagnosed Mrs. Boatman's condition. Subsequently the treating osteopathic doctors in the hospital had negligently failed to administer necessary and lifesaving blood transfusions.

The suit had been filed against numerous defendants because, until testimony was taken, it was practically impossible to know exactly "who had done what" for Mrs. Boatman. The hospital, Dr. Willis Yeamans, and Dr. Leon Shore were all represented by Paul R. Larkin of the Blackwell firm, a fine trial lawyer and a gentleman. Dr. Glazer's lawyer was George V. Lanza, and Dr. Stanley Newman was represented by Raymond Dwyer of Carey, Dwyer, Austin, Cole and Selwood.

As the testimony at trial was to disclose, Mrs. Boatman had seen two physicians before her admission to the hospital on March 27, 1971, the day she died. On February 27, a month before her death, Mrs. Boatman had had a severe bout of lower abdominal pain. She went to see her osteopathic physician, Dr. Stanley S. Newman, who had taken care of her for the previous two years. He sent her to the emergency room at Osteopathic General Hospital, in North Miami Beach, suspecting a kidney stone. She began to feel better and did not need an overnight hospitalization.

Mrs. Boatman felt fine for the next several days, but because she had missed one menstrual period, on March 2, 1971, she went to see Victor Glazer, a doctor who specialized in obstetrics and gynecology. Dr. Glazer judged her to be approximately eight weeks pregnant.

This was Mrs. Boatman's first visit to Dr. Glazer. She advised him that she was a Jehovah's Witness and could not receive another person's blood under any circumstances. According to Dr. Glazer, at the trial, he told her that he could not accept her as a patient unless she allowed him to give blood if in his medical opinion a dire emergency existed. After thinking this over, and without any pressure being exerted by the doctor, Antoinette agreed that she would accept blood, but only if it was absolutely necessary. Dr. Glazer accepted her as a patient on this basis, although their understanding was never formalized in writing. This conditional consent was known only to Dr. Glazer and was never made known to the other physicians, the osteopaths who came into the case on March 27.

Antoinette saw Dr. Glazer a second time on March 15, giving a history of vaginal bleeding since March 13. He saw her again on March 16 and 17 because of continuing complaints of bleeding and pain. On the morning of March 17, she called him excitedly from home saying that she had passed a blood clot or some tissue. He had her come to the office immediately. After examining her, he made a diagnosis of "complete spontaneous miscarriage" or abortion. He told her to come back in one week.

Mrs. Boatman returned on March 25, 1971, two days before her death. This was the last time that Dr. Glazer ever saw her. He examined her and found everything to be normal and corroborative of his diagnosis that the pregnancy had terminated. He discharged her, seeing no need for treatment.

Dr. Glazer was wrong. Mrs. Boatman did not have a complete or even incomplete miscarriage. What she had was an ectopic pregnancy, a term which refers to any kind of abnormal pregnancy in which the fetus forms outside the womb; most commonly in one of the very small fallopian tubes. The diagnosis of ectopic pregnancy in the early stages is very difficult because it is almost impossible to feel or "palpate" a very young fetus either in the uterus or in one of the tubes. Once an ectopic pregnancy ruptures, which it eventually must, the diagnosis is simple, but by that time a true medical emergency exists.

March 27 was a Saturday. Jim Boatman had left the house for an hour or so that morning. Mrs. Boatman suddenly had pain which became so bad that she had her ten-year-old daughter call Dr. Glazer's office. There was a mixup on this call, since Dr. Glazer was in his office occupied with patients. The mix-up was fatal. The little girl thought she had been told by the receptionist that Dr. Glazer was not there. Mrs. Boatman then told her to call Dr. Newman's office. Dr. Newman responded very quickly, making a house call at approximately 11:30 A.M. Because of her pain, Dr. Newman could not perform an adequate pelvic examination. He had Mrs. Boatman come to his office, which accomplished nothing as he was also unable to perform a thorough examination there. He decided to have her admitted to Osteopathic General Hospital, after first giving her a shot of Demerol to kill the pain.

Dr. Newman was unsure of the diagnosis. He thought it was probably "anemia and/or pelvic inflammatory disease," which is a pretty broad general diagnosis. Mr. Boatman took his wife from Dr. Newman's office to the hospital, where there was approximately an hour's delay before she was admitted to her room at 2:35 P.M. The admission was "routine"; not designated as an "emergency" admission. In nine hours and ten minutes she was dead.

Once Mrs. Boatman was admitted to her room, apparently resting comfortably, Jim Boatman went home to look after the children. Nobody seemed to think there was any cause for undue alarm. Dr. Newman waited at his office for the hospital to call him before he gave any orders. Two hours after Antoinette's admission, at 4:30 P.M., the hospital called. Dr. Newman ordered routine tests. He arrived at the hospital at 5:15 P.M., reviewed the results of the tests and conducted an examination at 6:00 P.M.

From the results, it was obvious to Dr. Newman that he needed a surgical consultation. He wrote a request in the hospital records. A hospital nurse then called and left a message with the requested surgeon's answering service. Dr. Newman did not call the surgeon, Dr. Willis Yeamans, personally, nor did he wait for him to arrive.

The hospital record reflected that Mrs. Boatman's blood pressure was taken for the first time at 3:00 P.M. when, significantly, it was near normal. There was no evidence in the chart that Dr. Newman took her blood pressure while he was at the hospital between 5:15 and 6:35 P.M. The next time her blood pressure was recorded by a nurse was at 7:00 P.M., at which time it was 60/30, which is abnormal and extremely serious. At the trial, I emphasized this fact, that during these four hours nobody recorded the patient's blood pressure. Dr. Newman and others testified that they did take the blood pressure during this period, but could not remember what it was, and, of course, they had not written it down.

The level of Mrs. Boatman's consciousness and lucidity in the hours after 7:00 P.M. was a critical legal issue in the case relating to her refusal to receive blood. Dr. Newman had given her a shot of 75 mg. of Demerol for pain at his office at 12:30 P.M. She received a similar dose at the hospital at 5:30 P.M. During this hospital visit, he testified, Dr. Newman did not discuss blood with Mrs. Boatman because it did not occur to him that she would require any. (As the trial unfolded, his opinion backfired on him.) He knew she was a Jehovah's Witness, though, because from the very first time he had ever seen her she had mentioned that fact, in connection with her religious convictions about blood transfusions. Part of my theory against Dr. Newman was that he should have considered the possibility of the need for blood at that time and discussed it with his patient.

In Mrs. Boatman's hospital chart there was a note made by a young intern shortly after Dr. Newman left, to the effect that Mrs. Boatman appeared "shocky." This intern took a history from the patient, performed a cursory physical examination, and wrote his diagnosis for the record: "Ruptured ectopic pregnancy." Somebody at last had made the correct diagnosis!

Later on in the trial, there was a great deal of disagreement between the witnesses as to precisely when the pregnancy ruptured. Most of the osteopathic physicians, testifying with hindsight, felt that it had ruptured before Mrs. Boatman entered the hospital. That made no sense to me. If it were true, certainly Dr. Newman and the hospital were negligent, first in misdiagnosing it, and second, in not discovering this medical emergency until after 7:00 P.M.

A second intern saw the patient at approximately 7:15 P.M,. found her to be in a "state of shock" with a blood pressure of 60/30 and a pulse reading of 140. From these signs it was obvious to the intern that the patient had to be seen by a surgeon *immediately*. It was also obvious to him that she needed blood. He telephoned Dr. Leon Shore, the younger partner of Dr. Yeamans, the surgeon who eventually was to operate on Mrs. Boatman later that night. The intern told Dr. Shore to get over there "on the double" because she needed surgery right away.

Dr. Shore arrived at the hospital at 7:45 P.M. He agreed that Mrs. Boatman needed blood and surgery as soon as possible. At about this time, Dr. Yeamans. who was at the Cocoanut Grove Playhouse in Miami, responded to his answering service message by calling the hospital. Dr. Shore explained the situation. Dr. Yeamans left for the hospital, a thirty-five-minute drive away.

Dr. Shore ordered blood to be cross-matched and readied. He did not "scrub" although as a surgeon himself he could have made the decision to operate without waiting for his partner to arrive. He notified an anesthesiologist who was on call, just a few minutes away. (Up until this time, Mr. Boatman had not been notified about any problem whatever.) Dr. Shore, a total stranger to Mrs. Boatman, discussed blood transfusions with her, using his best bedside manner. He asked her detailed questions about her family, her children and her activities. They discussed religion and the "meaning of life." He testified that he made it perfectly clear to Mrs. Boatman that if she refused to accept blood, she would die. According to him, she could understand everything, and her conversation was entirely rational.

One problem with "death" cases as distinct from cases where one's client survives, of course, is that in the "survival" case, there will be two sides to the testimony, and the defense knows it. In the "death" case, all the plaintiff's lawyer has to go on is the hospital chart, what little a surviving spouse may know and the usually undisputable testimony of the defendants as to what was done and said.

The defense was built around Mrs. Boatman's Jehovah's Witness religion. On her admission to the hospital, she and her husband had signed a form on Osteopathic General Hospital's stationery which said:

Because of my religious faith and believings, I will not consent to a blood transfusion. I hereby release the Osteopathic General

Hospital and all attending physicians from all responsibilities and liabilities for any ill effects and untoward results would a blood transfusion become necessary.

I contended that this was a mere formality since no one had advised the Boatmans that she might require blood. I knew that Antoinette had given Dr. Glazer (but not the osteopathic doctors apparently) an authorization to administer blood to her if absolutely necessary. From the pretrial depositions, the defendants knew this too.

Dr. Shore testified that Antoinette was not excited, but was calmly resigned to any fate that the Lord might choose for her. She had told him that she could not receive blood under any condition or circumstances, and "if it was God's will" that she die, "so be it."

Dr. Shore insisted that he pleaded with her about her children, emphasizing how terrible it would be for them to be left at their ages without a loving mother. Mrs. Boatman replied, he said, that she would not be doing her children any good by taking blood and being forever doomed, and if it was the Lord's will that she die, "He would look after her children."

By now, several physicians were trying to impress upon Mrs. Boatman the absolute necessity of her accepting blood. According to them, her answer was always the same. Mr. Boatman was finally called by the hospital, arriving there at 8:30 P.M., just about the time of Dr. Yeamans's arrival from the Cocoanut Grove Theater.

Jim was amazed to learn how critical the situation had become. Even though he, too, had been converted to the Jehovah's Witness faith, he tried to talk his wife into accepting blood, but without success. There was, however, a significant contradiction between his testimony and that of the various physicians about Antoinette's mental condition. Mr. Boatman would later testify that Antoinette was "not herself," that "she was out of it," meaning that she was not making any sense at all. He admitted that she could carry on a conversation, but she was hazy and did not seem to appreciate her true plight. Jim did not know of her earlier agreement with Dr. Glazer.

Several of the doctors discussed giving Mrs. Boatman blood even against her consent in order to save her life, but they vacillated. Not one of them would assume the responsibility. At one time, according to the testimony of one of the interns, several doctors thumbed through a medical-legal textbook to ascertain what their position was. This self-appointed Supreme Court then made the determination that they could not give an adult blood in the face of an express refusal.

Dr. Shore had the bright idea of asking Mr. Boatman whether he would sign a consent permitting them to give his wife blood. When it came down to the hard choice between his religious belief and saving the life of his beloved wife, he said, "Give me anything and I will sign it." More time was then wasted in drawing up a form for his signature which said:

I, James E. Boatman, husband of Antoinette Boatman, give permission for blood to be given to my wife. I further release the Osteopathic Hospital and all physicians from all responsibility.

According to the testimony, one or two of the doctors felt that this would be good enough, but then they got cold feet again. At the time of trial, Paul Larkin tried to impress the jury with the fact that his clients had greater respect for Mrs. Boatman's religious beliefs and the United States Constitution. I was to argue that this was nonsense. The reason they didn't give blood was that they were worried about their own hides. This was one of my main themes throughout the trial (during the first four days especially), and to this day I strongly feel that they were wrong not to transfuse blood in view of her condition and her husband's consent. To me it bordered on the obscene to be discussing legalities while a woman's life was ebbing away. I was to discuss with the jury the whole question of motivation as to why one chooses to be a doctor in the first place. In my summation I said:

The money and the prestige are fine, but hopefully the primary motivation is because you want to help people and save lives. I don't want a brilliant technician who does not revere life to be my doctor. In every country on the face of the globe; in every language, there is a toast to life. I hope I never hear a toast to death. The Talmud says that "He who saves one life is considered as if he had preserved the whole world."

. . . Don't talk to me about constitutional niceties. The greatest judges in America frequently disagree on what certain phrases mean. Have you noticed that there is some minor dispute going on in the country now having to do with the question of what is an "impeachable offense"? Yet these men, trained in another field, were going to resolve the matter on their own. Terrific! Not one of these legalistic purists could name a specific case where a doctor had ever been sued successfully for giving blood to preserve life. It was okay with them for Antoinette Boatman to commit suicide; yet suicide is illegal in every state of the United States.

During the trial, George Lanza, on behalf of Dr. Glazer called as a witness Dr. Joseph A. DeCenzo. He was to give my case a lift even though he completely exonerated Dr. Glazer. I kept nudging him on cross-examination until finally he said, "That is why I won't treat these people. If it had been me, I'd have given the blood."

I was to tell the jury later that DeCenzo was "my kind of guy." "If someone had gotten mad, if someone had the guts to say, 'Damn it, I'll take the responsibility for giving blood. I refuse to stand by helplessly and watch a wife and mother die.' If someone had said that, and done that, Antoinette Boatman would be alive today and everyone could apologize very graciously to her for having violated her religious principles."

A little knowledge is a terribly dangerous thing. These geniuses had perhaps heard through the grapevine of situations where a physician had been sued for giving blood against someone's wishes. How I would love to be in the position of defending a physician who is being sued by some ingrate for saving a life! Moreover, even if some insane jury somewhere found the doctor to be liable in such a situation, the potential damages would be legally nonexistent. You cannot collect for being made well, but this is what the doctors were *really* worried about.

Even though the medical-legal hotshots decided not to give blood, they nevertheless went ahead with the surgery. Anesthesia was administered at 9:55 P.M. The operation lasted from 10:20 P.M. to 10:45 P.M. It went very quickly because technically it is a breeze. It is a very easy matter for the surgeon to stop the bleeding with a clamp. It was significant, I thought, that surgery was performed by Dr. Yeamans even though all the doctors were convinced that surgery alone could not save her life. Mrs. Boatman had always consented to the surgery (which indicated to me that she was far from completely resigned to meeting her Maker).

Antoinette Boatman died in the recovery room at 11:45 P.M. on the day she was admitted to the hospital. When her finger was pricked it was not blood, but saline solution, which oozed forth. She was just twenty-eight years old. She had literally bled to death in a supposedly modern American hospital in the year 1971.

How strong she must have been to survive the blood loss, the anesthesia and the surgery! In a situation where time was of the essence, the operation was not begun until eight hours after she was first admitted and eleven hours after Dr. Newman first saw her that morning.

What right did these medical men, supposedly scientists, have to debate the ethics of religious freedom and its application to the First and Fourteenth amendments to the U.S. Constitution where a patient of theirs was needlessly dying? Instead of acting as amateur lawyers, they should have done their duty as physicians. To my simple mind, it may have been a complex issue for theologians, but the choice should not have been difficult for doctors.

After many depositions and much discovery were taken, the case came to trial before Judge Milton A. Friedman and a jury consisting of four women and two men from Monday, April 1, through Friday, April 5, 1974.

I put Dr. Allen Shepard, the expert anesthesiologist who had testified in the Elease Morris case on the witness stand. He had been a general practitioner, faced with the same type of situation that Dr. Newman was in, and was also an expert on the effect of the medications and Antoinette's severely lowered blood pressure on her consciousness and lucidity.

Dr. Shepard said that Demerol is a narcotic which affects both mind and body. A person can seem lucid in terms of ability to respond to simple questions, but this does not prove that they are functioning with any real intelligent judgment. Dr. Shepard felt that considering the medications she had received, her blood loss, her dangerously low blood pressure, and her anxiety, she was in no position to think for herself or give an informed consent or refusal. She was, in fact, in a state of shock.

It was Dr. Shepard's opinion that Dr. Newman had abandoned his patient. Dr. Newman admitted Mrs. Boatman to the hospital and she remained his responsibility. Just asking for a surgical consultation was not sufficient;

he had a duty to make sure that it was accomplished promptly.

None of the other doctors had the presence of mind to insist that Dr. Newman come to the hospital in order to reason with Mrs. Boatman. None of them called Dr. Glazer, who testified that if he had received such a phone call he would have come to the hospital immediately, even though medical doctors do not generally practice in osteopathic hospitals. He would have then been able to tell the osteopaths about her agreement with him to accept blood in an emergency. He most certainly would have been able to remind Mrs. Boatman of that understanding.

The agreement Mrs. Boatman had made with Dr. Glazer was crucial in allowing me to argue that the osteopathic physicians were lying about Mrs. Boatman's state of lucidity at the time blood was being discussed with her. Why, less than a month earlier, would Mrs. Boatman in a very calm atmosphere have agreed to receive blood in a dire emergency and then refuse it when her life depended upon it?

Through my witnesses, including the hospital interns whom I called, I implied to the jury that if any of these doctors had really been gutsy, they could have made a note in the hospital record to the effect that they were unable to communicate with her, and therefore they administered blood with the husband's consent. (This was a dangerous business because the jury could be offended that I was even suggesting a dishonest means to accomplish a noble end.)

When Jay Swidler had originally filed the lawsuit, his sole theory had been that the hospital and the doctors were negligent in not administering blood to Mrs. Boatman. That certainly was the thrust of my testimony throughout the first four days, but Judge Friedman made a ruling at that point which changed things fast. He ruled that the doctors were legally correct in *not* giving Mrs. Boatman blood without her personal consent. This was, of course, based upon the document she and her husband had signed when she first went into the hospital in the afternoon.

This ruling was absolutely devastating to my case! I argued, cajoled, and pleaded, but it did no good. Judge Friedman further emasculated my case by ruling that Osteopathic General Hospital, its nurses and interns had done nothing wrong either. This meant that he would not let the question of whether or not the physicians should have given Mrs. Boatman blood be considered by the jury at all. Judge Friedman had pulled the rug completely out from under me.

A trial lawyer needs to be quick on his feet. I could, of course, appeal Judge Friedman's ruling, but after four days of trial, plus countless hours of preparation, I refused to give up. Stubbornness is one of my outstanding qualities! I decided to forge ahead, even though I was now restricted to a very narrow area of negligence—the paper-thin theory that if they had operated soon enough, they could have saved Mrs. Boatman without any blood transfusion at all.

I had to do a complete flip-flop, which is always embarrassing in front of a jury. On my opening statement, I had said that I would show them that Antoinette Boatman had needed blood to save her life. For four days, I had pounded away on that theory. Judge Friedman's ruling left me with only one choice. I had to show that prompt action —instead of indecision—would have saved her.

At this point, I also had to decide which of the defendants I could most reasonably show to have been responsible for the delay. I zeroed in on Dr. Newman, not only because he had missed the proper diagnosis of ruptured ectopic pregnancy, but also because he did not make sure that a surgeon saw Mrs. Boatman while he was still in the hospital. He had already testified that when he saw her in the afternoon, in his opinion, she would not need blood. I intended to prove that even without a transfusion Antoinette should have been saved.

My "ace" on the subject was Dr. Courtlandt D. Berry, the chief pathologist at Naples Community Hospital in Naples, Florida. Dr. Berry had received his medical degree from Duke University in 1938. He had practiced obstetrics and gynecology in Orlando, Florida for many years, and was, in addition, board certified in two separate fields, obstetrics and gynecology as well as clinical and anatomic pathology. Dr. Berry testified if Mrs. Boatman had been operated on at any time before 8:15 P.M., she could have been saved without a blood transfusion.

This testimony was critical to the only theory of malpractice left in the case. As a practical matter, it just about destroyed my case against the surgeons, because Dr. Shore had arrived at the hospital only shortly before 8:00 P.M. and Dr. Yeamans not until 8:30 P.M.

Naturally, all the defendant osteopathic physicians disagreed with Dr. Berry. They testified that Mrs. Boatman could not have been saved wtihout blood even if they had operated hours earlier. To support this contention, they put on several medical doctor experts, who said the same thing. On cross-examination of each of the defendants and their experts, I was able to emphasize that these men would have been crazy to cut Mrs. Boatman open at 10:20 P.M. if they were certain that there was no possibility of saving her life.

They knew before they opened her up that they were not going to transfuse blood. I had to assume that they did not perform the operation for practice, or for kicks. (Of course, they had to agree with that.) Not one of the doctors could give a satisfactory answer to the question of precisely how much blood Mrs. Boatman had lost between 8:00 P.M.—while they were talking and debating—and the time of actual surgery, two hours later.

The basic structure of the lawsuit had been set before I came into it. This included the names and number of the defendants. Because of Judge Friedman's rulings, I had to decide what to do about Dr. Glazer.

During the first four days of the trial, when I was trying to prove negligence on the part of at least one, and as many as all, of the defendants, Dr. Berry testified that Dr. Glazer was *not* negligent to miss the diagnosis of ectopic pregnancy during such an early stage of development. After Mrs. Boatman's initial visit to Dr. Glazer, however, all subsequent visits were abnormal because of the pain and bleeding. Dr. Berry felt that Dr. Glazer should have done blood studies, particularly so because of her religion. In addition, although this was not malpractice, in itself, Dr. Glazer had made an inaccurate diagnosis of "complete spontaneous abortion."

The difficulty with a case against Dr. Glazer, though, was that even though he missed the diagnosis it was extremely difficult to prove that this caused Antoinette's death. On March 27 the osteopaths still had plenty of time to save her life. Also, by pushing against Dr. Glazer, I would be diluting my case against Dr. Newman—my prime target.

When you are dealing with a Jehovah's Witness, speed is particularly important because the doctor should seek to do whatever will make a blood transfusion most unlikely. My approach was that if Dr. Newman felt that the results of certain tests were important, he should have ordered those tests immediately rather than waiting for the hospital to call him at 4:30 in the afternoon. If Dr. Yeamans was not immediately available through his answering service, Dr. Newman should have arranged for a consultation with another surgeon. He should have remained at the hospital until that surgeon arrived and examined the patient.

The defendants contended that Mrs. Boatman remained lucid during the discussions about blood on the evening

of her death. I used numerous notes in the medical chart
to contest that:

Two interns described her as being "shocky" and "in a
state of shock."

Dr. Shore wrote the word "shock" in a 9:00 P.M. note in
the chart, and at 9:00 P.M. Dr. Yeamans's note referred
to the patient as being "semi-comatose"; probably the most
damning reference of all. Further, in a 9:10 P.M. note, by
the anesthesiologist, he also referred to Mrs. Boatman as
being "in obvious clinical shock."

Mrs. Boatman's mental condition had really become irrelevant by virtue of the judge's ruling. He felt that the
form which was signed on admission got everyone off the
hot seat on this point. However, the jury had already heard
all this conflicting testimony. If they felt the doctors were
lying about her mental state, this would affect their deliberations even though the purely "legal" issues had been greatly
narrowed by the judge.

A jury will frequently decide a case on peripheral matters
if those are what move them emotionally. They will often
decide the case against "liars" because this fact alone
may anger them. If this jury felt I was wrong in one basic
contention—that blood should have been administered in
view of the wife's condition and the husband's consent—we
might very well lose the case. And this could be true regardless of whether they believed Mrs. Boatman could have
been saved without blood.

The interns who saw Antoinette Boatman at 6:00 P.M.
and 7:15 P.M. were hospital employees. They had certainly
provided enough warnings to the private physicians, but
Jay Swidler had joined the hospital, their employer, as a
defendant for one very good practical reason. Cases have
often been tried where the defendant will avoid liability
by arguing to the jury that the plaintiffs have sued the

wrong person. A defendant can often lay the blame on an absent party. Hence the plaintiff's lawyer, when in doubt, will generally bring several defendants into the suit and ask the jury to decide which is responsible. This must be weighed against the possible disadvantages of the "shotgun" approach.

One of my theories in Mrs. Boatman's case was that there had been no organized decision-making process in the hospital. Jehovah's Witnesses are not so rare that hospitals and doctors should not be expected to have procedures to care for them. Amazingly, there was no hospital rule at Osteopathic General Hospital nor any general standard among the osteopaths of Florida, dealing with this kind of situation. I called David Collins, the administrator of the hospital since 1953. He was forced to admit that there was no policy whatever concerning Jehovah's Witnesses. In fact, he could not recall their particular problems ever being discussed at his hospital.

Mr. Collins was the senior administrative officer of a large and busy hospital. Nevertheless, he had no idea of the hospital's legal position concerning giving blood to Jehovah's Witnesses. The unusual circumstances of Mrs. Boatman's death had never been brought to his attention until the filing of this lawsuit, many months later. He was totally unfamiliar with the form which had been signed by the Boatmans upon admission to the hospital and did not know how it came to be worded. Nor did anyone else in the hospital. It was so poorly drawn that no one wanted to take "credit" for it.

This is one of the many tragic things, which is so exasperating about hospital procedures. Even after a tragedy occurs, in my experience, hospitals almost never investigate the matter carefully, with the aim in mind to prevent recurrences. They are so quick to accept an explanation that absolves medical personnel that they do not look very hard or very critically. Because of this, lawyers bringing cases on behalf of plaintiffs have an added incentive.

Dr. Shepard testified that Dr. Newman abandoned his patient. Dr. Newman admitted Mrs. Boatman to the hospital. She should have remained his responsibility. Just calling for a surgical consultation was not sufficient: he had a duty to make sure it was accomplished.

I was to tell the jury that because of Dr. Newman's past relationship with Mrs. Boatman, he was in the best position to persuade her to accept blood. Even when he was finally advised of the drastic drop in blood pressure, he did not rush to the hospital to talk to Mr. or Mrs. Boatman. He did return later, but by then she was under anesthesia.

I had to be careful in proceeding against Dr. Newman since he was a very sympathetic witness. In fact, his interest in his patients was shown by the house call he made during the morning. On the other hand, Dr. Glazer was a handsome, charming guy who seemed to me to have impressed the women on the jury.

By the close of the testimony, I had spent four days proving that all of the doctors should have diagnosed Antoinette's condition and given her blood in order to save her life. I had then backtracked and tried to pin liability primarily on one of them: Dr. Newman. Obviously, the closing arguments would be viciously fought.

Dr. Newman's lawyer, Raymond Dwyer, is one of Florida's finest trial lawyers. He did not fail to point out Dr. Newman's conscientiousness in making the house call, and also the inconsistency in my position relative to the blood issue (which was now out of the case).

Dwyer's style meshed perfectly with mine. He is a man who likes a fight. Righteous indignation is a very natural emotion for him. He is a "yeller," which I love, because that means I do not have to restrain myself. George Lanza, eloquent and aggressive, also comes on very strong, and thus the trial was a lively one.

Dwyer pointed out how terrible it was for his client to be "accused" of being a malpractitioner. I countered by saying, "I do not 'accuse' Dr. Newman of being a bad doctor. All I have to prove is that on March 27, 1971, he was negligent in caring for Mrs. Boatman. He may have treated all his other patients that day perfectly. He may have treated Mrs. Boatman perfectly on all other occasions.

"We doctors and lawyers are not holy. We can and do make mistakes and when our errors cause harm, we should pay for them, just like any other group in our society. Raymond Dwyer has attempted to make Dr. Stanley Newman the object of your sympathy."

Pointing to an empty chair, I continued: "Who speaks for Antoinette Boatman? The defense lawyers tell you over and over again that you shouldn't decide this case on sympathy for Mr. or Mrs. Boatman, but they very cleverly imply that you should be sympathetic towards their clients because their reputations will be ruined.

"Well, their reputations will not be ruined. They may learn something and become better doctors, which will benefit all their patients. Besides, Mr. Dwyer's concern is phoney since he was hired by an insurance company and probably never met Dr. Newman before this case. Ray Dwyer and I and every lawyer in this courtroom have liability insurance to afford protection to our clients for our mistakes. Yes, folks, the secret is out—doctors and lawyers are not perfect. We make mistakes. And, there is nothing venal or underhanded in asking that a professional person pay an innocent victim for his mistakes. The law, in fact, demands it."

After discussing the case with Jim Boatman, I decided not to proceed any further against Dr. Glazer. Because we had been in trial such a long time, though, I could not afford to give the defense attorneys an opportunity to point to an "empty chair." They could then imply that I had settled with Glazer since he was the one really at fault. I therefore did an almost unheard-of thing during my summation. This was possible only because I trusted George Lanza.

I called George at his home at 6:45 A.M. on the final day of trial and told him that I intended to tell the jury that I could not in good conscience ask them to return a verdict against his client. I had to tell Lanza this in advance, or Dr. Glazer was liable to get up and walk out of the courtroom upon hearing my statement or display an attitude which implicitly said, "If you feel that way, why the hell did you sue me and keep me in court and away from my patients for five days?"

Lanza was more than happy to agree that both he and his client would remain in the courtroom and look appreciative. In a performance worthy of Marcello Mastroianni, George almost fell out of his chair when he heard my "shocking" announcement.

This could have backfired. If the jury thought that I was playing games, or letting out a doctor who should have been kept in the lawsuit, they could easily have found against my client. On the other hand, if I had kept Dr. Glazer in, and the jury had the opinion, as I had, that the proof simply did not show that his part in Antoinette's treatment caused her death, they could have found against my whole case. If I guessed wrong, I was going to look bad.

In spite of what I had told the jury, when George's turn came for summation he got up and talked for twenty minutes. After spending five days in trial, he was going to have his say even though there was no way this jury was going to find against his client. Trial lawyers must talk as musicians must play. To this day I call George the "Italian ham."

The jury returned a verdict of $160,000 against Dr. Newman, and $15,000 against Dr. Shore, for a total of $175,000. I believe that they found against Dr. Shore because they felt that he was a surgeon, the first one there, and that he should have operated almost immediately, whether he was going to give blood or not. There was no need for him to wait for Dr. Yeamans. This, at least was the thrust of my argument against Dr. Shore. Neither of the defendants nor their insurance companies had made any offer of settlement at any time.

The fragmented practice of medicine leads to disastrous results for many patients. Everyone is "doing their thing" (and perhaps doing it very well), but there is seldom a unified approach to the problems of a particular individual. This fact worked to the disadvantage of Antoinette Boatman.

She used both an M.D. (Dr. Glazer) and a D.O. (Dr. Newman), and there is a woeful and historic lack of communication between these two professions. The doctors of Osteopathic General Hospital never knew Mrs. Boatman had agreed to let Dr. Glazer give her blood in a dire emergency. They were unaware of Dr. Glazer's diagnosis of "spontaneous abortion."

Dr. Newman admits Mrs. Boatman to the hospital on a routine basis. The hospital wastes an hour in admitting her. The hospital wastes two more hours before calling Dr. Newman for his orders. Dr. Newman saw her at 11:30 A.M. at home, but it is not until 6:00 P.M. that he decides his patient should be seen by a surgeon.

It's Saturday evening and Newman assumes there will be no problem in locating Dr. Yeamans. He goes home. A hospital nurse calls the surgeon's answering service. No one tells Jim Boatman that surgery is contemplated. An intern, observing that Mrs. Boatman is in a state of shock, calls Dr. Shore. This intern was the first one to make the correct diagnosis of ruptured ectopic pregnancy.

Shore shows up at 7:45 P.M.—five hours after the patient was admitted. All this time Mrs. Boatman is bleeding to death, yet her admitting physician never discussed with her or her husband the likely need for blood. Newman had nothing to do with getting Shore to the hospital. The consultant he requested was Yeaman, who didn't arrive until 8:30 P.M.

Shore and Yeamans are now acutely aware that a life-or-death emergency situation exists. They don't call Dr. Glazer. They don't call Dr. Newman. They try to persuade a medicated and anxious woman, who has already suffered a substantial blood loss, to violate her religious beliefs. They do this despite the fact that she is in an obvious state of shock.

They don't call the hospital administrator, the hospital lawyer, or a judge. They waste precious time having Mr. Boatman sign a silly form and then decide not to give blood despite his consent. Shore leaves the hospital before the operation begins. Newman comes to the hospital after his patient has been anesthetized. Yeamans does the surgery even though he and all the other doctors are convinced that it will not do her the slightest good by that time (10:20 P.M.). This is one thing they were right about all night.

The patient is a Jehovah's Witness, yet her blood pressure is not recorded anywhere from 3:00 P.M. to 7:00 P.M., by which time she is already in serious trouble. A major osteopathic institution in south Florida has no policy whatever for dealing with this type of situation or with Witnesses generally. I think it is a safe bet to say that the hospital still has no policy, particularly since the trial judge endorsed this glaring omission.

Jerry Burke, Elease Morris, and Antoinette Boatman were

all young and healthy when they sought medical help. Their deaths were unnecessary and were caused by medical malpractice combined with poor communication. Linda Powell was young and healthy when she went to see Dr. Fagan and contracted aplastic anemia. The medical profession can learn a great deal from these and loads of other cases which point the spotlight at negligence. Hopefully, they will make an effort to do so!

Death cases generally do not have anything like the damage potential of cases where the plaintiff is seriously injured. With a seriously injured plaintiff present in the courtroom, the real meaning of permanent suffering and the destruction of the ability to enjoy a happy life is evident to the jury. Jurors are generally not motivated to make a surviving spouse wealthy. Further, juries tend to be practical. If the survivor is relatively young, they will assume that such a person will remarry and have substitute companionship. Jim Boatman remarried in early 1972, but the jury never learned this. In all honesty, the new Florida law on this subject is an improvement, because the jury should know about remarriage.

The cases that have the most damage "potential" are those where an individual is badly injured, requires medical or custodial or nursing care for a period of years, and has a normal life expectancy. Such a person is, in addition, entitled to be compensated for loss of earnings, loss of future wage-earning capacity, pain and suffering, mental pain and anguish, and the loss of the capacity to enjoy life.

There were several interesting legal aspects to this case. At the time of the trial, Florida law did not allow the Boatman children to be parties to the case. If the case were tried today, under a modernized law, they would have separate claims for their own loss. This jury could consider only the loss of the surviving spouse.

Jim Boatman was expelled from his church for bringing

this lawsuit and signing the consent for blood. Antoinette, too, would have been expelled if her agreement with Dr. Glazer had been known. That is how rigid the Jehovah's Witnesses are about blood transfusions.

With all the complicated constitutional questions raised by this case, it was not surprising that there would be some grounds for appeal. Ray Dwyer, who is the type of combative lawyer who would have liked to retry the entire case before another jury the following Monday morning, appealed the decision. I "cross-assigned" as errors the judge's rulings which absolved the hospital and said all doctors were correct not to give blood. However, we settled the case before the higher court could render a decision.

Many questions remain about the issues raised in this case. What is the doctor's duty concerning Jehovah's Witnesses? In similar circumstances, should a doctor rely on the consent of the spouse, where the patient is in a state of shock and in no condition to make a sensible decision for herself? Does a person have the right to die or commit suicide? In the Karen Quinlan case a New Jersey judge in November 1975 denied her parents' request to have her disconnected from "artificial" life-support devices. The judge ruled that Miss Quinlan did not have a "constitutional right" to die.

On March 31, 1976 the New Jersey Supreme Court overruled the lower court and said that Miss Quinlan could be removed from extraordinary life support equipment. By late May, the respirator which had sustained her breathing was removed. But, to the surprise of doctors, she continued breathing.

What is the duty of a hospital with regard to Jehovah's Witnesses? There is no excuse for any hospital in the United States not to have a policy whereby persons known to be Jehovah's Witnesses are treated promptly with every effort being made to avoid the need for blood transfusions. There should also be legal guidelines so that doctors and hospitals would not have to work on a "trial and error" basis. Better "communication" between the legal and medical professions would work to the advantage of the consumer, and far fewer patients would end up being clients in malpractice cases.

The only thing certain about litigation is its uncertainty. That is why the vast majority of cases are settled before trial. This uncertainty is one of the things which fascinates me about the practice of law.

VI

Johnnie Lee Williams
—————VS.—————
The Sheriff of Miami-Dade County
Professional Negligence by the Police

Johnnie Lee Williams, age thirty-five, a bus driver for Metropolitan Dade County, went to watch a card game in a black ghetto area of Miami's decaying central city on August 13, 1968, at approximately 1:30 A.M. This spur-of-the-moment decision resulted in his death. The Dade County Sheriff's Department was particularly touchy at this time because it had been involved in quelling several mini-riots that accompanied the Republican National Convention, which only days before had nominated Richard M. Nixon for president, on Miami Beach.

On this particular night, there were no disorders of any kind, but the deputy sheriffs still possessed the shotguns which had been issued to them in connection with the convention. The card game was uneventful until the lights went out. When they were restored, six dollars was missing from the table. Titus ("Schoolboy") Walters accused Lonnie Johnson, one of the players, of stealing the money. Johnson pleaded innocence, but Walters said he was going to get his gun to teach him a lesson.

Johnson knew Walters well enough to know that he was not indulging in an empty threat. He therefore went looking for some police protection. He located a police car on routine patrol and advised the two white deputies of what had transpired. Instead of telling Johnson to go home, they followed him through winding dark streets and alleys, parked the car and proceeded to walk a block and a half to the home which was the site of the card game. Deputy Cribbs took along his twelve-gauge automatic Browning Hunt shotgun. In addition, each officer carried a .38 Smith & Wesson revolver.

Walters carried through his threat. He returned to the scene of the card game with a sawed-off shotgun—the brandishing of which is a felony in Florida. As the deputies followed Johnson, they approached a cluster of blacks —players and spectators—who were simply milling about in an entirely peaceful fashion. Pointing to the group of eleven or twelve men Johnson screamed, "There he is." Deputy Cribbs shouted: "Police. Freeze."

From this point on there was almost a total conflict in the testimony between the witnesses and the police. The deputies said that in response to the "Police. Freeze" order, Johnnie Lee Williams (not Walters, who had gone for the gun) whirled and pointed a shotgun at them. Deputy Laurie fired his revolver and missed. Cribbs killed Williams with a shotgun blast, he was to testify, as Williams was facing him. The only problem with that story was the fact that Johnnie Lee Williams was shot in the back with eight holes, slightly to the right of the midline.

As the testimony in the case developed the following facts were completely uncontradicted:

1. The sawed-off shotgun was not fired and, in fact, was on "safety."

2. No fingerprints were ever discerned on the sawed-off shotgun, the stock of which was covered with waterproof plastic tape.

3. Only the deputies and Titus Walters said that the deceased, Johnnie Lee Williams, had had the shotgun. All the other witnesses testified that Walters had it.

4. The group of blacks were extremely passive before, during and after the shooting. With the exception of the sawed-off shotgun, none of them had any weapons.

5. Police investigation was never able to ascertain ownership of the shotgun, but there was no evidence whatever linking it to Williams.

The information I had from several witnesses was that Johnnie Lee Williams had been peacefully minding his own business, that he had been unarmed, and that he had been shot in the back by one of the two policemen.

I was retained by Dorothy Williams, and filed suit for wrongful death against the officers' employer, the sheriff of Dade County and the county itself.

The trial began on Monday, June 30, 1969, before the late Circuit Judge J. Fritz Gordon. Since circuit judges are paid from county funds, as are sheriff's personnel, the person bringing suit often has one strike against him in this type of case. Because of the particular judge assigned to hear the matter, Mrs. Williams and her children began with two strikes against them. I knew that Judge Gordon, who had been a brilliant lawyer in his day, would not be receptive to the plaintiff's position.

Judge Gordon was an elderly, cantankerous, conservative jurist who had at one time represented Al Capone when the underworld king maintained a palatial estate on Palm

Island, off Miami Beach. In his youth, Judge Gordon had been a motorcycle cop. He was on good terms with Dade County's chief policeman, Sheriff E. Wilson Purdy.

My opponents were both from "establishment" firms. William M. Hoeveler of Knight, Peters, Hoeveler, Pickle, Niemoeller & Flynn represented Dade County. Joseph W. Womack of Dixon, Bradford, Williams, McKay and Kimbrell represented Sheriff Purdy and Deputies Cribbs and Laurie, whom we had also sued.

Hoeveler was the perfect choice to represent Dade County in court. He is a Harvard law graduate who practices with a large firm specializing in insurance company defense work. He is six feet three inches tall, handsome, suave, and is particularly dangerous because of his smooth manner and exquisite courtesy.

I had my work cut out for me, particularly since we ended up with a solid middle-class jury. Just the type of panel that defense counsel wanted. In addition to the problems inherent in a case of this kind, I would also have trouble proving that Dorothy Williams was Johnnie's legal wife at the time of his death. He and Dorothy had been married in 1955, but she had obtained a divorce in 1962. There was also a question of bigamy.

During the period shortly before his death, Johnnie and Dorothy were living together in a common-law marriage, holding themselves out to the community as man and wife. Because of their long relationship, they did not feel it was necessary to go through another marriage ceremony. Common-law marriages were declared invalid by the state of Florida on January 1, 1968, but the law did not void such marriages if they had been entered into, as this one had, before that date.

The county's attorney, Hoeveler, told the jury at the outset that what was done by Cribbs and Laurie was done "reasonably" and in self-defense. Their lives were in immediate danger because a shotgun was being pointed at them. Attorney Womack adopted a less subtle approach, hinting broadly that the incident was connected in some way with the need for "law and order." He told the jury that on the Thursday night preceding August 13, 1968, the governor of Florida, Claude Kirk, gave Sheriff Purdy a precise order to send our men into northwest Dade County to assist the National Guard in keeping the peace.

My first witness was Officer James Cribbs.

Q. Isn't it correct that this was the first and only time you ever fired your shotgun while on duty?
A. That is correct.
Q. When Lonnie Johnson came over to the car, you did not call headquarters?
A. No, sir.
Q. Before you got to the area where the actual shooting took place, you saw quite a few people, didn't you?
A. Yes, sir.
Q. These other individuals were just standing around talking in a peaceful fashion, weren't they?
A. Yes, sir.
Q. When you finally got to the group of men where the killing took place, it was very dark, wasn't it?
A. Yes, sir.
Q. What happened as you approached this group of men?
A. Johnson pointed at Williams and said, "There he is, he is the man with the shotgun"—and then Johnson jumped quickly back behind the building. I think my exact words were, "Police. Freeze."
Q. Who did Johnson point to?
A. He was pointing to Mr. Williams.
Q. How do you know that?
A. I saw the direction he was pointing in.
Q. Well, weren't there several other men very close to Williams?
A. I would say to my left there were two or three more.
Q. Well, if Williams was standing like this [*gesturing*], and an-

other man was directly in front of him, how did you know
Johnson wasn't pointing at the other man?
A. It is possible.

The area is dark, the eleven or twelve men in close
proximity are all black—yet Cribbs decides that Johnson is
pointing to a specific person in the group.

Q. What happened after you screamed, "Police. Freeze"?
A. Williams whirled in a counterclockwise motion very swiftly
and faced Officer Laurie and myself. I noticed an object in
his hand. It was a sawed-off shotgun. Officer Laurie obviously noticed it also, and started to the ground. I heard
his gun go off. The deceased still had the shotgun in his
hand when I fired my shotgun.
Q. So when you fired your shotgun he was facing you?
A. When I fired my shotgun he was still whirling.

The Sheriff's Department was aware of the medical
examiner's photographs showing the entry wounds in the
middle of the back. Therefore, the "whirling" explanation.

Q. How far would you say you were from him at that moment?
A. Eight to ten feet.
Q. Both during and after this shooting, no other person attempted
to shoot or attack you or even yell at you?
A. No, sir, nobody did anything.
Q. What happened to Officer Laurie's shot?
A. I don't know sir.
Q. As far as you know his bullet was never found?
A. That's right, sir.
Q. And he shot first?
A. Yes, sir.
Q. But whoever was holding the shotgun never fired a shot?
A. As I understand it, the shotgun had the safety on.
Q. Of course, with the safety on, you can't fire the gun?
A. That is correct.
Q. You couldn't see Williams's face when you shot him?

A. I don't remember seeing his face. I saw the shotgun.

Q. You never saw any other weapon in this group of approximately twelve people, did you?

A. No, sir.

Q. When you left your car to follow Johnson, you didn't take the flashlight with you, did you?

A. No, sir, I didn't want to make a target of myself.

Q. You didn't turn on the rotating spotlight on the car to light up the area, did you?

A. No, sir.

Q. Was there anything resembling a riot or a civil disturbance in the area that you were patrolling before this incident?

A. There were groups of young black males in different areas. There appeared to be a little unrest, but there was no actual violence that I saw.

Womack's questions were designed to make Cribbs look noble and brave—or at the very least quite human.

Q. Can you recall for this jury your feelings as you looked at that shotgun?

A. I was scared. It is hard to explain a feeling like that unless it actually happens to you.

This was a central theme for the defense. The argument was—it is easy for Rosenblatt to say this valiant police officer was negligent, but unless you are in that situation yourself you cannot judge the actions of another person who may be faced with immediate death. We all have 20/20 hindsight, but Cribbs did not have the luxury of reflecting and choosing between alternatives. It is an appealing and telling point.

Q. Can you recall now the feelings that went through your heart and mind at that moment?

A. I think my first thought was I couldn't see how my partner was going to get out of it, being he was in between two shotguns. I couldn't possibly shoot at that point without hitting him. I felt that neither one of us was going to come out of it.

Q. Did you truly fear for your life at the time you fired your weapon?
A. Yes, I did.
Q. Is that the reason you fired?
A. I fired to protect both of us.

I had a few more questions for Cribbs.

Q. Because of your concern for your partner, after he fired his revolver, you waited for him to get completely down and out of your range of fire so that you could shoot safely?
A. Yes.
Q. About how long after he went down did you fire your weapon?
A. As soon as I had a clear view I fired.
Q. But whoever had the shotgun never fired, right?
A. That is correct.

I then called Officer James T. Laurie, Jr.

Q. When you were following Johnson, all you knew was that some person had a shotgun, but you had no idea who that person was?
A. Yes, that is correct.
Q. You didn't feel it was necessary to call headquarters for instructions or help in view of the problems a few days earlier?
A. No, sir. I did not.
Q. As you were walking, you were very apprehensive about being ambushed by someone in between those buildings?

I had a reason to show that both officers were "apprehensive" since one of my theories was that they panicked upon seeing a weapon in that crowd.

A. Yes, we had had a great deal of trouble in that area. We are good targets. I have been to innumerable shootings and cuttings and assaults in that area. I was apprehensive. *(He was giving the white jury a subliminal message.)*
Q. Did it ever occur to you to say to Johnson, "Well, since there

is someone with a shotgun looking to shoot you, go home!"

A. I didn't see it my duty to do that. It was my duty to seek the man with the shotgun and disarm him.

Q. About how far would you say you walked with Johnson?

A. About 125 yards.

Q. When you finally saw this group of men, is it correct that Johnnie Lee Williams had his back toward you?

A. I saw four men; two of them had their backs to me and the other two were facing the two whose backs were to me. The two whose backs were to me were obstructing my vision of the two who were facing them.

Q. Officer Laurie, if you have two men standing side by side and two men facing them and Johnson is pointing and says, "There he is"—how in the world do you know who he is pointing at?

A. At that time that's all I knew.

Q. He was pointing at a group of several men?

A. That is correct, sir.

Q. What happened next?

A. After Cribbs yelled, "Police. Freeze," a man then whirled around with a sawed-off shotgun in his hands.

Q. And who was that?

A. I never saw his face—I was looking at the shotgun. The minute I realized it was a shotgun I started going down. I was six feet away from him. He couldn't miss me.

Q. You knew he was going to fire at you; but he didn't.

A. No, sir, he didn't.

Q. But you fired your gun?

A. Yes, sir, I did.

Q. What did you hit?

A. Apparently nothing.

Q. Where was Cribbs when his shotgun went off?

A. He had to be immediately behind me because the shotgun deafened me.

Q. Even after the shooting, the crowd was still very orderly—they followed your instructions?

A. That is correct.

Q. You didn't see any other guns around you, did you?
A. No, sir.
Q. When your statement was taken on the very morning of the shooting, it was your belief that your bullet had struck Williams, wasn't it?
A. Yes, sir.
Q. What caused you to think that?
A. I fired right *at the center of his chest,* and at six feet I didn't see how I could have missed.

I was to argue that this was further evidence of apprehension and a panic-stricken reaction. This may be an understandable response in an ordinary person, but may constitute negligence by a professional police officer.

Q. You thought the holder of the sawed-off shotgun would shoot, and he didn't. You thought you couldn't miss from six feet, but you did.

Hoeveler and Womack both objected to the question as being argumentative. I withdrew it since it had served my purpose.

Q. Do you think in your apprehension you might have gotten Schoolboy and Williams confused? *(I knew how he would respond but the question itself contained my point.)*
A. No, sir. I fired at the man who had the shotgun.
Q. But isn't it correct that until Johnnie Lee Williams was killed you had never seen his face?
A. That is correct.

I next called Lonnie Johnson, who had unwittingly started this tragic business.

Q. When the police officer yelled "Halt" or "Police. Freeze"— in what position was Johnnie at that time?
A. Johnnie was standing still, facing the four men with his back turned.
Q. And when he got shot, how was he standing?
A. With his back turned.

Q. Did Johnnie Lee Williams ever turn and face you and the police officers?
A. No, at no time.
Q. Did you ever see Johnnie with a shotgun?
A. No, I didn't.
Q. Who had the shotgun?
A. Schoolboy.

In cross-examination, Womack continued with his "hero" theme.

Q. Do you know how many people you can blind and murder with one blast from a sawed-off shotgun?
A. Yes, sir, that's true.
Q. Several?
A. It is a possibility.

This was obviously improper questioning. I objected: "Are you qualifying Mr. Johnson as an expert on ballistics, Mr. Womack?" Judge Gordon shot me a withering glance. I sat down. I had irritated the judge, but the interruption served to stop Womack's dissertation.

My next witness was Bo Coney, another participant in the card game.

Q. Did Johnnie Williams ever turn around to face the police officers before he was shot?
A. No, sir.
Q. Do you know if he had any weapon in his hand at the time he was shot?
A. No, sir, he didn't.
Q. Are you sure of that?
A. Yes.
Q. Was anyone pointing a shotgun at the police at the time Johnnie was killed?
A. No, there wasn't.
Q. After the police said "Halt," how much time went by before the officer shot Johnnie?
A. No sooner than he spoke.

Q. In other words, "Halt," then "bang"?

A. Right. No sooner he said that—you know how everybody may be flinched up—he shot that quick, didn't nobody have no chance to move or run or nothing.

If anyone was going to cast a southern black Damon Runyon story, our witnesses would be perfect. Their dress, their manner on the stand, their speech, and their street names kept everyone wide awake. I had witnesses nicknamed "Bull," "Red Cat," "Greasy," "Colt 45," and "Creep."

These men were vulnerable because many of them had criminal records, although not for crimes of violence, and their average formal educational background was only through the sixth grade. They were worried, for by testifying, they could easily be exposing themselves to trouble and harassment at the hands of the police.

They said that Johnnie Lee Williams never had a shotgun or other weapon, never threatened the police officers, and was shot in the back. Of course, the defense attorneys were able to confuse these uneducated men on numerous peripheral points relating to distance and position.

Each of the witnesses was asked: How far were you from Bunk Bailey? What were the lighting conditions? Where were you in relation to Johnnie and the other witnesses? What was Johnnie wearing? Where were the police officers in relation to each other and in relation to Lonnie Johnson? Of course, on many trivial details, the answers were often at odds.

Hoeveler and Womack used numerous photographs of the scene to create additional contradictions. It would be difficult for well-educated and sophisticated witnesses to be consistent on so many minor points, but for my crew, it was well-nigh impossible. Because they didn't want to appear stupid, they would answer questions even though they were guessing, which just led to more inconsistencies.

After the shooting, all the witnesses were taken down to

the Sheriff's Department, where they finally gave statements at approximately 5:00 A.M. Several of them said they went to headquarters in handcuffs although they were obviously guilty of nothing. As far as I was able to determine, the main objective of this so-called "investigation" was to white-wash Cribbs and Laurie in short order. It was hardly the atmosphere in which to obtain impartial eye witness testimony.

In addition to these statements, many of the same wit-nesses testified before the peace justice and also before the grand jury allegedly investigating the shooting. As expected, these official bodies completely absolved the police officers of blame. I was not at all interested in saying that Cribbs was guilty of any *crime*—I was merely charging him with negligence, which is simply the failure to use reasonable care under the circumstances.

It was child's play for Hoeveler and Womack to develop contradictions between the grand jury testimony, the peace justice testimony and the statements given the Sheriff's Department. The witnesses never had the opportunity to reread their previous testimony. (It wouldn't have helped much if they had.) There was also the gambling and drink-ing atmosphere in which the killing took place. Defense counsel were obviously hoping this would not sit well with the "solid citizen" jury that we had.

I called Dr. Joseph H. Davis to the stand. Although a county employee for many years, Dr. Davis has the reputa-tion of being a straight arrow. He doesn't try to be cute or shade his testimony in a way which will make his superiors happy. He is a scientist who never tries to impress the jury with witticisms or phony "regular guy" slang in an attempt to ingratiate himself. He is therefore very effective because once he starts explaining things, it becomes obvious to almost anyone that he is just laying it on the line in a dispassionate, professional manner.

Dr. Davis is a pathologist, board certified by the American Board of Pathology in the subspecialty known as forensic pathology, which deals with injuries and sudden and unexpected deaths.

Q. By whom are you employed?
A. By Dade County. I am a separate department of the county, being one of the department heads, and I work directly under the county manager and county commission.
Q. What is your basic function as the medical examiner?
A. My basic function is to determine the cause of death in certain cases that are defined by law.
Q. When was the first time that you had contact with the body of Johnnie Lee Williams?
A. I actually commenced my autopsy at approximately 9:00 in the morning.

Now I zeroed in on the nub of the case. I wanted the "middle of the back" point to be crystal clear.

Q. Doctor, you mentioned an area of the back. I would like for you to specify either on my back or on your own the area where the gunshot wound was. I will stand here so that everyone on the jury can see it
A. Approximately 10 inches below the top of the shoulder or 43 inches above the soles of the feet, there was an area, a circular area of holes in the *back*. These were located to the right of the midline, for the most part, and measured approximately 3½ inches across by 4¾ inches vertically. These consisted of eight holes that are characteristic of pellets or projectiles entering the body.
Q. This man was shot in the back?
A. Yes.

No qualification or excuse of the type that you would get from 90 percent of medical experts being asked this question under these circumstances. Just a straight, short and truthful answer. I could have kissed him. Since a picture is often worth more than a thousand words, I sought to introduce the most important demonstrative evidence of the trial.

"Your Honor, on behalf of the plaintiff, I will offer these photographs in evidence at this time. They are all of Johnnie Lee Williams."

Womack and Hoeveler bounced out of their chairs sputtering objections with machine-gun rapidity.

The Court: Take the jury out, Mr. Bailiff, until we decide a question of law.

Mr. Womack: The defendants object to the proffered photographs on the ground that they are designed solely and exclusively to inflame and prejudice the jury against the defendants. The identity of the decedent is not in question. There is no dispute about it. The cause of death is not in question.

Mr. Rosenblatt: Your Honor, obviously if the photographs are relevant, the fact that they may be gruesome or inflammatory, is not a good objection. In this case, the place where these bullets entered the man's body is directly in issue, and that is exactly what is portrayed. One defense is that the bullets couldn't have entered his body where these photographs demonstrate that they did.

These pictures are not in color. They are not posed. They are Dr. Davis's own photographs and they portray to the jury the precise location where the pellets entered. There is no point in the jury speculating about position when they can view this graphic demonstrative evidence.

The Court: I am going to admit this one photograph and that's all. Just to show the point of entry of the wound.

Judge Gordon kept out nine photographs, but the one he admitted confirmed Dr. Davis's testimony that Johnnie Lee Williams had been shot in the back.

The defendants called Edward Bigler, a firearms expert with the Dade County Public Safety Department. He had examined Laurie's .38 special revolver and described it as the type that will hold six live rounds of ammunition. When he received it, it had five live rounds and one fired cartridge case. He examined the twelve gauge automatic shotgun used by Cribbs to kill Williams.

Bigler described the twelve-gauge sawed-off shotgun, explaining that the barrel and stock had been cut down substantially. He said it was a Savage, Model 220. The length of the barrel was 7½ inches. He pointed out that it was a violation of the National Firearms Act to have a barrel of that length.

Womack questioned his witness:

Q. How many weapons have you examined for fingerprints in your career?

A. I would say it would run into several hundred.

Q. If you examine one hundred handguns for prints, how many times will you find a readable, legible print?

A. The percentage would be very small. Maybe you would find it on one or two or three weapons.

Q. What is the reason for that low number?

A. Well, I think principally there are two reasons. First of all the physical characteristics of the firearm—due to the shape, some rough surfaces are not conducive to finding latent fingerprints. And the second reason is the manner in which the normal gun is handled. You have to load the gun, unload it, and break it open. This tends to smear any good prints that may be there.

I only had a few questions:

Q. When the sawed-off shotgun was retrieved from the scene it was on "safety," wasn't it?

A. Yes.

Q. If the gun is on "safety," a person pulling the trigger cannot shoot it, is that right?

A. That is true.

Q. The first thing you have to do is take it off "safety"?

This sounds like a silly question, but I had no idea how much or how little these particular jurors knew about firearms. My philosophy is—when in doubt, repeat and re-emphasize.

A. Correct.

Q. Did I understand you to say that simply holding this weapon is a crime in Florida?

A. It is illegal to have it in your possession. It is an illegal firearm.

I wanted to show Schoolboy's motivation for laying the blame on my client. Walters was a previously convicted felon, who would certainly lie to save himself from an additional criminal penalty.

Several officers of the Sheriff's Department had testified that they had conducted a wonderful investigation and that Cribbs and Laurie were fully entitled to exoneration. On cross-examination, I showed that the investigation had been sloppy from its inception. The departmental report indicated that Williams had been shot both with a twelve-gauge shotgun and a .38 caliber revolver, which was half wrong. Their report also said that Williams had been shot in the front left shoulder, whereas this was obviously an exit, rather than an entrance, wound.

Although the department interviewed a total of twelve witnesses concerning this incident, there was only one, other than Cribbs and Laurie, who said that Williams had the shotgun. That individual was Titus (Schoolboy) Walters, the person who, everyone else said, was carrying the sawed-off shotgun. Yet, in spite of the contradictory accounts of the shooting the sheriff reached the conclusion, on the very same day, that Cribbs acted in self-defense. Was the sheriff being objective, or was *he* also acting in self-defense—protecting his department? Even after they ascertained that Johnnie Lee Williams had been shot in the middle part of his back, it did not prompt anyone to conduct an additional investigation.

The only witness called by the county who was not a county employee was Titus Walters. Hoeveler questioned him:

Q. Tell me about the card game.

A. Lonnie Johnson was talking loud, annoying the game. I had a knife, so I take it out and put it on my lap. So Johnson moved to the side of me. We played a bunch of hands and Johnson kept moving around from one side of the table to the other. Next thing I knew the lights went out and the money was snatched off the table.

Q. Was any of that money yours?

A. None of it was mine. I think some of Johnnie's money was taken and he went away for a while and he came back with a sawed-off shotgun. After the shooting the officers handcuffed some of us and put us in the car and then they brought us down to jail.

This last statement was unresponsive to the question, but excellent for my case, because obviously a number of innocent bystanders had been handcuffed and hauled off to jail for no good reason.

Q. Did they release you?

A. Yes, sir.

Q. Who was holding the gun at the time Johnnie Lee Williams was shot?

A. Johnnie.

I cross-examined:

Q. What was it exactly that caused you to take the knife out and put it in your lap?

I wanted to stress his propensity for violence. He admitted that he and Johnson were already in conflict, and Johnson stated that he went for the police because of Walters' threat. Would the plaintiff have gone for a weapon over a measly six dollars? Walters was the only person to even suggest that some of Johnnie's money had been taken.

A. I took it out 'cause Lonnie came up to the side of me. I was already told about him.
Q. What were you told about him?
A. He was a gorilla. He takes people's money. When the table gets full of money, he and a punk named Pluto take it.
Q. Afer you took the knife out what did Lonnie say to you?
A. He asked me, "Would you hurt anybody with that knife?" I said, "No, if they don't take my money, but if they do gorilla me, I don't know what I'll do."

I could not shake Schoolboy from his story that Johnnie had the sawed-off shotgun. He did say, however, that Johnnie never pointed it at anybody.

Q. Were you and Johnnie in the same group of men at the time he got shot?
A. We was probably three foot apart.

This was very helpful. It showed how easy it would have been for Cribbs and Laurie to mistake Williams for Schoolboy in their apprehension. My theory and belief was simply that they saw a shotgun, panicked, and fired into a crowd.

Q. Mr. Walters, isn't it a fact that you gave two statements to the Sheriff's Department?
A. If I did it was that same night because that's the only time I have been there. That night everybody was afraid and I can't recall what was said then.

Yes, people do have a tendency to become frightened when they are hauled off to the sheriff's department in handcuffs after seeing one of their friends blasted by a shotgun.

Q. But you gave two statements that same morning. You gave one, and they weren't too happy with it.
Mr. Womack: Wait a minute, I object to this insidious remark.

The remark may have been insidious but it was true.

The Court: It will be stricken. Ladies and Gentlemen, you will not consider the statement just made by counsel.

Q. Why was it necessary for you to give two statements?

A. First, I was trying to cover up. Next, I didn't know what to say. I didn't know what anyone else was saying. They questioned me for about an hour, an hour and a half. I was the last one released, I think. In my first statement, I denied knowing anything.

Q. If you didn't know anything—then what happened in between the first statement and the second statement—that all of a sudden you knew something?

A. Well, after they kept questioning and I was standing in a group with the rest of them, I had to see something or know something, so I up and told what I knew about it. At first I had given some kind of wild statement.

Q. You gave some kind of wild statement which means that the first statement you gave to the police was a lie?

A. I don't know whether it was or not. I don't know what the first one was.

If that didn't discredit Schoolboy with the jury and if they didn't understand the department's desire for a whitewash, then I had the wrong jury. During my cross-examination of Walters, I did several things to provoke him. He was a big man—rugged, with a violent temper.

Shoolboy was the type of witness who is very sharp, streetwise and coy in answering questions as long as he can maintain his composure. I worked on this composure, returning to the different statements he had given to the Sheriff's Department. Hoeveler and Womack were objecting because I was being repetitious. I was getting on Schoolboy's nerves, hoping that, in a flash of anger he would say something useful to my client. (I was getting on Judge Gordon's nerves as well, but all he could do was put me in jail for contempt. Schoolboy could remake my features with

one punch—and he was getting angry. I therefore stood
behind the counsel table, some fifteen feet away.)

Q. Isn't it a fact that when you gave your first statement to the
sheriff, you said that you did not know who had the gun at
the time of the shooting?

A. He asked me about a gun and I said, "I don't know nothing"
or something like that. They questioned two or three more
and then called me in again and talked to me and then I
gave the statement.

Q. So the first time you talked to the police, you said you didn't
know who had the gun at the time Johnnie was shot, and the
second time you told them Johnnie had the gun?

A. They called everyone in and questioned them two or three
times until they got the *right* statement, I suppose.

There it was! He had made my point for me. The police
wanted the "right statement"—one which was consistent
with the account of Cribbs and Laurie. And they could exert
great pressure on Walters with the threat of prison for
possessing an illegal firearm.

Womack called the Great White Father next: Dade
County's police chief.

Q. Give your full name and office address and present position,
please.

A. E. Wilson Purdy, Director of Public Safety and Sheriff of
Dade County.

Q. How long have you held that position?

A. Since 1966.

Q. Tell the jury please your training and your qualifications for
the office which you now hold.

A. Bachelor's degree in police administration from the School of
Police Administration, Michigan State University. Four years
as an officer in the military police. Twelve years as a special
agent with the Federal Bureau of Investigation. Four and
one half years chief of police of St. Petersburg, Florida.

Three years as commissioner and head of the Pennsylvania
State Police. *(All very impressive to the jury.)*

Q. Did there come a time during August, 1968, when extra men
were put into the northwest section of Dade County following orders from the governor?

A. Yes, sir.

Q. Would you please tell these ladies and gentlemen how it
came about, why your men were sent there?

A. On approximately August 7 a condition appeared to escalate
in the northwest section, a part of which is within the City
of Miami and part of which is in the unincorporated area of
Dade County. The following day the conditions again esca-
lated to a point where apparently the governor felt that
additional forces should be deployed in the area, and on
August 8, Governor Kirk instructed me to take over the
supervision of law enforcement activities there.

Q. Following this occurrence involving Johnnie Lee Williams,
was an investigation made by your department?

A. Yes, sir.

Q. Would you tell these ladies and gentlemen briefly what
investigations were performed?

A. Actually two investigations were performed by the department. A regular homicide investigation as would be conducted in the case of any unexplained or unnatural death. In
addition to that, a departmental investigation commonly referred to as an "internal review investigation."

His responses indicated that he was perfectly satisfied
with the conclusions reached by his men. I had a few
questions.

Q. Are you aware of the fact that Johnnie Lee Williams was
shot in the back?

A. I don't recall whether I was advised as to the entrance wound
or not.

Q. Did you ever read the autopsy report by Dr. Davis or see
his photographs?

A. No, sir.

He was satisfied with the conclusions but had no idea of the facts upon which they were allegedly based.

Q. Is it good police work to leave the car 125 yards away and walk in a very dark area without a flashlight, to an uncertain destination, without any idea of how many persons will be present with what, if any, weapons?

A. It would depend on the judgment and discretion of the officers depending on the situation that existed at the time. These officers are well qualified and are fully capable of exercising good judgment.

Sheriff Purdy gave a typical political answer of the type we hear every night on the news—nice-sounding, vague generalizations which say nothing. Purdy's position was that these highly qualified police officers were there at the scene and had to make a judgment under the existing circumstances—and almost anything they did would have been proper.

Q. You simply assume that every member of your department, whether you know them personally or not, is qualified and capable?

A. Each member of the department has had the training and experience which would make him qualified for the situation which was presented.

Q. You haven't answered my question. My question is, is it not a fact that you regard every member of your 1,400-man department as capable and qualified?

A. Yes, sir.

Q. If a man comes over to a police car in an agitated state and says to two officers, "There is a crazy man back there with a shotgun looking to shoot me," what should the officers do?

A. The officers, based on their experience and ability, should evaluate the information which they have just received, and act in accordance with their judgment.

Q. What should they do specifically?

A. It would depend on the situation that existed and they would be called upon to exercise their judgment, based on their experience and training to make a decision as to what police action they would take.

It all "depends." There are no guidelines. Purdy just assumes that all his people have sound judgment and a cool nervous system. Well, it would be for the jury to determine if the killing of Williams was reasonable under the circumstances, and it would be up to them to decide what the true circumstances were.

The county had raised the defense that Dorothy Williams was not Johnnie's "legal" widow. If that were so, she had no legal "standing" to bring the case.

Q. When did you first start to use the name Dorothy Williams?
A. May 27, 1955. Johnnie and I were married.
Q. Did you and Johnnie ever get a divorce?
A. Yes.
Q. What year was that?
A. 1962, I think.
Q. What were the circumstances surrounding the divorce?
A. Well, Johnnie and I had quite a bit of ups and downs. Our marriage wasn't all peaches and cream. So although we were still very close to each other and everything, I applied for a divorce because I thought maybe this would change him.
Q. What did he do that you didn't like?
A. Well, he has always played cards for money and well, there were other women.

Their two children had been born years before the divorce. She and Johnnie continued to see one another occasionally but, according to Dorothy, he came home for good in mid-1967 and the family lived together from that time up until Johnnie's death.

Q. Did you handle the burial and the funeral?
A. Of course.

Hoeveler's cross-examination was gentle on the surface but ruthless.

Q. Let me make it clear to you, Mrs. Williams, that if any question I ask is one that you don't fully understand, will you please ask me to repeat it?

A. I will.

Q. Let me say that I dislike having to ask you these questions but I am sure you understand that in a case of this type it is necessary, so I apologize in advance for what I must do. Could you tell us whether or not there was more than one time that you were separated for over a year?

A. Well, sir, there could have been, but I definitely can't say.

Q. Isn't it true that you told Welfare at the inception of your payments that you could not find or you did not know where Johnnie was?

A. Right.

Q. If I understand correctly and certainly it is not my intention to cast any stones, I hope you understand that, I gather it was your intention to have the Welfare people think that Johnnie had a separate address from you?

A. That was the general idea.

Q. So that you could continue with your program and your Welfare payments?

A. That's right. Not necessarily with Welfare payments because Johnnie was supporting me. But to tell them the truth all my training would have been thrown out the window and I never would have received my high school diploma.

Hoeveler established that when Dorothy went to work for Southern Bell (where she was still employed at the time of trial), she had said that she was divorced. But in the same application form, she listed her "nearest relative" and the "person to notify in case of emergency" as none other than Johnnie Lee Williams.

The defense next called a lady named Lillian Williams. She testified that she and Johnnie were married on August

24, 1957—at which time he was still legally married to Dorothy. Lillian added that they lived together from the date of the marriage until some time in 1964, and they had three children. Johnnie supported her and the children while they were together, she said, and he continued to support the children even after they were separated.

Another lady named Mozelle Pollard testified that she had lived with Johnnie from January 1963 until May 1967. She and Johnnie were never married; she was merely separated from her husband. Her three children by Mr. Pollard lived with them, and Johnnie supported the children during the years they lived together.

Johnnie must have been quite a guy. I was already formulating my final argument, to the effect that although my client may not have been a great husband, he was certainly an outstanding provider, since he supported all his own children as well as another man's.

At the conclusion of all the testimony, the defendants moved for a "directed verdict." This is a decision that the judge can make in favor of one party, taking the case away from the jury.

Hoeveler and Womack had three points to make. The first was simply that from the evidence Dorothy Williams was not shown to be Johnnie's legal widow. They had been divorced and there was no subsequent marriage, common-law or otherwise. Second, they argued, we had failed to offer evidence proving that there was a negligent killing by the police officers. Third, the officers were acting in self-defense. They were assaulted by either Johnnie Williams or the holder of a sawed-off shotgun. They were in mortal danger, and their actions showed no negligence.

I opposed their motions vehemently. "Who had the sawed-off shotgun? Was it pointed at the police officers? Why was it on safety? Why would a bus driver, with no prior criminal record, threaten the police?" There surely were enough unresolved questions so that the case should be submitted to the jury. (For many centuries in our law it has been the job of the jury, not the judge, to decide cases where there are conflicts of fact in the evidence.)

Without any preliminary comment at all, Judge Gordon granted the defendants' request. We were stunned. What a letdown after four days of trial! Judge Gordon called the jury back into the courtroom and announced that he was directing a verdict of "not guilty" for all the defendants. He had the jurors go through the charade of rubber-stamping his decision.

That was it. I was enraged after expending all that time and energy. If the jury had decided in favor of the defendants, that would have been disappointing enough, but at least we would have known that our client had her day in court. It looked as though the defendants were correct in never offering anything to settle.

I couldn't help wondering if the judge's desire to begin his July Fourth weekend early influenced his ruling. He made his decision on Thursday, July 3, 1969.

We appealed Judge Gordon's decision to the Third District Court of Appeal. That court said that he was correct in deciding that Dorothy Williams did not have "standing" to bring the suit since she was not Johnnie's lawful widow. At the same time, though, the court also decided that the case against the officers alleging negligence was one that should have been submitted to the jury. The court said "a jury of reasonable people could find that Johnnie Lee Williams had been shot in the back when he did not have a weapon at hand, and while there was no riot or affray in progress."

The appellate court agreed with me that Judge Gordon had usurped the proper role of the jury. Dorothy Williams couldn't bring the suit, but her children could. At this point a "funny" thing happened. Lillian Williams hired a lawyer who in turn referred her case to me. So now I was representing all five of Johnnie's children: Lillian's three and Dorothy's two!

I felt that our case was strengthened. The defense could no longer "muddy the waters" about Johnnie's life-style or his sexual virtuosity. I was raring to go, particularly since I had already done all the tedious preparation in getting ready for the first trial.

But it was not to be! On the morning the second trial was to begin, the county's attorneys offered to settle for $22,500. I recommended that my clients reject it. I believed that I would prove negligence. All my instincts said "go to the jury."

The clients asked the classic question. "Can we lose and get nothing?" Of course, my answer had to be yes. It is impossible to guarantee anything with that eighth wonder of the world—a jury. To me, we were gambling peanuts, but to my clients this sum was at least certain, and represented money which would be set aside for the children for educational purposes. Fear prevailed, and my clients instructed me to accept the offer.

Defense attorneys are well aware of the pressure to take a settlement offer which exists in the minds of poor people, and they use it to their advantage; offering little and late. I had been all cranked up, and now I was wiped out emotionally. I think the situation is analogous to an actor preparing for an important role and then being told that the play will never open. How would the audience have reacted? What would the jury have done?

The summation which had been gestating would never be delivered. There were so many things I wanted to say. For example:

The alleged civil disturbance was a totally phony issue. The Republican convention was over. Governor Kirk's order to the sheriff was issued five days earlier and related to a completely different area of Dade County. On this particular night, in this particular area there was certainly no riot. This "crowd" was very tame. If the deputies had really been worried about unruly crowd behavior then their actions were doubly amateurish because Lonnie Johnson could have been leading them into a trap.

Cribbs and Laurie did not call headquarters or use a bullhorn or the car spotlight. They walked in the dark and saw several blacks clustered about. They saw a shotgun. They were sure "Williams" would shoot, but he didn't. They were sure Laurie couldn't miss with his revolver, but he did. Were they just as wrong when they said the plaintiff had the shotgun pointed at them?

Laurie said he fired "at the center of plaintiff's chest." If so, how could Cribbs shoot Williams in the back a split-second later? Why did the sawed-off shotgun remain on safety?

I believe the police officers saw a shotgun. I further believe that *if* someone had pointed it at them, they had the right to shoot first in self-defense and ask questions later. However, if someone "whirled" after the order to "freeze"—it figures that person would have shot immediately. He would not have stood around with an illegal weapon on "safety."

I think police pride got in the way of the truth here. I think Cribbs meant to shoot Walters but got Johnnie instead. Police pride didn't want to admit two things—that the officers reacted unprofessionally to the sight of a shotgun which was not pointed at them, and that one of them shot an innocent bystander.

It was much more likely that someone with Walters's criminal background (someone who had a knife at the card game) would have more immediate access to a sawed-off shotgun than would a Dade County bus driver. The jury could have become angered at the unseemly speed of the police investigation and at taking witnesses to the station in handcuffs. I felt it was eminently provable that the "internal review" of this tragic incident was political and not objective.

Yes, I could have said a lot of things. Maybe we would have won big. But perhaps the jury would have felt that the officers acted reasonably under terribly difficult circumstances. We'll never know.

Johnnie Lee Williams died because he was in the wrong place at the wrong time. I wished the children and both Mrs. Williamses well, and went on to the next case.

VII

Richard Adams and Michael Robinson
———VS.———
the Miami-Dade County Jail
More Police Negligence

Across the street from the Dade County Justice Building, which houses all the criminal courts and the district attorney's offices, is the Dade County Jail. There is a police precinct building next door. The inmates are "right under the nose of the authorities."

I

On May 31, 1968, in a cell in the Dade County Jail, Raymond Rhome, an inmate, murdered Richard Adams and proceeded to mutilate his body. Rhome and Adams were the only two in the cell. The adjacent cell was empty.

Both men were young and black. The similarities stopped there. Richard Adams was in jail awaiting trial on charge

239

of armed robbery of a supermarket, but the evidence against him was weak. He had no prior convictions at all. He was from a hard-working family and lived at home with his mother and brothers and sisters. Ever since he dropped out of high school, he had always worked and contributed a portion of his earnings to the household. His father, A. G. Adams, had been employed by the same paper company in Miami for over thirty years. There was a bond of only $5,000 on Richard, but his family was still trying to raise $500 to pay the premium to get him released, pending trial.

In contrast with Richard Adams, who was merely accused of a crime, Raymond Rhome had been convicted. For him, the Dade County Jail was a mere holding facility, before he was to be transferred to a maximum-security state prison at Raiford, in North Florida. His crime was rape, and his sentence was life.

In connection with his rape trial, Rhome had a psychiatric evaluation at Jackson Memorial Hospital, Miami, on June 6, 1967, a year before he was put in the cell with Richard Adams. The history taken by the psychiatrists reflected repeated arrests and convictions for burglary and related crimes. The final diagnosis by the psychiatric staff was "sociopathic personality disturbance with deep-seated antisocial feelings, and strong elements of sexual deviation."

Rhome's defense to the rape charge had been insanity or mental aberration. The court-appointed psychiatrist, Dr. Albert C. Jaslow, submitted his report to Circuit Court Judge Jack A. Falk on February 10, 1968. Dr. Jaslow said:

He is an eighteen-year-old who states that he makes his living by robbing and stealing. His formal education ceased prior to the seventh grade. He is an admitted homosexual and feels there is not much difference between male or female sex objects. His judgment is poor and his entire thinking process is deficient and distorted. His orientation and philosophy is entirely sociopathic, and he feels he can and should do whatever is necessary at any given time to gratify himself or respond to a given situation. There is nothing to indicate that this boy was unaware of the nature and consequences of his behavior at any time, although he is undoubtedly of borderline mental intelligence. Within the limits of his deficient mental capacity, I feel he was sane at the time of the commission of the alleged rape.

Rhome had a history of disruptive behavior while in jail. Adams had given the authorities no trouble at all. Rhome was constantly being placed in punishment cells for infractions of a variety of rules; he had been found with razor blades on several occasions and had even attempted suicide more than once.

Adams and Rhome were alone in their cell, which they had occupied for four days. There were no witness to the strangulation. In fact, it was Rhome who had to advise the authorities of what had occurred. He gave this account.

Early in the morning of May 31, he was sleeping with a towel across his eyes because the light was on, when he was awakened by Adams standing over him with a razor blade. Adams allegedly said, "I want a little of your behind." Rhome's reply was that he wasn't that kind of fellow and Adams should leave him alone.

As Richard Adams started to walk away, Rhome hit him from the back, knocked him down and choked him till he was nearly unconscious. Rhome then dragged his victim to the cot, knotted three towels together and put a toilet paper core on one end. He continued to choke Adams until his body was limp.

According to Rhome, he next took a razor blade and carved his name in Richard Adams's back. The autopsy report, in describing the defaced body, said that in an area commencing from below the left shoulder and extending down to the low back, the name "RHOME" had been inscribed in three-inch-tall bold capital letters. Rigor mortis was complete by the time the medical examiner saw the body. The cause of death was listed as "asphyxia due to strangulation."

Rhome took a shower and began to read a book. When the odor got to be too much for his delicate sensibilities, at around 4:00 A.M., he notified a guard that there was a "dead guy" in his cell. Rhome was moved to the cell next door which had been empty all the time.

This fact was a compelling reason for my acceptance of the case. I just could not believe that jail personnel could be so lacking in classification standards that they would place a convicted rapist and homosexual sociopath in a cell with another young man who had no history of sexual deviation or prior criminal record, when there was an empty cell right there.

During the course of preparing this case for trial, I was to take photographs and measurements of the murder cell. I was to learn a great deal about the inner workings of this institution, which I had seen so many times from the street. The inner depth dimension from the bars to the back wall, was 9 feet 3 inches. At the far end, or innermost part of the cell, there was a shower on the left as you faced inward, 3 feet 6 inches deep by 2 feet 8 inches wide. There was a 6-foot 6-inch metal bunk bolted to the wall on the left as you faced in.

Sergeant Isaac Johnson of the Mobile Crime Laboratory of the Sheriff's Department described his findings in the death cell:

On the floor directly across from the bunk, and against the opposite wall is a mattress. Above the mattress, on the floor bolted to the wall, is a metal table and a metal chair. There is a lavatory seat attached to the far wall, opposite the side of the shower. On the floor in front of the toilet seat are three towels tied together, with a third towel tied through a wet roll of toilet paper. On the bunk end, or edge nearest the shower, there is a blanket. I observed the victim lying face up on the bunk suspended from the wall, dressed in white boxer-type undershorts with his head up.

Three more psychiatrists examined Rhome. Circuit Judge J. Gwynn Parker found him mentally competent to stand trial for the murder of Richard Adams. Killing in response to a homosexual attack, if believed, could be a valid defense to a charge of first-degree murder. However, even by Rhome's own account, Adams was walking away as he jumped him from the rear and strangled him.

Rhome was found guilty on April 29, 1969. The jury recommended mercy, which made a life sentence mandatory. So now Rhome was still on his way to Raiford State Penitentiary, but with *two* life sentences facing him rather than only one. (It is a well-known fact in Florida penal circles that "life" sentences generally result in time actually served of seven to twelve years.)

The *Miami Herald* had been editorializing for a long time about the atrocious conditions in the Dade County Jail. In response to the Adams murder, the *Herald* had this to say:

Even with the jails crowded, it is hard to understand how an inmate can strangle another man in a cell, carve on his back with a razor blade and complete the deed without interference. With other prisoners on hand, with guards about, one would assume an alarm of some kind would be sounded and the murder prevented. It is carrying noninvolvement too far to permit murders to happen in a jail cell.

On another occasion, this editorial appeared:

What goes on in the Dade County Jail is an abomination. The *Herald*'s Charles Whited has told the story of homosexual abuse that goes beyond and pales the terror that was part of America's chain gang era. It is a story that needs to come down hard on the conscience of the community. It would be easy to blame a

long-gone County Commission for awarding the architectural
contract for the jail on a "politics as usual" basis. That happened
a dozen years ago.

What good does it do to point out a bad design that makes it
difficult to keep the cell blocks under surveillance? What is
needed is a community task force to deal with the problem of
prisoner protection immediately. This is no time for any prolonged investigations by the grand jury or any other public
body. The facts are clear. The recent articles by Mr. Whited
must be credited for the sudden alarm of the criminal court
judges and the public defender's office. There must be a better
system of arraignments and easier bond procedures for relieving
the overcrowding of the jail.

If there is manpower for protecting only six hundred prisoners
from abuse, then there should be only six hundred persons in that
jail. To put the six hundred and first man behind bars is to
invite the unthinkable to continue to occur. The terror in the
jail must end!

I agreed with the editorials. That is why I accepted the
case, knowing full well that there would be no real money
here and that I would make enemies in the "power structure."

I filed suit against Miami-Dade County on the theory
that they had a responsibility to protect persons in their
custody from physical abuse and death. My familiar adversary, Bill Hoeveler, once again represented the county. The
suit was for wrongful death. Unfortunately, though, in the
eyes of the law, the death of an unmarried person ap-
proaching adulthood has very little value. If you have a
wife who becomes a widow, she has a good claim, and if
you have children, they have a good claim; otherwise the
potential is terribly limited.

There was some evidence that Richard was twenty-one,
rather than nineteen, as his mother asserted. If he was
twenty-one, the case would be worth absolutely zero. The

law in Florida has changed since that time, so that today an eighteen-year-old is regarded as an adult for all purposes. Today nobody can recover one penny for the death of an unmarried person above the age of eighteen with no dependents, such as Richard Adams.

I had several hurdles to overcome. The first, obviously, was a possible prejudice against blacks. The second was the presumption which the average middle class WASP juror will normally make—that a person is in jail because he deserves to be there. In theory, we say that a man is innocent until proven guilty, but in practice the jury may ignore that. People are very conscious of the expenditure of tax dollars. When you start talking about inadequate supervision in jail, their reaction is that they don't want their money spent to give prison a "country club atmosphere." Such jurors rarely choose to empathize with persons who are incarcerated, even those presumably innocent.

Richard's parents were separated. They were poor. Mr. and Mrs. Adams were not on good terms. They had not visited Richard often during the time he was in jail. These facts, too, militated against a substantial damage award.

I knew that Mr. and Mrs. Adams did not want to go to court under any circumstances. As a practical matter, they would have accepted any offer. This willingness to settle is an attitude plaintiff's lawyers frequently confront, even where the facts of the case are not controversial and tragic to the extent that people would be emotionally overwrought in the course of a trial.

Under these circumstances, one must be an extremely artful negotiator, because if your opponent senses this attitude, he will make no offer at all. If the defendant is unaware of the plaintiff's fear of the courtroom, you can frequently bluff an insurance company into a decent settlement. They are apt to mistake the aggressiveness and confident pose of the attorney as indicative of the state of mind of the client.

Shortly before trial, the county offered $7,500 to settle. Naturally, my clients accepted it. Even in death, the poor and the poorly educated often receive a shafting from our judicial system and the insurance industry. Sometime after this case was closed another outrageous murder was committed in the Dade County Jail. I became the attorney in that case as well.

II

I once wrote a book about our so-called criminal justice "system," which is no system at all, which deals out far more injustice than justice and which is a disgrace to a civilized nation.

After Richard Adams was killed, you would think someone in authority would take steps to prevent further killings. To allow violence to prisoners, who are trapped, is intolerable. In this case, as in Adams, the person murdered had not yet been tried. He was in danger, and he knew it. He told the authorities, and they ignored it. He was caught and killed.

Michael Robinson, an eighteen-year-old mildly retarded black youth, was murdered by a southern white man in a Dade County Jail cell on Friday, July 3, 1970. As in the Adams case, the murderer here, Bobby Barfield, was a hardened and convicted criminal, whereas Michael had never been convicted of anything. As in the Adams case, too, Michael was there to be killed only because his family did not have the wherewithal to raise a minimal bond premium.

However, in stark contrast to the Adams murder, where there were no witnesses, the Robinson killing took place in front of fifteen inmates in a sixth-floor cell with measurements of 39 feet by 17 feet. There was absolutely no classification in this cell as to age, race, previous criminal or mental records, or anything else. Including Michael, there were three blacks in the cell.

Barfield ran the cell. A tough, hardened criminal, and a friend of Murph the Surf, of "Star of India" infamy, Barfield possessed a "shank," a sharpened-down spoon that served as a homemade knife. Two of Barfield's underlings who assisted him in the enforcement of his wishes also had shanks, and had had them for several weeks prior to the killing.

Residents of the death cell were interviewed in the sixth-floor lobby of the jail. It was a classic case of "hear no evil, see no evil, speak no evil." It seems everyone was preoccupied in one fashion or another.

Seven of the men insisted that they were sleeping, even though the murder took place during daylight hours. Two others said they were reading the newspaper; two more were reading books; another was playing cards—solitaire. Yet another said that he had been reading his Bible and had no knowledge of the incident. Barfield said he was reading the sports section of the newspaper and had absolutely no idea as to what caused Michael Robinson's untimely demise.

There was one hero in the drama. His name was Nicholas Zarnbus, a young man who had been convicted of numerous assaults and breaking and enterings. He was awaiting transfer to the Sumter Correctional Institution in Bushnell, Florida, to begin serving a ten-year sentence. Zarnbus was from Cincinnati, where he had also been convicted of several crimes. He was the key to the case. Without him there would have been no possibility at all of a civil suit. He was the only individual in the cell who said from the outset that Barfield had murdered Michael Robinson.

Zarnbus had written Mrs. Robinson a very poignant letter expressing deep sympathy for her son's death. Michael's mother gave me that letter. I made contact with Zarnbus, who immediately said he would be willing to tell the truth in court. He didn't ask me for any favors in return.

Zarnbus, who was white, met Michael a week or so before the murder, when Michael was moved into this multiple cell. Michael had been in Dade County Jail over two months, since April 21, 1970, and, like Richard Adams, was there on a charge of armed robbery. By virtue of a court order I obtained, Zarnbus was transported from Sumter to Miami for the trial. He was housed once again in the familar surroundings of the Dade County Jail, the very institution we were suing, where the authorities gave him unending grief because of his willingness to stand up and tell the truth.

I had filed suit against Dade County on several theories of negligence. First, all types of person were crowded together in one large cell. There were felons, men not yet convicted but accused of felonies, psychopaths, men accused of minor matters, men convicted and waiting to be transferred to other institutions. There was no attempt made to classify them or separate the dangerous from the harmless.

In addition, it developed that three men in the cell had weapons, and there were no means employed in the jail for periodic searching to prevent this from happening. There was obviously overcrowding in the jail and inadequate staffing by prison guards. There was no effective supervision of the prisoners. My basic job was to convince a jury that Michael Robinson was killed because of a total lack of supervision and protection by the county. I put Zarnbus on the witness stand.

Q. What was Mike's relationship to Barfield?

A. He was pretty much the same as the way Barfield treated some of the other younger fellows, but he picked on Mike worse. He made Mike do all his stuff, like make his bed, you

know, and stuff like that, take his tray and clean up after
him.

Q. Did the jail have any search system at all, either searching
individuals or searching the cell?

A. I spent a year in the Dade County Jail, and I never seen
them shake down any cell I was in.

Q. What happened on the day of the killing?

A. Barfield ordered Mike to pick up a cigarette butt and he
refused. I think Mike had just gotten sick and tired of following all his crummy orders. Barfield threw a punch at him
and the boy punched back and he got in a good lick and this
was embarrassing for Barfield. So he said, "I'm not going to
fight you. I'm just going to kill you." He said, "I have something for you." Then he went and got the shank, and it
wasn't really a fight, 'cause Mike didn't have nothing, and
the other two guys had their shanks keeping everybody out
so they wouldn't interfere. He got Mike hemmed up between
the table and the wall, over by the television, and when Mike
started to come out, he just stabbed him.

Q. On July 3, 1970, before the stabbing, had Mike complained
to anyone?

A. He told the guard Barfield was threatening him and he
wanted to be taken out of the cell. The guard looked at Barfield
and looked at the boy, and said, "Don't worry about it, I'll
take care of it, I'll come back around." He never did come
back. I heard Mike ask different guards to be taken out of
the cell on other days, but they always wanted a specific
reason, and Mike was leery because he didn't know how
much Barfield could do.

Q. Did anyone in the cell come to Mike's aid?

A. Well, Barfield's two buddies were there and they also had
shanks, and he told everyone that if they tried to interfere
the same thing would happen to them.

Q. No guard came around?

A. If you would see a guard come by once in every two hours,
you were lucky.

Q. After Michael got stabbed, what happened?

A. He moved around for I guess three or four minutes, and he tried to pick up a brush—a scrub brush we use to clean the sinks with and he put it on the table, but Barfield kicked it out of his hands. Mike stumbled around a little more and finally he leaned against the far wall and slid down. Blood started coming· out of his mouth. Barfield made everyone wait about three or four minutes and then they beat on the table to call the guard.

Just as in the *Adams* case, the inmates had to inform the guards that a murder had taken place.

Q. On those occasions when a guard would come by what would he generally do or say?

A. Just walk on by as quick as he could, because they hate to stop and talk to anybody—afraid they'll have to do something for somebody.

Q. How long had Mike and Barfield been arguing before Mike was actually stabbed?

A. About half an hour.

Q. How long before the stabbing had Mike notified the guard that he wanted to get out of there?

A. About the same time—a half hour. *(The county, through an employee, had notice of an explosive situation but failed to protect Michael Robinson.)*

Now I had to get into a very tricky area. Barfield's first-degree murder trial had ended in an acquittal. That's right, fifteen eyewitnesses, yet no punishment for the killer! Zarnbus had testified truthfully before the Dade County grand jury, and it was his account which laid the groundwork for the indictment. By that time two other cellmates, having Zarnbus's courage as an example, came forward to corroborate him. However, they all remained in the Dade County Jail pending that trial, and they had very good reason to fear for their lives. Zarnbus had not been completely truthful at the criminal trial.

Q. Did you testify at Barfield's trial?

A. I testified as far as I could without getting the same thing happen to me. I played kinda dumb. Even though I did that, my first day at Sumter I got jumped with rocks and everything else and spent two weeks in the hospital.

Q. How did you know that beating was related to the Barfield matter?

A. The same guy that jumped me was one of the guys that held the shank on the rest of the cell and told them not to interfere. He and two other guys jumped me my first day there.

Bill Hoeveler made much of this on cross-examination in the usual fashion. "Well, you admitted you lied at the criminal trial when you told that jury you did not see Barfield stab Robinson. Why should we accept your present version as the truth?"

One reason was the fact that this truthful testimony couldn't hurt Barfield any longer since he could not be tried again under any circumstances. I think Zarnbus was seeking redemption for his failure to help Michael. He was the only one in the cell with the decency to feel guilty about that.

The two cellmates who had corroborated Zarnbus before the grand jury refused to help in the civil trial. They felt that there was still danger of retribution from Barfield's friends. Hoeveler made much of Zarnbus's criminal record which I, of course, had brought out first. It would be very foolish of me to permit the cross-examiner to make a bigger thing of it by not mentioning it. By laying out that which may be harmful on direct examination, you take a great deal of the sting out of the "cross."

I was prepared to argue to the jury later—"Who does Hoeveler expect me to get as witnesses, choirboys?" Sarcastically, I would say, "When a murder takes place in a jail cell, it is likely that the eyewitnesses will be convicts." My star witness's criminal record was a complete red herring. The only pertinent area of inquiry would be whether he had any motivation to lie. And he did not. Actually he was telling his story at substantial personal risk since he was blasting the Dade County Jail as well as Barfield.

Zarnbus became very angry at Hoeveler's interrogation and the implication that the Dade County Jail was really a marvelous facility with interested and enlightened personnel. He knew better, from bitter experience. This insurance company lawyer was not about to tell him the facts of life. His demeanor on the stand might not sit well with the jury, who knew as much about jail conditions as they knew about the migration habits of the Alaskan seal, but I gave him a full head of steam.

Zarnbus's testimony was tough and arrogant, but straight. His contempt for the flag-waving, establishment approach of Bill Hoeveler was something to behold. I could only hope that his attitude would not turn the jury against him and, by implication, against my clients. He simply refused to pander to the jury, which in his circumstances, I had to admire.

Once the guards were notified of the stabbing, they rushed Michael to Jackson Memorial Hospital, a county facility, which is located within shouting distance of the jail. He arrived there at 7:26 P.M. with no pulse or blood pressure. Surgeons cut his chest open and gave internal heart massage, but he was pronounced dead at 7:56 P.M. The shank had lacerated his heart.

To prove negligence by the county, I desperately needed expert testimony. The county would argue that there is no way to prevent a sudden assault, since you cannot have a guard at each cell constantly watching what the inmates are doing. I had to show that the conditions at the jail did not conform to reasonable and proper penal standards, and if they had conformed to those standards, that a murder would not have been committed.

I corresponded with many law-enforcement agencies and universities. Finally, I was lucky enough to locate George L. Kirkham, a professor in the department of criminology at Florida State University in Tallahassee. Less than a month before the trial was to begin, Professor Kirkham agreed to testify. Without him, I had every reason to believe that the judge would direct a verdict against us, kicking us out of court.

Professor Kirkham was not just an academic. He had spent three years as a correctional counselor at Soledad State Prison in California. He had also been the director of a federally supported project in a big California jail system.

At the trial, I established certain facts through other witnesses to lay the foundation for my crucial question. I asked Dr. Kirkham to assume the following facts:

That the Dade County Jail contained a total of seventy-six cells for eight hundred seventy-eight men on July 3, 1970, and that there were sixteen multiple cells on the sixth floor. That there was only one guard to a floor. That no provision was made for the separation of convicted inmates from those persons who had only been charged with crimes. The lack of a classification system made it likely that persons convicted of drunkenness might very well be placed in the same cells with individuals convicted of murder or rape. That on July 3, 1970, in the murder cell there were a total of seventeen men—that these men remained locked up for twenty-four hours a day, leaving the cell only for a serious illness or to visit with their attorney for a few minutes.

There were more inmates than bunks; jail personnel were aware of the fact that Barfield was the boss in this cell. Barfield and two of his cronies possessed shanks which they had for at least several weeks prior to the murder of Michael Robinson.

No weapon of any kind was found in the cell or on anyone's per son following the murder.

Now came *the* question:

Was the behavior and actions of Dade County personnel, as I have described them, in conformity with reasonable penal standards in metropolitan communities of comparable size to Dade County?

Of course, Professor Kirkham said they were not! I didn't bring him down from Tallahassee to say that the jail was a first-class operation. He said the county was grossly negligent in permitting such conditions to exist.

Dr. Kirkham testified strongly about the lack of a prisoner classification system, the lack of an adequate system to prevent the use of shanks and a preposterous ratio of one guard to sixteen multiple cells. It was a situation he said, which fostered the creation of a boss in each cell, since someone had to be in charge and it obviously couldn't be a guard who walked quickly by each cell two or three times on his particular eight-hour shift.

Naturally, jail personnel testified that they had a very thorough "shakedown" system to ascertain the existence of weapons. This was ludicrous. The fact of the murder made it very obvious that the "system" did not work.

The defense witnesses denied that Michael had asked any guard to be removed from the cell. The only testimony I had was Zarnbus's word for this, as well as for nearly every other part of the case. If Hoeveler could succeed in discrediting Zarnbus, then he could succeed in diminishing the effect of Professor Kirkham on the theory that the information I gave him in my question was neither accurate nor complete.

Try as I might, I could get no testimony from the other men who had been in the cell at the time of the murder. It was plain that they still had a great fear that the County would not be able to protect them against Barfield's power. This was certainly the underlying reason why he was acquitted on the murder charge.

Prior to the beginning of the trial, Hoeveler had offered only $2,500 to settle the case, which suited me fine. O. C. Robinson had been a garbage man, and his wife, Ida Mae, a maid for many years and I knew they were anxious to settle. If the defense came up to $15,000, they would undoubtedly tell me to grab it. Like Richard Adams's parents, they were hard working and steady citizens, and in my view were perfectly entitled to compensation for this ridiculous and avoidable waste of a life.

I went through my usual routine of being obnoxious (which comes very easy to me) and avoiding settlement negotiations so as to discourage a decent offer, one which my clients would accept. At $2,500, there was no decision to be made because that was so low that after the payment of fees and costs, the clients would wind up with very little.

Insurance companies correctly figure that a certain percentage of litigants will "chicken out" at the courtroom door. They frequently wait to see how a trial is going before offering any substantial money. This is one of the main reasons why court calendars are clogged and years behind in many jurisdictions. The insurance company usually has enough information to evaluate the case and dispose of it on a reasonable basis within a few months of the incident, but all too frequently, they wait till the moment of truth nears.

During the trial insurance company representatives frequently sit in the public section, observing the impression that the parties and their witnesses make upon a given jury. A lawyer may have a $100,000 case if it is being tried before *one* combination of six or twelve people, and a big ugly goose egg if it is tried before a different combination. Much of that is completely beyond the control of a lawyer. Once he has utilized all his "challenges" (three in the usual civil case), he and his clients are stuck with whoever is left. Somtimes you get such a bad "juror panel" that you would like to excuse ten of them. But you can only get rid of the "worst" three and hope for the best.

Hoeveler and the Continental Casualty Company obviously became concerned as the trial moved along. He may have felt that my sense of outrage over the violent murder of this youngster had permeated the jury box. They were impressed with the testimony of Professor Kirkham and had to have at least some grudging admiration for Nick Zarnbus.

The case was settled before it was to be given to the jury for the sum of $25,000. Even though the jury looked fairly conservative, I felt there were one or two members who could be aroused over the blatant negligence of jail personnel. This anger could have translated into a big verdict.

During my entire legal career, I have settled only eleven or so cases during the trial itself. I dislike doing that immensely. By the time the trial begins, I am all geared up emotionally, intellectually, and dramatically. All the hard work and preparation has been done. The battle lines have been drawn. My curiosity and ego want to know the verdict. Was I able to persuade the jury to accept our point of view?

Many lawyers talk settlement throughout the trial. My attitude is that I have been hired to try the case, not negotiate it. On the other hand, being ridiculously stubborn would be a disservice to one's client.

Rear-end collision automobile cases and "slip and fall" accidents in supermarkets can be awfully boring. Cases like Robinson, Adams, and Williams are tragic and aggravating, but they are also fascinating and instructive and challenging. Through questioning witnesses, viewing the scene, reading all the pertinent documents, you can sink your teeth into a case like this and get to the bottom of it. After all, I didn't go to law school to read abstracts of title or prepare people's wills.

The frequency of homosexual rapes, beatings, and murders which occur in our "warehouses" is a national disgrace. As a matter of fact, the Dade County Jail is regarded as a relatively modern institution. Sheriff Purdy is considered to be a man of impressive credentials, as well as a man of integrity. It does not take any great imagination to realize what goes on in places with even worse physical facilities and where there is no community pressure to improve things.

I strongly believe that civil trial lawyers with guts enough to take cases like this can have a useful social impact. I am criticized by some of my colleagues for being a sucker for some of these so-called "cause" cases. They generally figure that the odds are too tough and the damage potential is not there—so why buck City Hall and make enemies?

A lawyer—and particularly one who is making good money—has a responsibility to take some of the tough cases. I hope I never reach the stage where I am looking only for the safe case—one that I will definitely look good in— which is a serious failing of too many of my brethren who call themselves trial lawyers. Anyone can try the case of a wage earner who suffers multiple injuries in an automobile accident, although the great lawyer will usually get a much higher award than the average attorney.

The point is that we should—at least sometimes—take cases simply because our client is right, and simply because we may be able to improve things by obtaining a good result. One of the best instruments of improvement of any unsafe condition or negligent procedure is the civil lawsuit which costs an insurance company money. Just as medical malpractice verdicts have started the insurance companies clamoring for hospitals to set up review committees and for medical associations to "clean their own house," so also will cases like this—and I am sure there are many more which never come to light—encourage insurers to insist upon better standards of housing, of discipline, of treatment, supervision, and above all, of protection of people incarcerated in jails and prisons.

By settling the cases of Johnnie Lee Williams, Richard Adams and Michael Robinson, Dade County admitted some degree of negligence or fault by their police and jail personnel. These cases involved a very emotional but still infant area of law—the responsibility of a community for negligent acts of its policemen. If being a policeman is a "profession" as it should be, there should be a professional level of duty, the breach of which is malpractice.

I do not want to hamstring law enforcement officers in the performance of their duties. I would not take a case where I was satisfied that injury or death arose from misfortune during police action by a reasonably prudent officer. However, just as the M.D. degree should not serve as a shield for malpractice, so the uniform should not be a screen for incompetence. Hopefully, governmental bodies and insurance companies will learn to seek improvement of police work and detention facilities without tragedies such as these having to act as a prod.

VIII

Arthur Dillon
——VS.——
Miami-Dade County
The Value of a Father's Love

The trial lawyer faces a different set of facts in each case. Tactics and style will be influenced by the ability of your opponent, the makeup of the jury, the personality of the judge and a hundred other variables. Considering the inherent drama of litigation, it is amazing to me how very few imaginative movies or TV programs there are nowadays which deal with the courts.

This case demonstrates how the trial lawyer must retain flexibility and the aptitude to adapt to circumstances. I was representing the divorced father of a dead little girl while the mother was being represented by J. B. Spence of the firm of Spence, Payne and Masington. I had never in my career tried a case together with a law partner, yet here it would be necessary for Spence and me to cooperate and mesh our respective approaches.

My client, Arthur Dillon, was divorced from his wife on March 19, 1973, after seven years of marriage. They had

two daughters—Darlene, affectionately known as DeeDee,
and her little sister Pamela. Sometime after the predivorce
separation in October, 1972, Diane Dillon and her two
daughters moved to the home of Mrs. Dillon's aunt.

It was a very convenient location for DeeDee, just two
blocks from the Benjamin Franklin Elementary School.
Mrs. Dillon had repeatedly shown DeeDee the safest route
to school, leading her up to a crosswalk on Northwest 135th
Street in North Miami where all a pedestrian had to do
was press a button for the light to change.

At 8:10 A.M. on Monday, April 9, 1973, six-year-old
DeeDee left for school alone, wearing a red and white
checkered blouse with three-quarter-length sleeves, a navy
blue skirt and white patent leather shoes. She was carrying
a storybook called *Walt Disney's Alice in Wonderland* and
a lunchbox decorated with Charlie Brown and Snoopy
characters. It was a clear, sunny day.

Since there was no paved sidewalk on the north side
of 135th Street, DeeDee had to walk off the roadway
on the grassy, sandy shoulder. The street is one-way, with
two lanes of traffic going east. DeeDee was walking in an
easterly direction, toward the crosswalk, on the north side
of the street.

A Miami-Dade County garbage truck turned the corner
form twelfth Avenue onto 135th Street, and began going
east on the same shoulder that DeeDee was walking on.
The driver went on the shoulder so as not to interfere with
the movement of rush-hour traffic on 135th Street, a very
busy thoroughfare. The two helpers on each side of the
rear of the truck had made a pickup from a garbage can
at the first home on 135th Street. They both noticed DeeDee
walking to the left or slightly north of the truck, and several
yards in front of it.

Dade County garbage crews work fast. They are paid
to cover a certain route, estimated to be an eight-hour-day's

work. The faster they work, the earlier they finish. They generally finish their day's work in about five hours.

After replacing the cans, the helpers returned to the back of the truck, and jumped on the rear step. The driver checked his rear view mirrors to make sure they were firmly situated, and then he proceeded, he said, at a speed of about five miles an hour towards the next garbage pickup.

When the truck came to a stop for the second pickup, the helpers looked back and saw DeeDee Dillon on the grassy shoulder behind the truck. Although he had a perfectly clear view, the driver had never seen DeeDee until the helpers pointed her out to him at that moment. This was almost certainly because his attention was focused on his two helpers in the back, looking through his rear-view mirrors. DeeDee had been crushed under the left rear wheels of the garbage truck, and was killed instantly.

It was a freak accident. No one knew exactly what happened. The crosswalk was still fifteen feet or so in front of the truck after it had come to a complete stop. The driver did not stop because of the accident, but simply in order to make the next pickup. One housewife looked out of her kitchen window because she heard a dog barking and saw what she thought was a "rag doll" being tossed through the air at a height of about four feet. She saw the "doll" land and the left rear wheels drive over her. But this witness did not see any other contact between the garbage truck and DeeDee. In the course of the lawsuit, in which the county denied fault, their defense was to make much of this, particularly since there was no firm evidence that any portion of the truck other than the wheels ever touched the child.

The autopsy on 3'10", forty-five-pound DeeDee Dillon was performed by the Dade County medical examiner. Her head and skull were severely crushed and she sustained multiple fractures of the face, nose, cheeks, and jawbone. Her brain was severely lacerated. The huge wheels of the truck had simply crushed and mutilated the little girl's head, chest, abdomen, and pelvis. The autopsy report was never allowed into evidence because there was no dispute as to how she died. The judge felt that the introduction of the report into evidence would have been highly inflammatory and prejudicial to the county. This did not concern us because any jury would certainly comprehend the effect of garbage truck wheels rolling over a small child.

We had a strong case against Dade County. DeeDee was walking on the shoulder, which had to be considered as the sidewalk area. She was walking toward the crosswalk so that she could then cross to the south of 135th Street. Even after the wheels passed over her, she was fourteen feet away or north of the north edge of the highway. In all likelihood the truck, angled slightly towards the highway as it approached the second garbage can, caught DeeDee, who was walking with her back to the truck, flipped her in the air and rolled over her.

The county's real reason for contesting the case, in my opinion, was that they did not think that I could "sell" Arthur Dillion to the jury. Nevertheless, they also contested liability, coming up with the theory that the little girl's lunchbox fell under the truck, that she tried to get the driver's attention, reached under the truck to retrieve the lunchbox, and was caught by the rear wheels.

Since I represented a father who had initiated the separation and divorce, I anticipated problems. Arthur was twenty-seven years old at the time of trial. Although he was not a hippie in any sense, he did have flowing locks down to his shoulder blades. He would have had a crew cut if I told him to get one, but I knew the defense would be able to show what his appearance was prior to trial. I decided to play it perfectly straight.

Arthur had quit school when he was in the eighth grade. He tried some commercial fishing with his stepfather and married Diane at age nineteen. He had worked for Sears, Roebuck & Company as a shipping clerk, a helper on a delivery truck, and finally as a truck driver. He had been in the employ of Sears a total of seven years, when he quit his job shortly before the divorce.

The opposition would try to make Arthur look irresponsible because he did not work for five or six months after leaving Sears. In truth, Arthur was in the process of attempting to find himself and adjust to a new life-style. He had lived with a girlfriend for several months. This certainly would not help his "image" if we got a WASP middle-class jury. Another problem was that Diane had brought him to court on one occasion following the separation because he was behind in his support payments. The defense was careful to get this into evidence, trying to make it appear that Arthur was not at all interested in his two daughters.

The case opened on Thursday, November 8, 1973, before Circuit Judge Raymond G. Nathan—the same judge who had presided over the original Linda Powell v. Dr. Fagan trial. The case would be over by Friday afternoon. Bill Hoeveler was defending for the county again.

Detailed depositions had been taken. The county had ample time and opportunity to evaluate the case, both in terms of liability where in my opinion it was obvious they were at fault, and also in terms of damages. My demand for settlement had been $150,000. Spence was seeking a far greater amount for Mrs. Dillon, but it was all academic since Hoeveler did not come close to our demands.

During the pretrial depositions and from talking with Arthur Dillon, I became impressed with the man. Although young and outwardly living a rather unconventional life, I soon learned that he had suffered a very real loss. He really loved his little girl and became emotional whenever we discussed her. My problem at trial would be largely that of persuading a jury of probably "straight" conventional people that this long-haired young man, although divorced, and not having custody of his daughters, had suffered acute grief at the loss of his DeeDee.

As my client was a man and a father, I wanted men on the jury. We wound up with a jury of five women and one man, which was perfectly okay with Mr. Spence. Two of the women were divorced. I figured that they might be bitter toward a man who had left his wife and two young daughters. Another disadvantage was that three of the jurors did not have children. But with a limited number of peremptory challenges, you are often forced to stick with jurors you feel are wrong for a particular case.

I faced the long-hair problems squarely in my voir dire questioning of the jury, where the attorneys have a chance to eliminate jurors who may have a prejudice against their client, or against their client's case.

Now, I am sure all of you have looked at Arthur Dillon and seen his long hair. There are some lawyers who would tell a client that some juror may not like a fellow with hair that long, so "cut it for the trial." I think that is absurd and I believe people have more common sense than that, and wouldn't make a judgment on a purely outward appearance. But on the other hand, I recognize that there are some people who just don't like a man with long hair, period. Do any of you have that feeling with respect to Mr. Dillon?

Naturally, as I fully expected, they all said no. Most prospective jurors, even if they had a blatant prejudice against long hair, would not admit to it. But by asking such a question, you hope to clear the air and make someone with that bias feel slightly ashamed, and therefore, unwilling in the privacy of the jury room to act upon the bias when considering your client's case. Through experience you sometimes get a "vibration" from a gesture or grimace which tells you intuitively to get rid of a certain individual.

Another problem was that some people feel that a woman automatically suffers much more in losing a child than a man does. I had to impress upon them that there is no scientific basis for such a generalization, since it depends fully upon the people and specific circumstances involved. I wanted Arthur's award to bear at least a reasonable relationship to the amount given his ex-wife.

Arthur had not been to see any physician or psychiatrist for treatment or medication. The jury would simply have to take his word as to his own mental pain and suffering, which is the basic element of damage in such a case. Mrs. Dillon, on the other hand, was under psychiatric care for severe depression and anxiety. I said to the jurors:

In, our society boys are frequently brought up to hide their emotions, whereas it is perfectly all right for a girl to cry and display feelings. These attitudes are being examined more and more in terms of the traditional roles of male and female. I think we all understand that there can be very deep feelings without necessarily demonstrating them on the surface. Do you agree? Do any of you have the feeling, as you sit here now, that a woman would automatically suffer more from this type of loss than a man?

I didn't get any bad vibrations from the answers.

The liability witnesses were two police officers, the truck driver, the two helpers and the lady who mistook DeeDee for a "rag doll." Teachers and neighbors testified about the type of child she was. To explain the relationship between Arthur and his oldest daughter, I called Arthur, his parents, and one of his married sisters. The testimony went about as expected and there were no big surprises. I was confident we would get a verdict, but the question was how much?

Spence and I had divided the liability witnesses between

us since our objective was precisely the same in this regard. He tried Mrs. Dillon's case on damages and I tried Arthur's. In his summation, Spence asked the jury to return a verdict in favor of his client alone in the sum of $2,000,000.

Trial lawyers frequently disagree on the strategy of asking for an "outrageous" amount of money. Some think this can offend the jury and result in the client being penalized with a low award. It also allows the defense attorney to use the standard argument that our system is designed to compensate and not create instant wealth. The insurance lawyer will nearly always say that the named figure is hard-sell salesmanship, and plaintiff's counsel will be overjoyed if you return one-twentieth of the request. Hoeveler characterized the $2,000,000 as a "commercial venture."

I nearly always ask for a specific figure in my cases or at least suggest a reasonable verdict range or neighborhood. Most personal-injury lawyers use a blackboard adding up bills and placing a dollar value for pain and suffering on a daily basis. I do not do this because I believe that in a potentially big case you want to prevent the jury from developing an overly analytical frame of mind. It can degrade the case to ask for $10 or $20 per day for intangibles such as mental anguish. Because "J.B." named a specific figure, I did not.

In summation, I said:

What are the real values of life? What do we work and struggle for, what do we really hope to achieve? It is not the Cadillac and it is not fancy clothes or a big house. Those things are okay, but that is not what life is all about. What life is really about are family and friends, and relationships based on trust and loyalty and love.

How do you put a price tag on going into your child's room, and watching the child sleep with a teddy bear, or having a child put her arms around you and say—"Daddy, I love you."

There is no way to gauge the value of hearing your daughter laugh or feeling that she is happy and content.

You know, a great poet once said—"For of all sad words of tongue or pen, the saddest are these: it might have been" . . . the saddest are these: it might have been!

When you look at Arthur Dillon's background, you see he quit school at an early age. But, for his daughter, the sky was the limit. And that is the beauty of this country. He did his best within his capacity. Parents can accept any heartache and any disappointment if they have the hope that their children will do better, and part of the reason they will do better is because I was a good parent, because I was a good father. That has been the whole history of immigration and the melting-pot concept of America—the dream that their children would lead useful and productive lives; that the children would do better than the parents and not have to struggle so hard.

We lawyers know how to read lawbooks and we know the rules of evidence. But you need a gifted poet or a great orator to bring forth the meaning and extent of this tragedy, and to try to translate it to six members of a jury. There is a sensitive and special relationship of love and devotion between a father and his girl. What does a father feel when his child gets married, when she is sweet sixteen, when she brings home her first boyfriend, when she wears her first long dress—these joys are immeasurable. You can take a bad boss or an uninteresting job or the aggravation of modern living, and it is all bearable when you have these things to look forward to.

Your verdict will be a message to Arthur Dillon and I think you should tell him—"we believe that you are a good father who loved your child and we know she loved you. We know that you suffered a grievous and tragic loss."

Bill Hoeveler, the prototype of the insurance lawyer, with the look and demeanor of a clergyman, began the type of argument of which he is a master. He can somehow make it appear that the decent, honest, courageous, and

American thing to do in cases like this is to give the plaintiff nothing, or "peanuts."

There comes a time when you are asked to be a juror, and all of a sudden, you rise to exactly the same dignity as his Honor. You don't happen to have robes on, but in this case you are as much judges as Judge Nathan. He has his function, you have your function. It is a great thing.

There is a lot of attack on the jury system these days in various quarters, saying juries do this and juries do that. I think we all believe that the jury system is one of the greatest defenses of our individual liberties, and I hope we will always have it, and it is great as long as we act reasonably. But every day the system gets a little bit better or a little bit worse, depending on whether or not huge awards are entertained or we act reasonably.

I don't think Mr. Rosenblatt or Mr. Spence have proved how this accident happened, and the burden is theirs. *(He was correct in that we had no actual eyewitnesss to the initial impact which sent DeeDee under the wheels).* Now if you believe they haven't met their burden of showing that our driver was negligent—and you recall I asked you on voir dire—"Did you have the strength to do a very distasteful job. Not distasteful because it is right, but distasteful because you have to say to somebody, 'I am sorry, but there is no liability'?" You all answered that you would be strong enough to do this if they failed to prove negligence.

I think as reasonable people we have got to talk about what is reasonable if you feel we are wrong on the question of liability. It is reprehensible to transform a tragedy into a commercial enterprise and by bringing back an unreasonable award you would put the plaintiffs in a position of never having to work, where they could just sit back and think about why they got all this money. I agree with Mr. Rosenblatt that the important things are not Cadillacs and big houses, but somebody wants those things, and that is why we have a case that involves a loss of this type turned into what I submit is a commercial venture.

What does the law say? The law says that up till the age of

eighteen a parent has the right of action for pain and suffering for the death of a child. And it goes as long as they sustain the pain and suffering—that is, for the life expectancy of the parent.

But the law also recognizes that in the ordinary course of events children leave home, they have their own lives, they have their own problems—so there is no cause of action for the parents of mature children who have died. If a child dies at eighteen years, one day, there is no longer an action on the part of the parents for pain and suffering. Realistically, since grief is the most intense of emotions, it is the shortest lived. The very intensity of grief makes it self-destructive so that one's survival instinct rises up to shield the mind and heart from it.

It is an interesting psychological fact that the good does replace the bad sooner or later. They grow up, they are out on their own, and the good does replace the bad—and this situation will taper out in like fashion.

Money does help to relieve a certain amount of stress, and to some extent that will help him, I don't know what is right, but if we want to be reasonable we would award Mr. Dillon something in the neighborhood of $25,000 to $30,000. We are not talking about a man who has lost his leg and can't work anymore. We are talking about a man who has sustained some pain and suffering, but who will recover and there is no indication he won't. He elected to remove himself from the household for reasons that may have been good to him.

The county's position and that of its insurance company really boiled down to a calculated gamble that the jury would be more or less *against* Mr. Dillon, both because of his long hair and the divorce. They were not shy about digging up any dirt, either. Because Diane Dillon's claim was largely based on her own mental anguish, the defense had been entitled to discover her medical history. At one time, Mrs. Dillon had been to the emergency room of a hospital, feeling very depressed and ill. Hoeveler referred to this incident, and pointed to an entry in Diane's chart where an intern had written something to the effect that the basis of Mrs. Dillon's problems with her husband was his drinking, and perhaps drugs. I had put on testimony to show that Arthur Dillon had never been arrested for either of these alleged problems and had been a very steady worker during his seven years with Sears, Roebuck.

Hoeveler continued:

I think really what I am trying to say, and this is a little flowery, so forgive me—but I have been a lawyer for a number of years and I love this work and the system. It is a real privilege to be able to talk to six people and say to you we have got a terrific system here. This is the greatest in the world. It is a system which is bedrocked on reasonableness. It is a system whereby the Continental Casualty Company can come in and sit in an empty chair and say to you, "we glory in the fact that we can ask you to do what is right not only in this case but in the interests of the jury system."

We are asking you not to succumb to the type of demand that throws the whole system out of kilter. It is only through you that we are protected. It is the greatest system in the world and I really mean that. In conclusion, it hurts me to say it and yet I have got to say it, that the plaintiffs have failed to prove a case of negligence. But if you feel they have, Mr. Dillon's damages should not be over $25,000 to $30,000 at the outside. *(Hoeveler suggestd that an appropriate amount for Mrs. Dillon would be $75,000 to $100,000).*

I could hardly sit still during his "holier than thou" argument with Spence and me as the unholy "thou." Here was the county's elegant, polished advocate who, day in and day out, minimizes injuries and settles cases cheaply, relying largely on the fear and conservatism of poor plaintiffs, unctuously talking about "the system." It is just impossible to out-nice-guy, or be a more solid American citizen than, William Hoeveler. He has perfected the mold on apple-pie virtue. Hoeveler's approach had been very effective, as it always is. I had a chance for rebuttal.

You know, members of the jury, I find it difficult to believe that Mr. Hoeveler could characterize what we have said in this case as an attempt to translate this tragedy into a commercial venture. We talk about inflation—about everything under the sun going up, up and away. If you have to put a price tag on something meaningful, then what could be more legitimate and real than mental pain and suffering. It is perfectly okay with Bill Hoeveler for a landlord to ask an outrageous sum for an apartment, or a grocer to ask an outrageous sum for a can of tuna fish, but it is somehow truly outrageous for a lawyer to ask for just compensation for a client whose innocent six-year-old daughter was killed on her way to a crosswalk so she could safely go to Benjamin Franklin Elementary School. It is reprehensible to ask for just compensation for her being crushed and mutilated by a Miami-Dade County garbage truck. How dare we do such a thing?

How does Mr. Hoeveler attempt to lower the value of Arthur Dillon's case? He takes a piece of paper allegedly written by some doctor whom he doesn't call to the witness stand, and without so much as offering in evidence the piece of paper, he mentions emotion-charged words like "drugs" and "drinking" to somehow prejudice you against Arthur Dillon. There is not one shred of evidence in this case that my client ever had a problem with drinking or drugs. The only evidence is that his wife used to get angry with him every once in a while when he would stop off and have a few beers with the boys and not call, and come home late. Big deal!

Bill Hoeveler hopes the jury will say, "Oh, he must be a hippie with that long hair—and now drugs." He says it all in his polite, sincere way. But he is trying to prejudice you against a man whose marriage didn't work out. The fact is you can't analyze a marriage in a day and a half of trial, and it is not our purpose here to know who was at fault.

The question is what kind of parent was Arthur Dillon? When the divorce came he said to Diane, "You can have the house and if you sell it, all the money is yours. I am going to take out health and accident and life insurance, and I agree to pay the children's medical and dental bills." No judge made him do this. He did it voluntarily.

Does this sound like a fellow who was irresponsible? His marriage ended, but the evidence is that Arthur Dillon is a man who recognized his responsibilities to his children. Mr. Hoeveler is saying that because of their difficulties as husband and wife, the case is worth less—that if they were happily married it would be worth more. There is really not an ounce of common sense to that, because a couple who is still together would at least have each other for comfort and for sustenance.

Talk about salesmanship. Mr. Hoeveler says that we haven't carried the burden of proof and his answer as to how this accident happened is some cockeyed theory about the child trying to recover her lunch box which unexplainably fell under the truck. He says he doesn't know how the accident happened but since the plaintiffs can't prove precisely how it did occur, give them zero. And if you believe somehow that we were negligent, then give them peanuts. That may be the Continental Casualty Company's idea of justice.

Mr. Hoeveler uses over and over and over again the word "reasonable." What he's really saying is that if you tell this community and this court and Arthur Dillon that—"We think your grief, your pain, your loss is significant. We think you have suffered a tragic and monumental loss"—that somehow this is not reasonable. But if you bring in a piddly amount, then you have met all his parsimonious criteria for reasonableness.

Am I talking about a piddly loss—to see a child that he nurtured and loved crushed into little bits without any explanation by the defendant except coming in here and saying, "We don't know how it happened." Well, that's just not good enough. Let me remind you that every teacher and every witness said this was a happy, adorable, loving, well-adjusted child.

You don't become a child like that unless you have good parents, unless you get love. And I think my client is entitled to a substantial verdict at your hands, a verdict that will be compatible with Arthur Dillon's loss.

J. B. Spence delivered his usual brilliant final argument.

The jury was interested and intensely involved in what all three of us had to say. It was difficult to "read them" or predict how they were leaning. After the Williams, Adams and Robinson cases, where the county had nickeled-and-dimed my low-income clients into what I considered low settlements, Bill Hoeveler and I were finally going to the jury.

The jury retired to deliberate at 4:20 P.M. on Friday, November 9, 1973. In an hour and fifteen minutes there was a verdict—$500,000 for Mrs. Dillon and $400,000 for my client. Arthur's verdict was a record amount for a divorced father who did not have custody of his deceased child. The blind refusal to face facts and admit fault by the insurance company, in the name of "reasonableness," cost them a total of $900,000.

I was very fortunate to have as my cocounsel, J. B. Spence, whose biggest reputation is in the field of medical malpractice. A colleague who did not have a flair for trying big cases could have been a disaster for both clients. The supposedly gigantic egos of trial lawyers presented no problem and our cases could not have been presented with more cohesion or less friction.

The fact that a jury consisting of five women could have given Arthur Dillon such a terrific award made me much less of a "male chauvinist pig" than I had been at the inception of the trial.

IX

Sears's Shocking Sewing Machine

Caveat Vendor—Caveat Emptor

A man whom I shall call Hyman Been took his wife, Gloria, shopping for a sewing machine on Saturday, March 21, 1964. The floor display in the sprawling Sears, Roebuck store in Fort Lauderdale offered many models, in a wide range of prices, but there was one used sewing machine which caught Mrs. Been's eye. The price was low and the style appealed to her.

As Mrs. Been circled the machine, casting a critical eye on its features, her husband sat in front of it, flicked on the switch and began testing the model. For a used machine, it didn't run badly. As the Beens were to learn much later on, this was a sewing machine manufactured in Japan which had been purchased in the mid-1950s. After seven years, the owner traded it back to Sears for a new model. Sears then put the old machine on display and stuck a low price tag on it for quick disposal.

The Beens, however, did not buy it—not after the way the fifty-year-old Hymie was almost catapulted from his seat while running the machine.

"What happened?" his wife asked, in bewilderment.

"I almost got electrocuted," Been managed to say as he gasped for breath. "I never got a shock like that in my life!"

Hyman and Gloria Been left the store and returned home to nearby Hollywood. The weekend passed, and Been could still feel the vibrations of the electrical shock he had sustained. On Monday morning he went to work in his novelty shop but spent the day in severe discomfort.

A few more days went by and Been felt progressively worse. He was experiencing an acute sense of inadequacy and—yes, his memory was failing him. He was also losing weight; yet there was no mark of any physical injury, whatever, from the experience at Sears.

"That shock has done this to you," Mrs. Been told her husband. "You have to do something about it."

Been did. Characteristically, he did not go to a doctor, but rather to a lawyer in Fort Lauderdale. A few days later, on April 27, 1964, the attorney filed a complaint against Sears, Roebuck & Co. in Broward County Circuit Court. I am at a loss to understand why the attorney filed the lawsuit so quickly. Perhaps he thought Hymie had such a great case that he did not want to run the risk of losing him as a client.

Depositions and other discovery procedures were followed in the usual manner. Sears was in no position to prove that Hymie was not shocked while using one of their machines. He and Mrs. Been had consistently told that to all the physicians he had seen. Based upon medical testimony, therefore, that the electrical shock caused Hyman Been to suffer severe psychological disturbances, the attorneys representing Sears, Roebuck agreed to pay a total of $20,000 to settle the case.

This was accomplished only a few days before the trial was to begin, in September 1965. The papers were signed.

Sears gave Been's counsel the $20,000 check. Case closed? Not quite. Been did not get his money!

As is customary, Been's lawyer deposited the check in his trust account. He then proceeded to issue checks in payment of Been's large outstanding medical bills, as well as legal fees and costs connected with the lawsuit. The total payments made were $10,544.40. That meant that Mr. Been was going to net $9,455.60. But before the lawyer could scratch out a check for his client, Sears stopped payment on their $20,000 check.

Why was this highly unorthodox action taken by Sears's attorneys? The lawyers advanced the reasons in court documents, which were designed to set aside the order, dismissing the case, the judge had signed pursuant to the settlement.

On September 15, 1965, the undersigned attorneys for Sears forwarded the settlement draft to Hyman Been's attorneys. On the afternoon of September 17, 1965, we first received access to certain documentary records which established that the settlement had been procured and induced by the plaintiff based upon false information and misrepresentations and concealment of material facts . . .

That the fraud perpetrated by plaintiff consisted of the following matters, although not limited to same:

A. Concealment of or false statements as to legal name or other names used by plaintiff.
B. Concealment of or false statements as to place of birth and places of prior residency.
C. Concealment of and misrepresentation as to prior employers and business activities.
D. Concealment of and misrepresentation as to prior medical and psychiatric history.
E. Concealment of and misrepresentation as to prior military service.
F. False statements as to his marital status.

. . . defendant shows that due to the plaintiff's fraud and false statements, it was effectively prevented from discovering that the plaintiff had for many years, dating to the early 1940s, been afflicted with various neurotic disorders which are precisely the same condition which he contends he sustained as a result of the electrical shock; Sears was further prevented from discovering that plaintiff had sustained no loss of earning ability since most of his life he had been a marginally productive or outright dependent person; and Sears was further prevented from discovering that Mr. Been may well have imagined or fabricated the very existence of the incident which forms the basis for this cause of action.

After Sears made these allegations, Been decided to switch counsel. With my luck, he came to see me.

Sometimes a lawyer has to represent people whom he cannot stand. This is very common among criminal lawyers, but fairly common also in a civil practice, such as mine.

The case appealed to me, even though Been didn't, and in spite of the fact the money involved could never justify the time which would be necessary to handle the matter properly. I felt that if Sears's contentions were accurate, the situation was rather funny. It meant that a mammoth corporation had been snookered by a "nut."

Sears had had more than sixteen months to take testimony and investigate Hyman Been and come up with the findings about his background. If they couldn't do it in that time, then let them swallow the bitter pill. I also figured it would be a lot of fun deposing the big shots at Sears and questioning them and their lawyers about why they entered into the settlement in the first place. I was not disappointed in watching them try to squirm out of their bad deal.

One of the greatest advantages in being a trial lawyer is that you are able to satisfy your intellectual and natural curiosity. It is great fun and very challenging to put the pieces together in an interesting and unusual factual situation. You get to play detective since witnesses have to answer your legitimate questions, and it is very instructive from a psychological standpoint.

The litigation attorney is given a marvelous opportunity to learn about people from all walks of life, what makes them tick, and how they react under a variety of circumstances. You learn that with one type of witness you can get more information with a kid glove approach; for another you need to come on strong and tough. This is invaluable information for the courtroom and as an aid in the selection of jurors.

I wrote to Sears's lawyers, demanding that they pay the balance of the $20,000 they had agreed to pay Been. They responded that they had no intention of doing so inasmuch as he had perpetrated a fraud upon their great and prestigious client. The lawyers contended that Been had deliberately lied about every aspect of his background, thus making it impossible for them to develop valid investigative material. They had a point, but they were not being very practical.

"Listen," I said to the lawyer on the phone. "Been is such a wacko that he is totally incapable of distinguishing the truth from fantasy. Are you actually going into court and permit it to become public knowledge that this kook conned one of America's biggest corporations?"

But like nearly all lawyers who represent corporate behemoths, he had no sense of humor concerning money. In fact, the poor fellow was all choked up over the $10,544.40 that had been paid out for Been's medical bills, legal fees, and costs. His position was that that money had been paid to "innocent third parties" who were not part of Hymie's alleged fraud. Sears had no intention of trying to recoup that money.

"But as far as your client is concerned," he said in his

most righteous manner, "we are not going to throw good money after bad."

"Very well," I replied with an equally original and scholary rejoinder. "I'll see you in court."

I sued Sears for the $9,455.60 that was due Hymie Been. Sears did me one better. They counterclaimed against my client for the $10,544.40 that they had paid out to those "innocent third parties."

Almost two years passed before we finally went to trial. Those twenty-four months will live in my memory for all time. Hymie Been never stopped phoning, never stopped dropping into my office, and never stopped being an unbelievable pain in the ass. He always had a new conspiratorial theory as to why he had suffered the electrical shock, and why Sears withdrew the money at the last possible moment.

"Sears was waiting for me," Hymie would say. "They knew I was going to test that secondhand Japanese sewing machine." He never could offer a logical reason why Sears was laying for him in particular. I shouldn't have been surprised, since Been felt the whole world was laying for him.

After his twenty-third unannounced and unwelcome visit to my offices, I declared in no uncertain terms that Hymie would henceforth have to deal with Jerry Burke exclusively. I hated to do this to Jerry, but I told him that this association could make him a world-renowned authority on the "litigation psychosis syndrome." The lawsuit was Hymie's whole life, but we had a few other cases to worry about as well. Jerry was actually able to keep him on an even keel.

Before we went to trial, scheduled to start on January 15, 1968, I had gotten some pretty good insight into the way Hymie Been's mind worked, as well as what I would be up against in my forthcoming square-off with Sears's well-prepared lawyers. This time they were really out to get the miscreant who had humiliated them.

It is my custom to have a detailed conference with my client prior to the time his pretrial deposition is taken, so that he will not be surprised by any question asked by the defense attorney. Meeting with Hyman and his wife was like attending a Marx Brothers rehearsal. Hymie Been was incapable of finishing a sentence. He was a master of the double entendre fragment, and he was the proud owner of a massive persecution complex. I have yet to decide if he is the world's champion put-on artist, or its greatest schlemiel.

The deposition taken by Sears' attorneys were hilarious:

Q. Is Hyman Been your legal name?
A. Yes—no, it isn't.
Q. What is your legal name?
A. Well, it's the same. Beenowitz.
Q. Where does your brother, Sol, live?
A. I am not sure where. Some place along the ocean near Long Island.
Q. Were you ever married before your present marriage to Gloria?
A. Yes.
Q. To whom were you married then, sir?
A. To a young lady.
Q. When and where were you married to her?
A. Well that I don't recall.
Q. Approximately?
A. I don't know.

He told the lawyer in our case that he had been born in Quebec, Canada. He told another lawyer in the original lawsuit that he was born in Asheville, North Carolina. In a log cabin, no doubt!

Q. What was the state of your health before this accident at Sears, Mr. Been?

A. I was in very, very good health.

Q. Had you ever been seriously ill, physically or mentally, before this accident in any way?

A. No.

But Sears's wily lawyers had uncovered information from Been's Army record in World War II, which indicated that he had enormous preexisting mental and physical problems which precipitated a medical discharge from the service. In the original case, Sears's lawyers had Hymie examined by a psychiatrist, who was questioned by his previous attorney:

Q. How far did Been tell you he went in school?

A. He told me he had a bachelor of arts degree from college, and asserted that he had graduated from high school in Asheville, North Carolina.

Q. Were his responses to your questions consistent with a college education?

A. They were not.

Q. What did he tell you about his service record?

A. He told me that he received a regular discharge, but there was something about the evasive nature of his response which caused me to be suspicious. I made an inquiry. I wrote to the area where the service records are kept. I haven't got the complete results yet because of involved governmental procedures and red tape.

That response was clearly a mouthful. It told me that back in the first lawsuit, Sears's lawyers had never attempted to get Hyman's military records. The psychiatrist had done this on his own.

Why didn't the lawyers think of this during the many months the original case was pending? Why didn't they use photographs or fingerprints to check on Hymie's background? Above all, after meeting Hymie, how could they have failed to see that his word under oath was meaningless? Considering these failures, I believed that the defense lawyers were guilty of malpractice.

If Sears's attorneys were so concerned about the military records, they should not have settled the case until they had seen them. The information that eventually came to the psychiatrist from the government would have fully justified Sears in not settling the original case for $20,000. These were the "documentary records" Sears referred to in their effort to void the settlement.

Been, who looked about as Gentile as Myron Cohen, told the psychiatrist that he was a Baptist. Of course, he was Jewish. Without question, Hyman told totally different stories on different occasions, under oath, about the most basic aspects of his background. He had lied about his birthplace, education, first marriage, work history, military record—ad infinitum, ad nauseam.

It would have taken the entire staffs of Johns Hopkins and Mayo Clinic to determine positively whether Hymie was lying deliberately or whether this was part of his sickness. I suspect it was a combination of both, but I believe most of Hymie's responses were on the level of conscious fabrication. As part of his paranoia, he was determined to outsmart everyone.

I decided upon the only strategy that was practically available to me—I would let defense counsel convince the jury that Been had lied over and over and over again. I was hoping they would indulge in overkill. I would also let them persuade the jury that Hymie had been mentally ill for many years before he had gotten that 110-volt charge from Sears' secondhand sewing machine. They would help me create a lot of sympathy for Mr. Been.

I was simply suing on a contract. When the settlement contract had been agreed to, Hyman had given something up (his right to have a case tried by a jury), and he had a

valid contractual right to $20,000, agreed to freely by Sears.
I did not have to like—or even believe—Hymie.

At the trial, I allowed Sears's lawyers to have their way.
In fact, I delivered an opening statement that was uncharac-
teristic of my style. Perhaps they would think that my
association with Hymie had taken its toll! I deliberately
fumbled because I didn't want to expose my strategy. The
case as far as I was concerned was eminently simple:

Sears had settled the case for $20,000. A settlement is
a contract. Sears reneged on that settlement and breached
its contract. Sears tried to justify its action on the ground
that Been had lied to them.

My position was "Pay up *and* shut up."

The case was short—funny and sad, all at the same time.
I summoned Hyman Been to the witness chair. In questioning him, I didn't ask one thing about his past medical
history, nor did I inquire about the effect the electric shock
had on him. My only aim was to project Hymie as a
plaintiff in a lawsuit who had received a $20,000 settle-
ment and who had been deprived of the proceeds by a
famous American retailer whose word could not be trusted.

When I sat down after a mere ten minutes of questioning,
I could sense the astonishment of the defense lawyers at
the brevity and lack of depth of my interrogation. Buoyed
by this seeming abandonment of my client by me, they
went on the attack.

Question after question was put to the plaintiff without
a single objection from me. Hymie's answers left no doubt
that he had given wildly conflicting testimony about every
aspect of his life. The bombardment soon had its effect.
In addition to the electric shock, he was now shell-shocked.
He kept turning to me with the hangdog look of an innocent
person being subjected to terrible persecution.

I could read the message on his face. "Why the hell aren't
you helping me?" I wanted the jury to get the feeling that

Sears never should have been taken in by this fellow. Naturally, Hymie hadn't the foggiest notion of what my strategy was. How could he? I had not talked to him in over a year. The defense counsel finally had their fill. Hymie returned to my side in a state of complete confusion.

As I went before the jurors at the conclusion of the brief trial, I felt the case was going to ride completely on the way we handled our summations. I told the jury:

I am not a psychiatrist. Therefore, I cannot satisfy your natural curiosity as to whether Hyman Been lied deliberately or because of compelling neurosis or due to a combination of the two. He may have lied from a sense of shame feeling that he had been legitimately injured, but fighting with every fiber of his being to deny his checkered and unhappy past.

In any event, I took the position that his falsehoods had nothing to do with his right to receive his share of the $20,000 settlement, because Sears had entered into that as an arms'-length business contract.

Sears is saying to you, "We made a bad deal—please, pretty please, rescu us." Well, maybe they did make a bad deal. But suppose they had made a great deal? What would Sears have done if, after they had settled the case for $20,000, they learned that Hymie really suffered a far more severe injury than the original diagnosis showed?

Would Sears Roebuck then add to the settlement to be totally fair about it? Or would they take advantage of a good deal? If you have any trouble at all with that question, then I might as well sit down right now. Just how naïve do they think you are? What would it do to a healthy person's psyche to have a case settled and then be told that everyone can keep their money except the injured party? And I'm not at all convinced that Sears did make such a bad deal for if Hymie was so sick, then this shock certainly had a much worse effect on him than it would have had on a normal person. He was functioning relatively well before this incident at Sears but fell apart following it.

It is not bad enough that Sears shocked him with a decrepit Japanese sewing machine; it is not bad enough that they didn't keep their word about the settlement. But now they want to add the ultimate insult to the ultimate injury—they want little Hymie Been to come up with over $10,000, which he doesn't have, to pay for their colossal goof.

The defense's basic argument was that it would be almost criminal to permit a fraudulent liar to benefit from his own misdeeds. The jury was out for about forty minutes when they marched back into the courtroom with a question. They wanted to know whether they could assess an attorney's fee over and above Been's share of the settlement! The judge said no, since that would be improper under Florida law. The question was nevertheless an electric shock to me. It meant that we were going to win in spite of the fact that I was absolutely convinced that this jury did not like or even believe Been.

In another few minutes, they were back in the courtroom with the final verdict. The jury said that Hyman Been was entitled to receive not only the $9,455.60 he had coming to him under the terms of the settlement with Sears, but that he had another $3,000 coming in punitive damages! This was obviously an independent jury! Even though the judge told them they couldn't tack on an attorney's fee to the award, they nevertheless decided to achieve the same result by calling the additional money "punitive damages." It was highly unlikely that that part of the award could hold up in an appellate court, but it made me feel good.

The trial was over, but my contact with Sears's lawyers didn't come to an end then. They put me on notice that they were going to appeal the verdict. These were the same guys who had told me they were "not going to throw good money after bad."

I pleaded with them not to expose me to another year of Hymie Been, for if they did I would end up footing the bill for Jerry Burke's sanitarium confinement. After a lot of back-and-forth nonsense, Sears's lawyers finally agreed to a settlement if we would permit them to reduce the punitive damage award by $1,000. We gladly did.

Sears issued a check in the total sum of $11,455.60, plus interest which had accrued since the time of the original settlement. The perverse part of my nature secretly hoped that they would stop payment of *this* check. If they had done that, I would have been in a position to ask for $1,000,000 in punitive damages.

Of course, Sears was not being altruistic. They were quite embarrassed by the whole thing. The defense lawyers in the original case were terribly chagrined that they had not obtained Been's military records far in advance of the trial date.

This kind of situation—where one party to a settlement becomes unhappy about it afterward—is not all that uncommon. In nearly all such cases, the shoe is on the other foot—it is the plaintiff who has the change of heart. But since a settlement agreement is a binding contract, the circumstances almost never permit abrogation of the deal.

I vividly recall my discussion with Jerry after our initial meeting with Been. We didn't need the aggravation of this small-money case. On the other hand, it presented a challenging opportunity. We knew how insurance companies operated in pressuring claimants who need money fast to accept settlements way below the true value of their cases.

Often the individual learns later that the injury was more serious than anticipated and the bills much higher. I have yet to hear of a company adding onto the settlement just to be fair. No, they rely on the legal "contract." The negotiations between an experienced insurance adjuster and a layman are a mismatch under the best conditions. Every personal injury lawyer knows of horror stories where a seriously injured but naïve claimant settled his case for peanuts.

Here an outfit as big as Sears was attempting to back out of a settlement which it considered bad. They had the time and the resources to check on Hyman Been from every standpoint. Jerry and I figured the point we could make with this case outweighed the disadvantages of putting up with Hymie. We were additionally incensed and motivated by the fact that Sears had the gall to sue Been for the $10,544.40 which had gone for medical and legal expenses. This stupid greed provided me with lovely ammunition for the jury trial.

I hope I don't have to destroy my Sears credit card after this book comes out!

X

Nobel Vega
—VS.—
City of Maimi Beach
My Flamingo Park
Becomes a Defendant

You may have seen the hippies on your TV set thrashing around in Flamingo Park's swimming pool during the 1972 Republican and Democratic national conventions. The huge park had been designated as an outdoor camping ground for the many protest groups that came to Miami Beach.

With so much activity and movement on your screen, you probably did not notice the ten-foot-high diving board at the deep end of the public pool. You would have seen just another high diving board with an aluminium ladder leading up to the platform and a protective 27-inch-high stainless steel rail running along the sides.

Today that high board at Flamingo Park's swimming pool has a different look. So does the one in the City of Miami Beach's other municipal pool—71st Street. Now, instead of just the horizontal rails flanking the diving platform, an eight-foot chain link fence encircles three sides of the platform of both diving boards. The city installed those cages as a safety device to protect the divers from slipping off and falling to the hard concrete pavement below. If someone falls off the boards today, he will land in the water.

A tragedy had to occur before this came about. It involved a little Cuban boy, with black hair and almond shaped eyes that were sparkling with the joy of an eight-year-old exhibiting newly discovered bravado on the high board—a little boy being watched by his mother and grandfather sitting in the bleacher section under a striped canopy, escaping the hot July sun.

The happy shrieks of laughter of children frolicking about the pool turned suddenly to cries of horror as little Nobel Vega lost his footing and plummeted headfirst off the high board. There was a sickening thud as Nobel's head struck the wet concrete, and his body sprawled limp and motioness. Fire Rescue, which is within shouting distance of the pool, was called immediately. The unconscious youngster was rushed to Mt. Sinai Hospital. He had multiple skull fractures and remained in a coma for nine days before he died on July 23, 1971.

Several months later I was sitting in my fourth-floor office in the Concord Building, gazing out of my window at the monster that is the Dade County Courthouse, across the street. My secretary buzzed to let me know that my good friend and fellow attorney Charles Appel was in the waiting room. I knew Charlie from high school, where he had been one of the roughest linemen in the history of Greater Miami football. He had been a Miami Beach policeman for several years before going to law school. Charlie always came to the point, and did so this time.

"I've got a case for you, but I'm going to level. Several attorneys turned it down before Mrs. Vega came to see me. It's a tough one. The boy's mother wants to sue the city, but all the lawyers told her she doesn't have a case."

"Does she?" I asked.

"I doubt it, but you've got to take a shot at it, Stan."

Elsa Vega walked into my office dry-eyed, but when she retold the story of how her son fell off the high board, she broke down and wept uncontrollably. She was at the pool with the boy's grandfather and her little daughter, Annette. As the boy lost his balance, she raced toward him but couldn't prevent him from hitting the concrete."

"Charlie," I said, "it's obviously a tragic accident, but where is the negligence on the part of the city? The child's mother was right there and she let him use the diving board. I assume the board was not defective in any way. The boy simply slipped and fell. You can't station a lifeguard on the diving board full time, and an accident like this must have happened in a split second."

"Damn it, Stan, you're probably right."

"Well, if I'm so right, why did you agree to accept the case?"

"Because," Charlie answered, "she pleaded with me, grabbed my hands and kissed them. I got carried away. What could I do?"

I had to smile as I pictured that scene. Soft-heartedness in the practice of law is generally a thankless commodity. Being as big a patsy as Charlie, I nevertheless agreed to speak with Mrs. Vega.

Although her explanation of Nobel's fatal fall was basically as Charlie had related it to me, she added details which suddenly opened my mind to a theory. Why did the boy slip and fall off the high diving board? Why didn't the platform have a protective device to protect children? I had discovered that children of any age were permitted to use the high board. The city charged a nominal fee for the use of the pool, and this created a legal duty to the customers to use a high degree of care for their safety.

This is one of the things I enjoy about representing plaintiffs, the little people. A set of facts is presented to me and, of course, at first I do not have anything but a brief, one-sided outline of the facts. On a first interview, I will decide that there is "no case" in over a hundred cases per year. Another hundred I may reject as too small or uninteresting, even though there may be a probable case of liability. Occasionally, however, I see a novel fact pattern which seems to me to justify filing suit.

Several attorneys had already declined to take this case. Based on the law as it then was, they were quite correct to do so. But negligence law—which in its wider aspects includes products liability, warranty cases, and malpractice cases of all types, all of the situations we here people may be injured—is still a creative field.

The stumbling block was that there appeared to be no responsibility on the part of the city. The diving board itself was well built. Thousands of children (and adults) had used it before. But Nobel Vega was killed at play in a city facility. This started me thinking. Could the accident have been avoided? Some sort of cage or fencing would have prevented his fall from a position above the concrete.

The city knew that small children used that board. The "legal duty" certainly increases when small boys and girls are concerned. If I were to win, not only would I have represented my client well, but I might well be the instrument for improving the safety of other children in my own city, and in fact, at the same Flamingo Park where I had played as a boy.

Having grown up in the shadow of Flamingo Park, from the time my parents brought me from Brooklyn till the day I went up to the University of Florida, I was intimately acquainted with it. It is a magnificent park, covering five square city blocks, and can be enjoyed by persons of all ages. It is one of the few areas left in the city which the politicians have not ruined yet. Older people can just sit on benches and enjoy the trees, the flowers, the birds, and, of course, the children.

The city's recreation department was, and still is, excellent. The idea of suing my city and my park did not appeal to me. Besides, in my early days of practice with Roland Granat, my first partner, we had represented the city and its employees in court on numerous occasions. But, corny as it might sound, I was representing a client and had to do my duty.

I knew that the pool was patronized primarily by young children and teenagers. To me it was foreseeable that accidents, such as the one which took Nobel's life, could occur very easily.

After filing suit and as I prepared for trial, I made a study of swimming pool design and safety standards. I could not find one pool—municipal, county or private— which had a protective fence or cage of the kind that I concluded could have prevented this tragedy. This posed a great challenge because now my task was clear: I had to establish a new safety standard.

There is a general principle of law that holds that all a business or a facility (such as the City of Miami Beach in this case) needs to do is meet the general and average community standards for safety. Operators or owners of pools are not held to higher standards than those which exist in the general community. As an advocate my own view was that when the need for a corrective device was so obvious, and its installation so inexpensive, it was wrong to allow a city-owned swimming pool to remain legally protected simply because other pools are in a similarly unsafe condition.

I made a point of revisiting Flamingo Park on a regular basis. Actually, I had never lost touch with the area. My mother still lives a mere three blocks away from the park, and when visiting I often stop and take a familiar walk. Now my attention was focused on the kids in the pool.

Interestingly, at the time of his death, Nobel was attending the same elementary school I had been to. When I went to school there, 95 percent of the population of that area known as South Beach was Jewish. The population in that area is now 50 percent Cuban, and the remaining Jews are mostly elderly.

I could recall the high diving boards in the many pools of oceanfront hotels where I had worked as a beach boy. They didn't even have a protective rail around the platforms. In my visits to pools, I saw children by the dozens scampering up the ladder, leaning perilously over the rail trying to get someone's attention, or just horsing around. Every time I saw this, my heart felt sick, thinking of what had happened to Nobel Vega.

I could not help wondering why more accidents did not occur on the wet slippery high diving platform. Yet the city maintained in sworn testimony that this had been the first serious accident on the high board. I was not able to prove otherwise.

We took the deposition of all known witnesses, including the two lifeguards. As the trial date neared, I was approached with an offer to settle the case. The Consolidated Insurance Company of New York, which provided coverage for the City of Miami Beach against accident suits, proposed to pay Mrs. Vega $5,000. We told them what they could do with their bounty.

The trial opened on January 15, 1973, before Judge Murray Goodman, who incidentally was presiding at his first civil trial. Until that day, Goodman had been a judge in the criminal division of the court, and ironically, he had presided at the perjury trial of Dr. Lewis Fagan, in which there had been an acquittal.

Interesting, also, was the fact that Judge Goodman, when

a practicing attorney, had always been closely associated
and identified with the City of Miami Beach. He had practiced law there for many years, had been a prosecutor for
the city and, in fact, had been its municipal judge. For
all those reasons, I seriously considered asking Judge Goodman to excuse himself, but after discussing the merits of
that in great detail with Charlie Appel, we concluded that
he would be fair—particularly since the insurance company
would pay off if we were successful.

The basic conflict in testimony had surfaced long before
the trial. The city would clearly be taking the position that
Nobel had slipped and fallen because he was waving excitedly for his grandfather's attention, that he was leaning
on the rail and in doing so, leaned too far and fell *over* the
rail. Our witnesses said that Nobel had walked out on the
diving board in a normal way, was making his approach
for a dive, and then slipped and fell *under* the rail. According to them he was not waving at all.

Obviously who the jury believed could make a big difference. If Nobel fell *over* the rail, it would indicate that it
was entirely his own fault. The position of the city, though,
seemed to indicate a tacit admission that a fall *beneath*
the rail should be prevented or at least preventable by a
railing and a cage. At least this is what I was to argue.

The city's star witness was a woman who had been at the
pool that day with her own children. She had since moved
to California, but the defense, feeling that her testimony
would lock up their case, flew her to Miami for the trial.
The city's contention that Nobel fell over the rail, not under it, was dramatized most effectively when the woman
took the stand and described how the boy was waving and
"showing off" and "leaning too far over the rail . . ."

The insurance company and the city made a brilliant
choice for defense counsel when they chose Arno Kutner,
a partner in the law firm of Preddy, Haddad, Kutner and

Hardy. Although he and Norton Preddy, who had defended St. Francis Hospital in the Morris case, are partners, their styles are totally different. Kutner has a tremendous courtroom record. He is youthful-looking and handsome; he dresses and grooms himself faultlessly. He is also a supremely effective purveyor of the "soft sell." He is polite and courteous outside of court, but even more so when doing his thing. Arno possesses one of the most valuable assets that any trial attorney can have—instant likability. He is devastating with old ladies on the jury.

My first words to the jury in summation were intended to dispel the notion that this was a "nice-guy contest" between the lawyers. "If that were the case," I told them, "I would never have walked into the courtroom with Mr. Kutner because he is nicer than me, better looking than me, and dresses better than me."

I told them I was not impressed with Kutner's "gee whiz" approach. "You know, we're sure as sorry as we can be that this awful tragedy occurred, but gee whiz, it certainly wasn't our fault."

In referring to Mrs. Vega's loss, I told the jury:

Children may be a heartache, but they are also a joy. How many people are millionaires and go to psychiatrists because they are unhappy and miserable? What is the real meaning of a full, good life? It is in watching a child grow to maturity. This pain will not end because when Mrs. Vega, four years from now or seven years from now, sees a teen-ager, she will say, "My boy would have been that age," or "My boy would now be graduating from high school."

The jury knew that Mrs. Vega was divorced. Her ex-husband, in fact, lived in another country. I don't usually quote from literary works during summation. Here I used a passage from Washington Irving because I felt the circumstances warranted such a reference:

A father may turn his back on his child; brothers and sisters may become inveterate enemies; husbands may desert their wives and wives their husbands. But a mother's love endures through all; in good repute, in bad repute, in the face of the world's condemnation, a mother still loves on, and still hopes that her child may turn from his evil ways and repent; still she remembers the infant smiles that once filled her bosom with rapture, the merry laugh, the joyful shout of his childhood, the opening promise of his youth; and she can never be brought to think him all unworthy.

I budgeted my time to leave as much as possible for rebuttal after the defendant's attorney had spoken. I did this because I knew that Kutner's argument would be very effective, and I had to do everything in my power to defuse it.

He did not disappoint me. He began his low-key argument:

Ladies and gentlemen, I would like to thank each of you for the kind attention that you have given me and to Mr. Rosenblatt on behalf of our respective clients. When we selected you as jurors, we asked each of you if you would decide this case on the law and the evidence and just decide it on those two elements—and you promised that you would.

Mrs. Vega has sustained a loss and I am deeply sorry for that. But sorrow is not a part of this lawsuit, sympathy is not a part of this claim and the judge will so instruct you. I want you to remember what the evidence was in this case. I believe that you, as a reasonable jury, can only return one verdict and that is a verdict for the defendant, and I told you that in the beginning, and I tell it to you now.

He argued that certainly the two lifeguards were not negligent, because the incident occurred in a split second. Just as Mrs. Vega was unable to reach her falling son in time, so would the lifeguards have been unable to react quickly enough to prevent or break his fall; even if they had been staring at him. Kutner made the point that there was no way to prevent a diving board from being wet, and the city did provide a "nonslip" material to cover it.

If Mrs. Vega thought anything was wrong with this diving board on that day, if she thought that this was a dangerous or negligent apparatus, she would not have let her child go on the board. The judge will tell you about Mrs. Vega's duty in this case—and, if she did anything that contributed to this loss or was negligent in the supervision of her son, then she cannot recover. A child of Nobel's age can be negligent, and if he was negligent in any way, that fact alone would prevent his mother from prevailing, under Florida law.

Please listen carefully to Judge Goodman's instructions. I don't think you will ever get to the issues of whether Mrs. Vega or Nobel were negligent since, once you determine that the city was not negligent, your deliberations would cease. But I owe a duty to my client to address all possible issues in this lawsuit.

I believe Nobel got his hands on the railing and leaned over to talk to his grandfather, who was out there under the canopy, and he leaned over too far and fell down. I don't think the accident happened the way Mrs. Vega has testified because I think that if he had been walking along the way she says he did, he would have fallen straight down.

When contradicting Mrs. Vega, Kutner's mild, polite manner was very effective. Not one of the jurors seemed to take offense at his argument which implied that she was lying.

As I always do during the other lawyer's final argument, I closely watched him and the jury. It is very hard to "read" most jurors since they try to keep a poker face, in keeping with their position and responsibility. I felt they were impressed.

Structurally the diving board was fine. It had no defect which required repair. The city had two lifeguards on duty who had not been negligent in any way. I could not show that the city had "notice" of prior accidents on this board. In addition to which Mrs. Vega allowed her son to use the high board.

I needed to come up with an attractive reason to motivate the jurors to find for the plaintiff. This is what I aimed for as I rose for my rebuttal argument.

Mr. Kutner talks about common sense. The City of Miami Beach is in the pool business. The Flamingo Park pool is 100 feet by 115, and they invited hundreds of children every week to use that facility.

Why does a parent repeatedly tell a child to be careful? Children believe themselves to be omnipotent. They are not born with fear; they learn fear. Children even younger than Nobel were permitted to use this high diving board. The city does not have to employ geniuses to realize that kids are kids—they will show off, they will engage in horseplay, they will run when they are supposed to walk——they will attempt other things over and above their abilities. They are full of energy and vitality and daring.

I used this argument so that we could still win even if the jury believed that Nobel had been waving to his grandfather and leaning over too far. What's so terrible about an eight-year-old doing that? The point is that if the city had the proper corrective device, it would have been impossible for the child to land on the concrete.

There is a well-known rule of law, which I believe applies in all the states of the Union, that the jury cannot receive evidence of subsequent repairs or improvements in a negligence case. The legal basis for this is that, as a matter of public policy, you do not want to remove the incentive to change conditions for the better. If the city or its insurance company knew that the jury would be told of this change, and it could be interpreted as an admission of guilt, there would be no incentive to change the diving board to make it safer for others. I was therefore not able to mention to the jury that the city, subsequent to Nobel's death, had installed around the diving platform the type of fence I was describing. I continued:

Don't say to the City of Miami Beach by your verdict that this [*I pointed to the photographs showing the narrow horizontal rail on the diving platform*] is good enough protection for our children. Tell them and other cities and other pool owners everywhere that they will have to do better, that it's not enough to send a talented, charming lawyer into court to say how sorry he is. You are the conscience of this community and by your verdict I implore you to let everyone know that you demand high, and not mediocre standards of safety—particularly when it comes to children.

At 5:15 P.M. on the second day of the trial, the jury retired to consider their verdict. They returned at 6:42 P.M.

The clerk read the verdict:

In the Circuit Court of the Eleventh Judicial Circuit in and for Dade County, Florida, Case No. 72-23030, Elsa Vega, individually and Elsa Vega, as administratrix of the estate of Nobel Vega, deceased, v. the City of Miami Beach, a municipal corporation, defendant.
Verdict: We, the jury, find for the plaintiff, Elsa Vega, as administratrix and individually, and assess her damages in the sum of $125,000.
So say we all.
Robert S. Hooker, foreman. Dated January 16, 1973.

Charlie Appel's comment was, "You're a pretty fair trial lawyer, Rosenblatt, but you sure as hell don't know how to evaluate cases. I told you we had a winner here."

I was so tempted to comment, but I never argue with Charlie when we win. We had the satisfaction of knowing we had secured "justice" and compensation for the bereaved mother. Of at least equal importance was the fact that the City of Miami Beach installed safety cages around the high diving areas of both its municipal pools. It feels good to know that there may be one—or fifty—children out there who will *not* be injured, maimed, or even killed, because of something we did.

Hopefully, other facilities will follow this example. This is the most meaningful extra dividend that the trial lawyer receives for his efforts. This case changed something in Miami Beach. I hope it doesn't take another death to change things in other communities.

XI

Olga Scarpetta
——VS.——
Nick and Jean DeMartino

The "Baby Lenore" Case

My law practice is focused very strongly in personal-injury law: malpractice, products liability cases, industrial accidents, and other types of accident cases. Occasionally, in special circumstances, something else comes along which is too interesting to turn down.

In late May of 1971, immediately after the final victory in the Powell case, and when I was looking forward to a rest, Olga Scarpetta asked me to represent her in a case of this type: a case which raised a basic question of the rights of a parent and a child, and also a serious question under the full faith and credit clause of our federal Constitution. It became the most widely publicized child-custody case in recent United States history.

Miss Scarpetta had not known the identity of the individuals who had her baby. The Spence-Chapin Adoption Agency refused to divulge this information. The adoption agency did not tell the DeMartinos, the foster parents, that

the baby's mother had changed her mind; in my opinion,
a grave breach of duty by a social service agency, both to
the mother and to the DeMartinos. When Olga Scarpetta
changed her mind about the adoption, her baby was only
one month old.

After several discussions at Spence-Chapin, which got
her nowhere, Miss Scarpetta decided to go to the New York
Public Library to research the law. She learned that in New
York, prospective adoptive parents cannot legally adopt a
child until *six months* after acquiring custody. She also
discovered that the mother is given the same period of
grace within which to change her mind.

Miss Scarpetta repeatedly asked Spence-Chapin for her
baby back, but got no results. On July 28, 1970, therefore,
she consulted with Manhattan attorney Joseph Zalk, of the
law firm of Zalk, Rubel and Perret. Mr. Zalk also found
great difficulty in ascertaining the identity of the custodians
of the child. On September 21, 1970, therefore, he filed a
writ of habeas corpus in the Supreme Court of New York
County. (Despite the name, in New York the Supreme
Court is the ordinary trial court, two levels below the actual
highest court, which is called the Court of Appeals.)

Olga Scarpetta, who had never been married, was born in
Colombia. Pregnant and alone, she came from Bogotá to
New York in November 1969 to look for a job and have her
baby. She had not confided in her Catholic family the truth
of her awful predicament. At the time of the initial hearing
in New York, at which she asked the court to give her her
baby back, Miss Scarpetta had a responsible position with
International Basic Economy Corporation, located at 30
Rockefeller Plaza.

The hearing in New York on November 2, 1970, was between the natural mother and the adoption service. It was
only on that very day that Mr. DeMartino was finally advised by Spence-Chapin that Miss Scarpetta had instituted

proceedings to get her baby back. Under New York law, the DeMartinos had no standing in court since they were mere custodians of the baby. The legal custodian was the adoption agency.

The hearing was held before Judge Alfred M. Ascione. Spence-Chapin's attorney asked Miss Scarpetta why she had consented to give up her baby for adoption. She answered:

Because I was ashamed. I never thought of the possibility of my being an unwed mother. I had planned to marry the baby's father and at the same time when I told him I was pregnant, he told me he was married. I did not know what to do. That is why I decided to leave home without telling my parents. I was afraid of hurting them. Then I came here. At the time, I had no intention of giving my child up for adoption. It was very hard to get a job and I started to feel it was due to my lack of capacity. When I did find a job the salary was very low and I felt that I would never do any better, and I felt guilty toward my child.

Gloria Laverne Daniels, a single twenty-two-year-old employee of Spence-Chapin, testified at the New York habeas corpus proceeding. Nearly all of Miss Scarpetta's contact with the adoption service was through Miss Daniels. Miss Daniels admitted that the mother came in to sign the surrender papers on May 29, 1970, but was in such an agitated and emotional state that she had to return three days later.

Miss Daniels knew on June 23 that Olga had changed her mind about going through with the adoption. This did not particularly concern her since, she testified, many mothers go through a similar period of doubt. She told Miss Scarpetta that these were normal feelings, but that the decision had been made and certainly it was in her best interest and in the best interest of the child for Lenore to remain with the adoptive parents.

Miss Scarpetta agreed to several counseling sessions with Miss Daniels before she ever saw attorney Zalk. Miss Daniels was unable to dissuade Miss Scarpetta from her decision.

The Spence-Chapin representative told Judge Ascione:

The *best interests of the child* can only be served and enhanced by Lenore's continuing in respondent's *[Spence-Chapin's]* custody, from which she will be adopted by her loving foster parents. A return of the child to the custody of the petitioner *[Miss Scarpetta,]* whose personal and familial future is so uncertain, is not in the best interests of the child.

Attorney Roy L. Reardon of the law firm of Simpson, Thatcher & Bartlett represented the adoption agency. He questioned Miss Daniels:

Q. At the time Miss Scarpetta signed the surrender on June 1st, was she calm, from your observation?

A. Well, she was crying, but it is normal. It is normal behavior for a mother when she signs a surrender, but she was not as upset as she was the previous week.

Q. When was the first time you personally met with Miss Scarpetta after you learned of her change of heart on June 23, 1970?

A. On June 29.

Q. Tell us what she said that day.

A. At the June 29 meeting, we talked about all of the things that we had discussed the past few months. I asked her if she felt coerced or forced into signing her surrender. She said, "no, it was my decision." She just changed her mind. She wanted the baby back.

Q. At that time did she mention any plans she had for the baby in the event she got her back?

A. I asked her if things had changed and she indicated that she had a new job, but other than that nothing had changed and she just wanted her baby back because she "loved her."

Mrs. Loyce Bynum, the associate executive director of

Spence-Chapin, who had been with that agency nineteen years, testified that she "participated in the decision to uphold the surrender and retain the custody of the child" in spite of Miss Scarpetta's change of heart. She admitted that she never had any personal discussions with the baby's mother; that was left to the caseworker, Gloria Daniels.

Judge Ascione filed his decision on November 17, 1970:

While it is true that the overwhelming majority of adoptive parents give of their love, many problems beset an adopted child. The knowledge of the adoption, ofttimes garnered through the thoughtless cruelty of preteen friends, the constant subsequent mental turmoil seeking reasons for their abandonment, the curiosity concerning the natural parents and possible brothers or sisters, and at times the search.

The mother had indicated her revocation quite timely and consistently. The record in this case sufficiently shows that petitioner has adequately stabilized her own relationships and has become stable enough in her own mind to warrant the return of the child to her. It appears that petitioner is motivated solely by her concern for the well being of her child. It appears that Miss Scarpetta is *fit, competent* and able to duly maintain, support and educate the child.

This court suggests that if respondent *[the agency]* desires to appeal, it do so as expeditiously as possible in order not to increase the sorrows of the prospective adoptive parents who have had the infant through this five-month period when the infant is so ingratiating with recognitions, smiles, and chuckles. In all probability, if they had known that the mother wanted the child, they would have voluntarily returned the baby.

After considering all the facts, the court is of the opinion that the child should forthwith be returned to petitioner, its natural mother.

Judge Ascione had found clearly in favor of Miss Scarpetta. He then made a decision which cost her dearly. Judge Ascione strongly urged the attorneys to enter into a stipulation "staying" enforcement of the judgment, which meant that the prospective adoptive parents would retain custody of the child until such time as the appellate courts acted on his decision. Miss Scarpetta voluntarily and trustingly agreed to this stipulation, which would not only delay her receiving the baby back, but unknown to her would also provide a ground for the DeMartinos to argue that they had become attached to the baby—and the baby to them—in the interval.

Spence-Chapin appealed. On January 28, 1971, presiding Judge Louis J. Capozzoli, as well as three associate justices of the New York Appellate Division, *unanimously* affirmed Judge Ascione. They agreed that Olga Scarpetta should get her baby back.

Spence-Chapin appealed this order to the highest court of the state of New York: the Court of Appeals. Another delay, with Miss Scarpetta's baby still in the hands of the DeMartinos, but on April 8, the court handed down its *unanimous opinion,* again in her favor.

The court said in part:

The resolution of the issue of whether or not a mother, who has surrendered her child to an authorized adoption agency, may regain the child's custody, has received various treatment by the legislatures and courts in the United States. At one extreme, several jurisdictions adhere to the rule that the parent has an absolute right to regain custody of her child prior to the final adoption decree.

On the other hand, some jurisdictions adhere to the rule that the parent's surrender is final, absent fraud or duress. The majority of the jurisdictions, however, place the parent's right to regain custody within the discretion of the court—the position which our legislature has taken. This discretionary rule allows the court leeway to approve a revocation of the surrender when the facts of the individual case warrant it and avoids the obvious dangers posed by the rigidity of the extreme positions.

In New York, a surrender . . . for the purpose of adoption

is expressly sanctioned by law. The statute nowhere endows a surrender *[of the baby]* with irrevocability, foreclosing the mother from applying to the court to restore the child to her. . . . Where the adoptive child is less than eighteen years of age, no order of adoption shall be made until such child has resided with the adoptive parents for at least six months. . . .

Inherent to judicial supervision of surrenders is the recognition that documents of surrender are unilateral, not contracts, . . . and are almost always executed under circumstances which may cast doubt upon their voluntariness or on an understanding of the consequences of their execution. Having the power to direct a change of custody from the agency back to the natural parent, *notwithstanding the document of surrender,* the court should exercise it only when it determines that the interest of such child will be promoted thereby and that such parent is fit, competent and able to duly maintain, support and educate such child. . . .

It has repeatedly been determined, insofar as the best interests of the child are concerned, that the mother or father has a right to the care and custody of the child, *superior to that of all others,* unless he or she has abandoned that right or has proved unfit to assume the duties and privileges of parenthood. It has been well said that the status of the natural parent is so important that in determining the best interests of the child, it may counterbalance, even outweigh, superior material and cultural advantages which may be afforded by adoptive parents. . . .

The change of heart by a natural mother is not an evil thing. Instead, the change of mind is to be accorded great sympathy, and, in a proper case, encouragement and favorable action. We conclude that the record before us supports the finding by the courts below that the surrender was improvident and that the *child's best interest*—moral and temporal—will be best served by its return to the natural mother. No finding of present or prospective unfitness has been made against the mother. On the contrary, the record discloses that she is well educated, financially secure, and in a position to properly assume the care, training and education of her child.

The DeMartinos had tried to intervene in the suit between Miss Scarpetta and the agency. The New York courts decided that they had no right to intervene. They had lost. Despite all the delay, the baby was to be given back to her mother.

On the very same day the Court of Appeals decision was enunciated, the DeMartinos commenced action in the United States District Court for the Southern District of New York. They sought an injunction to prevent Olga Scarpetta from enforcing the judgment of New York's highest court. Federal Judge Constance Baker Motley said that the same arguments presented before her had been made in the New York courts. She denied the injunction and dismissed the DeMartinos' complaint. Olga had won in federal court, too.

Spence-Chapin Adoption Service and the DeMartinos were ordered to surrender Olga's infant daughter to her on May 3, 1971. Lenore was not given to her mother on that date. Joseph Zalk filed a motion in New York Supreme Court to punish the DeMartinos for contempt. The court entered the following order on May 28, 1971:

It is ordered, adjudged and decreed that the motion to punish Nick F. DeMartino and Jean DeMartino for contempt of court be granted to the following extent; and it is further

Ordered, adjudged and decreed that Nick F. DeMartino and Jean DeMartino shall return the said Baby Scarpetta forthwith to the temporary custody of the Spence-Chapin Adoption Service, 6 East 94th Street, New York, New York; and it is further

Ordered, adjudged and decreed that if the DeMartinos fail to comply with this order they shall be adjudged guilty of contempt of this court in having willfully disobeyed its provisions; and it is further

Ordered, adjudged and decreed as punishment for said contempt, the said Nick F. DeMartino and Jean DeMartino be imprisoned in the county jail for a period of thirty (30) days.

This order meant the DeMartinos would be jailed *only if* they failed to return the baby. As everyone was to learn, the DeMartinos had already fled to Miami. The fact that Mr. DeMartino was an attorney was ironic. He had specifically taken an oath to uphold the law and respect the courts in New York.

Olga Scarpetta retained me to represent her in Forida. After the Powell victory, I had been looking forward to a rest, but within a month I was to be trying the "Baby Lenore" case in a glare of publicity, and in the most emotional circumstances.

It became obvious that the DeMartinos were not going to take any steps to legally adopt Lenore in Florida. They figured the longer they kept the baby, the better their chances would be for ultimate success. On June 10, 1971, at 3:50 P.M., the Clerk of the Dade County Circuit Court stamped my petition for writ of habeas corpus.

Through our "blind" filing system, the case fell in the division of Circuit Court Judge Ralph O. Cullen. Our legal position was perfectly sound. Olga Scarpetta and the De-Martinos were residents of the State of New York, and all their courts had unanimously ruled in my client's favor. Miss Scarpetta was Lenore's mother. The DeMartinos were not related to the baby, and had never adopted her. Therefore, my petition to the Florida Circuit Court was simple: "Enforce the order of the highest court of New York and return the baby to her mother." To us it was that clear-cut.

The DeMartinos' attorneys urged that they were entitled to a full scale hearing on the merits of the case—on the issue of what was in the "child's best interest." They argued that the DeMartinos never had their "day in court" in New York, and now wanted the opportunity to present medical and other evidence. (Under New York law, of course, they had no right to a "day in court," any more than I would have a right to a day in court to try to take your child from you.)

Mallory H. Horton, the partner of my good friend Alan Schwartz, was working with me and Joe Zalk on behalf of Miss Scarpetta. Mallory had been an F.B.I. agent and a former assistant attorney general of Florida. He was also a former chief judge of the Third District Court of Appeal of Florida, and is a top expert in family and child law. He pointed out that the natural mother's rights had already been litigated and that she should not have to compete with strangers. He called Judge Cullen's attention to the New York decisions which had found Miss Scarpetta to be "fit and competent" as a mother. Judge Cullen weakly disagreed with our clearly correct legal position and scheduled a comprehensive hearing for June 22. We had no choice but to get prepared.

The DeMartinos had enlisted top-notch lawyers. Their New York counsel, Jacob Fuchsberg, had called in Bill Colson, a nationally known trial lawyer. Colson, in turn, called in his appellate or technical expert, Robert Orseck.

This was the first courtroom confrontation between the DeMartinos and Olga Scarpetta. The atmosphere was filled with electricity. It would have been even more tense if the baby had been there. The tenth-floor corridor outside Judge Cullen's office was filled with photographers and reporters from all over the country. Television stations in New York and elsewhere had sent special film crews. The blaze of lights and tons of equipment were enough to unnerve anyone. The hearing was held in the judge's chambers, which were little bigger than an average living room. The chambers were packed with lawyers, witnesses, the judge, the court personnel and members of the press.

I began by questioning Olga Scarpetta:

Q. Please tell us something about your educational background.

A. I came to the United States and started junior high school in Cleveland, where I lived with my family for one year. After that we moved to New York but I went to boarding school in New Jersey. On weekends I came to visit with my parents, who lived in Flushing.

Q. During what period of time were you going to school in New Jersey?

A. This was between 1950 and 1954. My parents had to return to Colombia and I had two more years of high school, so I lived with relatives until I graduated. I returned to Colombia and studied philosophy and literature; then I went to France where I studied at the Sorbonne for a year and a half. Then I worked for two and a half years in Bogotá. I came to California and majored in social science at the California State Polytechnic College, where I graduated. After that I returned home and started working toward my master's degree in Latin-American affairs at the University of the Americas in Bogotá.

Q. In addition to speaking English, do you speak any other languages?

A. Spanish and French.

Q. Please tell us about some of the jobs you have held.

A. I worked as a teacher for three years, teaching English and Spanish. In California I worked at a mental institution where I was involved in helping people who were leaving make the necessary adjustment to society. During my last year of schooling in California, I worked at the foreign student desk, counseling foreign students on adjusting to life in the United States.

Q. What did you do after you returned to Colombia?

A. I worked at the Bank of Bogota, which is the largest private bank in the country.

Q. What did you do there?

A. I was the head of the social services department, which involved counselling for the employees and their families, and programming various activities. During the last year I was in

Bogota, I was teaching at a secretarial school and a junior college.

Q. What type of work does your father do?

A. He owns his own company in Colombia, which imports heavy equipment for road construction.

Q. As you were growing up in Colombia did you have one home or more than one?

A. We had one home in the city and one home in the country and spent weekends in the country.

I knew they would not be able to prove anything detrimental relating to Olga's background. My questions were designed to demonstrate that she was highly educated, well rounded socially and culturally, and came from a fine family with substantial economic resources. Her parents were two of the loveliest and most refined people it has ever been my privilege to meet. Like their daughter, they were extremely courteous, patient, and most unassuming.

Colson questioned Miss Scarpetta:

Q. Now, the father of this child lives in Bogotá, is that right?

A. As far as I know.

Q. Well, at the time you went with him you both lived in Bogotá?

A. Yes.

Q. And did you know at the time that you were going with him that he was married?

A. No, I did not.

Q. And how long did you go with him?

A. I knew him for about two years. We started going seriously for about the past eight or nine months.

Q. And you talked about getting married, did you not?

A. Yes.

Q. And yet you had no idea that he was married?

A. No, I did not.

Q. And at the time you were over thirty years of age, correct?

A. Yes.

Q. And you had a college degree and a master's degree, correct?

A. Yes.

Q. This was not your first love affair, was it?

A. Yes, it was.

Q. You never had any other love affairs in California when you were out there?

A. No.

Q. You never had any love affairs in Paris when you were there?

A. No.

Q. This is the first love affair, at the age of thirty-one, that you ever had in your life?

A. That is right.

This crap made headlines all over the country the next day. Colson, a native Miamian, was shrewdly bringing in all this nonsense because he knew that 'it would impress the elderly and conservative Judge Cullen. I had not asked Mrs. DeMartino if she was a virgin when she got married, and I didn't ask her if she ever had an affair after her marriage. Such questions would be cruel and pointless. Whether this was Olga Scarpetta's first love affair or her tenth was totally irrelevant to the legal or factual issues. Colson continued:

Q. During the four days that the child was in the hospital, she was not brought to you, was she?

A. Yes, she was.

Q. Did you actually feed the child?

A. I gave her the bottle, yes.

Q. On how many occasions?

A. Every day.

Q. Did you take the child personally to the adoption agency?

A. Yes.

Q. And your sister went with you?

A. Yes.

Q. Your sister came up and stayed with you throughout the birth, did she not?

A. No. She came up a week before the baby was born.

Q. Now on May 29 you came back to the adoption agency to sign the formal surrender document, did you not?

A. Yes.

Q. Did you sign the document at that time?

A. I could not sign because I could not stop crying. I could not physically sign the document.

Q. Then you came back on June 1?

A. That is right.

Q. And on June 1 you signed it?

A. Yes.

Q. At that time you were over thirty years of age, is that correct?

It was time to object and make a little speech.

This is at least the fifth time that Mr. Colson has asked Miss Scarpetta if she was over thirty years of age. Yes—she was thirty-two, she could understand the surrender and she signed it. She also revoked it twenty-three days later and only five days after the DeMartinos got the baby. And perhaps Mr. Colson might be interested in knowing that not everyone over the age of thirty has the same amount of experience or worldliness. I object to the question because it is repetitious.

The Court: Sustained.

Colson went on:

Q. And no one ever told you that you had six months to change your mind?

A. That I found out by myself when I checked the law.

Q. The reason that you wanted to go with the adoption was that you felt it was for the best interest of the child?

A. I felt that by putting my baby up for adoption, I was putting her away from every problem she could ever have in this world. I wanted her to have complete happiness.

Q. You don't have any suggestion in your mind that she has not been completely protected and happy, do you?

A. I think she has been hurt an awful lot.

Q. By whom?

A. All the propaganda in the press.

Q. You think that she is aware of the propaganda in the press?

A. She will grow up and will be very much aware of it.

Q. There is no question about that. No, ma'am, I am asking you, do you have any ideas that anything has changed since you wanted the child put up for adoption?

A. Yes. I realized that adoption is a hard thing for a child to face. I realize that as long as the mother is capable and loves the child and wants the child, the best place for her is with the mother because a baby has a right to her own heritage. She has a right to know who she is, to be among her people. If the mother is able to take care of her and if the whole family wants and loves and desires to have the child next to them, that child should be with them and not with strangers.

Q. At the time you signed this formal surrender document, didn't you feel that the best interests of the child were that she should have a home and a family and for that reason you were giving your child up?

A. At the time I signed those papers, I was under tremendous strain. I was feeling guilty, guilty of not providing my baby with a home.

Q. Now after you signed this document you changed your mind. Is it fair to say that no circumstances—as far as any marriage or your job or your home or anything changed?

A. As far as my work, it obviously changed. I had a very hard time when I came to New York finding a job. Before the baby was born my take home pay was $48 a week and I had been turned down in many jobs, and I was beginning to feel that I was not capable of holding a job that would bring in a decent salary. After the baby was born, I saw that I did have the capacity to get a good job. I secured a job which has good opportunity for advancement and I realized that I was capable of taking care of my child.

Q. Other than that, circumstances had not changed?

A. Circumstances had changed because I was no longer pregnant, and I looked at the situation and understood that the adoptive parents were just plain people like everybody else and she would have the same problems with them as she would have with me or with anybody in the world.

Q. When did you notify the agency for the very first time that you were thinking about revoking your consent?

A. I called the agency on June 23rd. They told me there was nothing that I could do. An appointment was made for me to come in on June 29th when I formally requested the return of my baby.

Q. All right, after the discussion on June 29th you had some more discussions with the agency, did you not?

A. On June 29th Miss Daniels told me that their main responsibility was with the adoptive parents and therefore they would do everything they could to dissuade me in my efforts. She told me it was very common for a mother to change her mind within the first thirty days after signing the papers and they were sure that with additional counselling, I would revert to my original decision. I agreed to go to that counselling and I went to four visits but I didn't change my mind. I was still insisting on getting my baby back.

I asked Miss Scarpetta about her state of mind at the time she agreed to give the baby up for adoption. How easy it was for the DeMartinos and their lawyers to say that Olga Scarpetta made a decision and should be forced to abide by it. The New York law has a grace period for precisely the reason that the signing of the surrender is nearly always done under circumstances of great stress and ambivalence.

Q. When you came to New York did you have a job waiting for you?

A. No, I did not.

Q. Did you have an apartment waiting for you?

A. No.

Q. Did you come to New York alone?

A. Yes.

Q. Mr. Colson asked you about all your visits with Miss Daniels both before and after the birth of Lenore. How old is this Miss Daniels?

A. I believe at that time she was twenty-one.

Q. And she is employed by and paid by the adoption agency?
A. That is right.
Q. And she told you their main responsibility was to the adoptive parents?
A. Yes.
Q. When you signed the consent on June 1, did you have a lawyer with you?
A. No, I did not.
Q. Before your experience with Spence-Chapin, had you ever had any previous dealings with any other adoption agency anywhere in the world?
A. No.

The Reverend Claire Anderson of the Redeemer Lutheran Church in Brooklyn came to Miami to tell Judge Cullen and the world what swell people the DeMartinos were. His church was next door to their home.

I objected:

Your Honor, it appears that Reverend Anderson's testimony is designed to go to the issue of fitness. We object to any testimony having to do with fitness as between the DeMartinos and the natural mother of the child. Mis Scarpetta, in New York, has already been adjudicated as fit and competent. I do not contend that the DeMartinos are unfit, and to have this witness and other witnesses say that they are a loving and nice couple is simply irrelevant to the issues before you.
The Court: Overruled.

I cross-examined Reverend Anderson:

Q. Do you know Miss Scarpetta?
A. No, I do not.
Q. You don't know her parents?
A. I have just met them outside.
Q. They seem like nice people?
A. Yes.
Q. You don't know anything about her apartment in New York?
A. No, I do not.

Q. Or her ability to take care of her baby?

A. No, I don't.

Q. Do I understand, sir, that you have come from Brooklyn specifically to testify in this case?

A. I was invited to do so.

Q. Who paid for your trip down here?

A. Mr. Fuchsberg.

Q. And what did that cost?

A. I have no idea.

Q. Where are you staying?

A. The DuPont Plaza Hotel.

Q. And Mr. Fuchsberg is paying for that as well?

A. Yes.

Q. Did the DeMartinos ever discuss with you their reasons for coming to Florida?

A. No, they did not.

Q. Weren't you curious as to why they were leaving their home in Brooklyn where they had all these close family and community ties—why all of a sudden, out of the blue, they picked up and moved to Florida?

Obviously, I was asking this question sarcastically, since I wanted a simple honest answer from someone that the only reason the DeMartinos fled to Florida was to avoid complying with the court orders of their home state. Such an answer was not to be forthcoming from anyone.

A. I understood they were leaving perhaps for the best interests of their child. But this is the decision that they made.

Q. During the entire period of time that you knew the DeMartinos prior to this adoption battle, had they ever indicated to you a desire to leave New York?

A. No.

Q. How were you contacted with reference to testifying in this case?

A. I was called last week by a committee which has worked on their behalf, and asked if I would come to Florida as a character witness.

Q. What is the name of that committee?

A. The Committee to Save Baby Lenore. *(From her mother!)*

Q. This is the very same committee that has been propagandizing in the New York area on behalf of the DeMartinos?

A. They may have.

This committee of "concerned citizens" aided and abetted by screeching and hysterical headlines of the New York *Daily News* (the famed subway throwaway) gathered 87,000 signatures from people—who all knew in their hearts that Lenore could achieve true happiness only if she remained with the DeMartinos. Olga Scarpetta was unable to launch any comparable public relations campaign.

Mr. Fuchsberg called Dr. Andrew Watson, a psychiatrist and professor of law at the University of Michigan, where he, Fuchsberg and Colson had participated together in several advocacy programs. Fuchsberg and Colson were both past presidents of the Association of Trial Lawyers of America. They were very influential and had powerful legal and medical connections across the country.

Although he taught law, the good doctor did not have a degree. He said it would be bad to remove a thirteen-month-old baby from the only parents she had ever known. Yes, thirteen months had already passed!

This is what all the DeMartinos' medical experts would say, in one fashion or another. I turned to Joe Zalk and whispered, "Insanity reigns supreme. They keep the infant illegally until she is thirteen months old. Then they contend it would be traumatic to give this Colombian baby back to her Colombian mother."

Being aware that Mallory Horton had known Judge Cullen for many years before he became a circuit judge, I asked him, "Could he possibly be buying this trash?"

Looking worried, Mallory said, "I never thought he would listen to such testimony in the first place. It is a purely legal question which is just as clear as it can be. Strangers cannot compete with a natural parent. The only evidence is that Olga would be a fine mother."

"Mallory—I repeat—could Cullen be buying this stuff?"

"Yes, primarily because it will take some fortitude to return the baby to her mother."

I knew exactly what he meant. I had tried several jury cases before Judge Cullen. Although he was always courteous and fair, he could be pushed around. He loved it when lawyers settled, because then he did not have to make decisions. He would let lawyers drone on and on, even when the answer was obvious. To him an unwed mother figured to be a pariah, and it was very doubtful that he would buck public opinion.

Dr. Watson, who reminded me very much of Sherlock Holmes's bumbling sidekick, said:

The child would perceive the removal as though a person was dying, and they have to go through a very profound grief reaction, which can leave very, very serious permanent scars. A whole new perception of existence would have to be accommodated, and it would be very, very difficult for the child to do so.

I cross-examined Dr. Watson:

Q. Where are you staying?

A. DuPont Plaza.

Q. A popular hotel. Who is paying for that?

A. I don't honestly know. I'm going to be reimbursed for my expenses. I don't know who is paying for it.

Q. How about your expert witness fee?

A. No fee.

Q. Why?

A. Because this case, as I mentioned before, I teach family law and I am very, very interested in the abstract social principles that are involved in this case and any like it. Therefore, I was very willing to participate.

Q. Were you influenced at all by the fact that with all the press coverage and attention, that testifying in this case might enhance your prestige?

A. No, not to my awareness. I am never willing to account for my unconscious . . .

Q. I understand that you worked for a private adoption agency and actually served as president of its board?

A. Yes.

Q. Have you ever "followed" a thirteen-month-old baby who was taken away from people and given back to her natural mother—to know what happened to a real, and not an abstract baby?

A. No, I have not.

Q. Have you ever "followed" any children whose parents died in infancy?

A. No, I do not treat children directly.

Q. So you have never "followed" a thirteen-month-old infant from any standpoint, have you?

A. No.

Q. What are the statistics on children, let's say thirteen months, or fifteen months, or seventeen months—whose parents are killed in accidents? You are not telling this court that all those children grow up and become manic-depressives, or psychotics?

A. I am saying all those children will grow up with a psychological scar which they will adjust to in various ways, depending on what kind of rearing, but always a scar.

This is the kind of glittering generality which makes many people despise the psychiatric profession. The simple truth is that we all acquire "scars" during childhood. What will scar one child will not scar another, and different people react in different ways to adverse experiences during the formative years.

What about the scars to children who learn they are adopted? What about those who spend years trying to discover their true identity? What about the scars that come from a deep-rooted sense of rejection—"Why didn't my parents want me?" It is valueless to talk about infants in the abstract.

In order to make even a semivalid prediction one would need an enormous amount of information about Miss Scarpetta, the natural father, the DeMartinos and the infant herself—and even then it would only be an educated guess. Anyone would agree, as a general proposition, that removing a thirteen-month-old infant from its foster parents would not do the baby any good. But if handled with love, patience, and understanding it is unlikely that there would be permanent ill effects.

I asked another practical question in an attempt to make Judge Cullen see that the defense medical experts were in a never-never land of speculation.

Q. Let me give you this type of situation. It occurs to me that when Jack Kennedy was president, his son was born. I assume that because of his position and wealth, his wife spent a lot less time with the infant than did the nursemaid. What would have been the effect if Jackie Kennedy decided to fire the woman after thirteen months? Would that result in a permanent scar to the child?

A. It would have a devastating effect.

To me that answer was absurd on its face. One would have to know a great deal before he could even begin to measure the impact of such a transfer. For all he knew, the child didn't like the nursemaid and maybe Lenore was sensitive enough to be uncomfortable with the DeMartinos' feeling that she belonged elsewhere. A silly hypothesis? Maybe so, but no sillier than saying dogmatically that the firing of a nursemaid would have a devastating effect on a child.

Q. Well, doctor, do you take the position that Jackie Kennedy or any other wealthy woman in a similar position would not have the right to fire the nurse?

A. I presume she does, but I think she would be very foolish to do so, extremely foolish. It would send an infant into a profound depressed state, which would leave a scar as it recovered.

Q. Isn't the question of identity—who am I, where do I come from, what is my lineage—isn't that one of the most basic psychological ingredients people possess?

A. Everybody has to develop a sharp, hard, clear image of those facts, yes.

Q. Isn't it normal for an adopted child at some point to feel that the adoptive parents are not the real parents, and to feel in a sense that they were obtained at a store?

A. All adopted children have that problem.

Q. Because although the parents have taken care of the child and provided for his or her material needs the feeling still persists—I am not of you, I have not come from your body.

A. That is true, that last is true.

Q. You have absolutely no way of predicting what the next eleven or twelve years hold for this child, what her family experiences are going to be, what her school experiences are going to be, what her intelligence is going to be, what her emotional level is going to be—do you?

A. One could make predictions, because some of the characteristics of any human relationship are susceptible to analysis in the abstract, without seeing the persons involved but it's a vulnerable position, and we both know that.

I turned to Joe Zalk and said, "He bets his ass we do. I only hope Judge Cullen knows it, too."

Q. Now, doctor, we've talked about rich people. What about poor people where the mother puts the child in a day-care center or has a relative take care of the child or has to go out of town to find work? Does that baby, if the mother is away for several months, always have permanent scars?

A. The baby will have very serious problems.

Q. Some children, as they grow older, are better able to cope with psychic damage than are other children?

A. Yes.

They brought in another doctor-lawyer named Ben Sheppard, who is, to this day, probably one of the best-known figures in South Florida.

Bill Colson, in introducing Dr. Sheppard, laid it on thick for Judge Cullen's benefit:

Everyone in the community knows Dr. Ben Sheppard, but I'll tell you he has been in pediatrics for forty years, that he was very active in the polio problems of this community, that he was a juvenile judge for seven years, that he is presently a member of the Dade County School Board—and I think that as the executive director of the Catholic Welfare Bureau he has charge of all the medical problems for adopted children in this community.

Colson started to ask Dr. Sheppard questions similar to those asked of Dr. Watson.

I objected: "The doctor is constantly using the word 'might,' which is speculative, and serves no useful purpose in this court."

Colson: Well, your Honor, six more doctors will testify. There are two from Yale, and the most famous lady in the country from Bellevue.

This was getting absurd, and I was becoming angry.

Rosenblatt: I think, judge, if they seriously intend to call that many doctors, that they are making a farce of this proceeding. We do not need Yale professors or "the most famous lady in the country" to tell us that it is bad for an infant to be taken away from the couple who have brought her up. The greatest doctors in the world can't tell us what the practical effect will be on this particular infant if she is returned to her mother.

Colson: May we proceed, your Honor?

The Court: I am inclined to think we are getting cumulative.

Rosenblatt: I am calling one psychologist and I am only doing that because your Honor has decided to hear testimony along these lines.

The Court: This could go on for a week.

Colson: No, sir.

Judge Cullen permitted Dr. Sheppard to testify. He volunteered:

It's my personal opinion that it would be very traumatic to take a child of thirteen months away from the environment which she knows so well, and put her in a totally alien environment. I think it *might* do damage, *might* scar. I think future interpersonal relations *might* be hurt.

I cross-examined:

Q. Doctor, you are talking basically about the odds and generalizations. You cannot, as a medical doctor, predict what will happen to this baby if she is returned to her mother. You are simply testifying in general that such a transfer is bad?

A. Yes.

Jake Fuchsberg, with a great flourish, called as the DeMartinos' next witness "the most famous lady in the country," Dr. Stella Chess. She was a professor of child psychiatry at New York University and was licensed as a practicing physician in 1939.

Her testimony boiled down to this: She "did not think it would be in the best interest of the child to move her."

I cross-examined her:

Q. You received a call from a gentlemen with the "Save Baby Lenore Committee," and he asked you if you would testify?

A. Yes.

Q. Did you ever do any psychological testing on him?

A. I never met him.

Q. You knew even without examining the DeMartinos or the child that you were at least philosophically in sympathy with their position?

A. Right.

Q. Of course, you have testified as a general proposition that it would not be in the best interest of the child to move her out of familiar surroundings. Are you able to predict with any real degree of certainty what would happen to this baby if she was given to her mother, assuming that Miss Scarpetta would give her love and meet all her other needs?

A. I can't predict in this case if a change were made whether Lenore would take it quite well, but I can predict that given a great many children who were moved at this time, that chances are it will not be the best thing for her.

An analysis of this answer says it all: "I can't predict in this case . . . " Well, this is the *only* case we're talking about. And the judge's ruling in this case will be the most important decision in the baby's life!

Lenore might "take it quite well." Sure, she might. And even if she takes it poorly, the odds are she will make a healthy adjustment in time to her own mother.

"Chances are it will not be the best thing for her." I agree, but that's a thousand miles away from saying that the infant will have a permanent psychological scar. Just how "iffy" can one get when you are talking about depriving a natural mother of her child?

Q. In your practice have you had occasion to treat or follow children whose natural parents were both Colombian, as opposed to America?

A. No.

Q. Of course, you have never examined or talked to Miss Scarpetta?

A. No.

Q. For all you know she might have better qualifications for motherhood than Mrs. DeMartino?

A. I can't make any statement on Miss Scarpetta.

Q. There is no way for you to predict the nature of the mother-child relationship between Mrs. DeMartino and Lenore as it may develop over the next several years, is there?

A. That is true.

Two psychologists and a pediatrician also testified for the
DeMartinos. Their answers closely paralleled the opinions
given by the others. In addition to all these medical wiz-
ards, the Yale professors and another New York doctor
were simply paraded before Judge Cullen on Colson's rep-
resentation that they would say approximately the same
thing.

Not one member of their learned chorus line ever met
or examined Olga Scarpetta. Not one of them had even
minimal experience with Colombian children.

I called only one expert, Dr. Leonard Haber, a Ph.D in
clinical psychology. He stated:

My opinion is that given a comparable experience, assuming the
same for the mother as for the parents who now hold the child,
there would be no permanent damage to this child.

Q. Could you explain the reasoning behind that conclusion?
A. Well, it seems to me that the pain and suffering belongs to
the adults in a situation like this. At the age of thirteen
months, even though the child does have a certain amount
of awareness and recognition, it is doubtful that it would
matter very much to the child who does the rearing if the
rearing is properly done. Damage in a situation like this is
much more likely to be related to the quality of the mothering, than to the question of who does the mothering.
Q. Do you feel, assuming Miss Scarpetta would be in a position
to give the child equal loving and equal material comforts,
that the transfer would cause even substantial temporary
problems?
A. Well, the child would be aware of the change in surroundings, and it would be difficult to predict what the individual
reaction of a given child would be or how long a child might
react with some discomfort or stress at being placed in a new
environment, and I expect there would be such a reaction. I
couldn't say how long it would last. My belief is that given
reasonably good handling, it would not result in any serious
or lasting difficulty.

Q. Dr. Haber, before I ever contacted you were you aware of this case from the press and from other sources?
A. Yes.
Q. Did you have occasion before I ever called you to take a public position on the very question that I have asked you today?
A. Yes. It came up as a question on a radio program I have conducted for several years and my response to that question then was essentially the same as it has been in court today.

I considered this an important plus from the standpoint of motivation. I had never met this man. He wasn't doing me any favors. He had expressed an opinion favorable to our position before he had any interest in the situation.
Colson asked very few questions:

Q. Doctor, you are not a medical doctor?
A. That is correct. *(Who the hell said he was?)*
Q. Do you know Dr. Stella Chess?
A. I know of Dr. Stella Chess.
Q. For instance, I have six books of hers, right here. Do you recognize her as an authority in this field, sir?
A. Yes.
Q. Did you see her standing outside?
A. I don't know who she is, but I know of her name.

We just had to hope that Judge Cullen would not be taken in by this sort of thing. Okay, Dr. Chess wrote books and she was well known and was probably a fine doctor. So what? All she said was that transferring Lenore at age thirteen months probably wouldn't be good for her.
Bill Colson called Mrs. Jean DeMartino as his next witness.

Q. What is your age, please, ma'am?
A. I am thirty-five years old.
Q. Mrs. DeMartino, where did you grow up?
A. In New York.

Q. How far did you go in school?
A. I went to college for two years.
Q. What religion are you?
A. Roman Catholic. *(The same religion as Olga Scarpetta and the natural father.)*
Q. Had you and Mr. DeMartino tried to have children of your own?
A. Yes, we did, sir.
Q. And what were the results?
A. Well, I was pregnant three times, but I was unable to carry them to full term.
Q. Linda is adopted?
A. Yes, sir.
Q. What agency did Linda come from?
A. The Spence-Chapin Adoption Service.
Q. Now, as to Mr. DeMartino, what is his occupation?
A. He is an attorney, sir.
Q. Did Mr. DeMartino follow you down here after you arrived with the children?
A. Yes, that is correct.
Q. What is your intention as to your future and your present residence as to the State of Florida?
A. Florida is my home.
Q. Regardless of the outcome of this litigation, that is your answer?
A. Florida is my home, sir.

It was clear to me, as it must have been to everyone else, that the DeMartinos had no intention of coming to Florida until the child-custody battle occurred. If we won, they would be on the next flight back to New York. I cross-examined:

Q. Are you still satisfied with Spence-Chapin as an adoption agency?
A. Yes, sir.
Q. You are not upset with the agency for not having told you in June or July or August or September or October of 1970

that Miss Scarpetta wanted her baby back? (*I wanted to
emphasize to Cullen how very early Miss Scarpetta had
changed her mind. The reason the witness had the baby thirteen months was because of the agency's malpractice.*)

Mr. Colson: Your Honor, I would object. I think her feeling
toward the agency is immaterial.

The Court: I will sustain the objection. (*I was getting ominous
vibrations from the judge's demeanor and rulings.*)

Q. But in any event, the agency never told you about any
possible problem until November of last year?

A. Yes.

Q. You and your husband have never adopted Lenore, have
you?

A. We have not legally adopted her, no, sir.

Q. Of course, with Linda there was a normal, formalized, legal
adoption—is that correct?

A. Yes.

Q. You had Linda some time before her adoption was finalized,
didn't you?

A. I think it was about nine months to a year.

Q. So you knew of your own personal knowledge, having already
adopted a child, that you could not legally adopt until at least
six months had passed?

A. I knew we could not get the legal papers.

Q. Where were you born?

A. In New York City.

Q. Have you ever lived any place other than New York City
until you came to Florida?

A. No, sir, I haven't.

Q. Throughout your marriage, you and your husband always
resided together in the state of New York?

A. Yes, sir.

Q. If the New York courts had said, "You can keep the baby,"
would you have come to Florida anyway?

A. We had talked often of coming to Florida, yes, sir.

Q. Mrs. DeMartino, I am asking you a very specific question.

If there had been no litigation and no problem, would you be a resident of Florida as you assert you are today?

A. Yes, sir.

I was happy to get that answer because it was patently false. Hopefully, it would make the judge angry. I said to Joe Zalk, "If Cullen believes that, he must be on a first-name basis with the tooth fairy."

Q. What is your husband's employment now?

A. He is doing insurance work, investigation.

Q. For which company?

A. For Colson & Hicks. (*How very interesting!*)

Q. Has Mr. DeMartino had any other job in Florida other than working as an investigator for the law firm of Bill Colson and Bill Hicks?

A. No, sir, he has not.

Q. What are they paying him?

A. I don't know.

Q. What date did you come to Florida?

A. It was early in April 1971.

Q. When did your husband come down?

A. He came down May 1.

Q. Did you ever meet Miss Daniels of the Spence-Chapin Agency?

A. No, sir.

Q. In addition to living all your life in New York, you have many relatives there?

A. Yes, sir, I do.

Q. New York is the only state in the country where your husband is admitted to practice law?

A. That is correct.

Q. What was your motivation in posing for all these photographs which have appeared all over the country, and in inviting photographers and reporters into your home?

A. Mr. Rosenblatt, there is nothing that I cherish more than my privacy, but I felt that I should inform the public what was happening. I phoned the newspapers.

Q. You and your husband made a decision to contact the press
in order to get public opinion on your side?
A. I thought the public should be advised.

Their public relations campaign had been a great success. Public opinion was overwhelmingly on their side in
New York and Florida, the more so as time went on and
they had more months of "parenthood" to use to gain the
sympathy of the press and public. Letters to the editor and
telephone calls to radio talk shows were nearly all in the
DeMartino's favor. Eighty-seven thousand signatures were
garnered by the "Committee to Save Baby Lenore." Incredible! They were trying to save Baby Lenore from the
terrible fate of being reunited with her mother. Their press
releases always failed to mention that Miss Scarpetta had
asked for her baby back only five days after the DeMartinos acquired her.

All the press coverage of this case was no accident. Jacob
Fuchsberg, a great public relations man, tried to ride his
publicity to the chief judgeship of the New York Court of
Appeals in the 1973 election. He lost that time but succeeded in becoming a member of that court in a later election.

I continued:

Q. Mrs. DeMartino, all these pictures which I now show you of
you and your husband cuddling the baby and with your
husband's head on Lenore's stomach, these are all posed pictures, aren't they?
A. Yes, as Miss Scarpetta did when she posed for pictures.
Q. Well, there was a minor difference. Miss Scarpetta, unlike
you, never posed for a picture with her baby, did she?
A. Miss Scarpetta signed away her baby.
Q. My question to you is, did Miss Scarpetta ever pose for a
picture with her baby?
A. You cannot pose with something you have given away, sir.

So much compassion for Olga Scarpetta's baby, but so little for her mother! Heredity and genes and carrying the child under difficult circumstances for nine months were all totally meaningless to the DeMartinos. Their attitude was, "Olga gave her away, and we just don't recognize the New York law or the New York decisions which say the natural mother has time in which to reflect and recant."

Q. What do you think Lenore's reaction will be when, later on in life, she sees all these photographs, and understands that her real mother fought long and hard to get her?

A. Well, she'll see the story of an adoptive couple who loved her greatly and who fought for her well being.

Q. Won't she also see the story of a natural mother who loved her greatly and fought for her? Won't the child see that also?

A. She'll see her mother sought to undo what she thought was a mistake. She'll also see there were parents who loved her greatly and who were concerned enough about her well being, so I think the stories will speak for themselves.

Q. So there is no doubt in your mind that when Lenore reads these stories and sees these posed pictures, it's not going to have any effect on her? She'll just know that the DeMartinos were right?

A. I think they will have very little consequence on her. The fact that she was given up is just a fact of life, and if she grows up in a home where there is love and security, she will be able to accept that fact. That scar does not change whether Lenore is in our home or in Miss Scarpetta's home. That scar will always be there. She was rejected. (*The lawyer's wife suddenly became an expert on psychic scars.*)

Q. You and your husband have never permitted Miss Scarpetta to see her baby, have you?

A. No. I checked with my pediatricians and they agreed with our attorneys. It would serve no purpose to Lenore. It would only be an emotional experience for the parents involved.

Q. How did the Miami newspapers learn of your whereabouts?

A. From Mr. Colson at his press conference.

Q. Have you or your husband taken any steps to adopt Lenore in the State of Florida?
A. No sir, we have not.

I had a few questions for Mr. DeMartino as well:

Q. You were born in New York?
A. Yes, sir.
Q. You went to high school, college, and law school in New York?
A. Yes.
Q. Would you have given the baby back if you had remained in New York?
A. No.

Judge Cullen had to be impressed with this answer. This attorney was saying that he was not going to obey the statutes and lawful court orders of his state.

Q. You knew that you would either turn the baby over to Miss Scarpetta or be jailed for contempt?
A. You are asking me as a lawyer. I am testifying as a father and a human being who never had a day in court.

He had the public relations patter down to a science. Mr. DeMartino and his wife played the media people beautifully, from their hand-holding routine down to their anguished expressions every time Lenore's name was mentioned. He was a "father," but Olga Scarpetta was apparently not a "mother," according to him. Olga Scarpetta made one mistake, so "to hell with her." So now he had his "day in court," and they established the earth shattering proposition that it *might* be traumatic or it *might* leave a scar to remove the baby from their sheltering arms.

Q. What was it about May 1, 1971, that after spending your entire life in New York and your wife spending her entire life in New York, that you suddenly decided to come to sunny Florida? Was there any compelling reason to come to Florida other than this situation?

A. Compelling reasons, no.

Q. How about three weeks earlier, when your wife came down—
was there any particular reason she came down at that time?

A. She came down because she wanted to see if it was as nice
as we had remembered it on our previous visits. And after
she came down she wrote a letter telling me she loved it—it
was wide open spaces, a lot of outdoor living, which in New
York is limited to a three-month period in the summertime.

A tough judge would have eaten a lawyer alive for giving
answers like that. "Yeah, folks, it was a mere coincidence
that we just happened to come to Florida at this particular
time in our lives."

At the conclusion of this testimony, Mallory Horton
quoted from a case which was decided by the Florida
Third District Court of Appeal when he was a member of
that court. The Court had said:

Without in any way minimizing the love and affection which
exists in a fostor home where the foster parents have loved and
cared for a child over a long period of time, there can be no
doubt that the law places the right of a parent on a different
level. This right of a parent has been described as a natural
God-given legal right to enjoy the custody, fellowship, and
companionship of his offspring. The right of the parents to the
custody, care, and upbringing of their children is one of the most
basic rights of our civilization.

As far as Mallory, Joe Zalk, and I were concerned, both
justice and the letter of the law were with our client. We
were all disgusted at the slop Judge Cullen had admitted
into evidence. Because of his background and general outlook, we were pessimistic.

Judge Ralph O. Cullen announced his decision:

There is no case a judge has to decide that is any more difficult
than one such as we have here. Many eminent jurists have written
eloquent opinions involving the same issues we have here which
I could refer to. I will not. I am constrained to the conclusion

that after all is said and done, analyzing everything, the petition should be denied and the writ discharged.

Judge Cullen's ruling meant that the DeMartinos did not have to give Lenore back to her mother. Olga Scarpetta was in a state of shock. The *Miami Herald* quoted her as saying:

I can't believe any judge would make a decision like that when they had fled the state where there were court orders telling them to turn the child over to me. I can not have any respect for Mr. DeMartino. He's a lawyer, a man sworn to uphold the laws. Yet he breaks the laws of his own state. How is he going to teach her moral principles and respect for the law?

Olga had retained her composure in the judge's chambers but she fell apart when she reached my office. The scene between her and her parents was so filled with pathos that Joe Zalk and I just had to go down the hall to Mallory's office for a few minutes. At no time did Olga or her parents or any of her relatives say anything really harsh about Judge Cullen or the DeMartinos. That is the kind of gentle, forbearing people they are. They vowed to continue the fight, and told us to appeal the trial court's decision.

Mallory was in charge of the appeal. He and Joe Zalk have judicial temperaments, and take things in their stride, whereas I tend to be a hothead when I honestly believe my client has received a screwing (judicial or otherwise).

I knew it wouldn't do any good, but we had to attempt to show Judge Cullen that he had made an abominable decision. Perhaps he would at least grant our client visitation during the months it would take us to travel the appellate road in Florida. Olga wanted more than anything in the world to see and touch her baby. We had to give it a shot. The hearing was on June 29. I began by saying:

Your Honor, this is a petitioner's request for a rehearing. More specifically, it is a request and attempt to discuss with the court what we feel are persuasive reasons as to why you erred in entering the judgment denying our petition for a writ of habeas corpus on behalf of Miss Scarpetta.

Lenore was born on May 18, 1970, and exactly one month later, the DeMartinos acquired possession of the baby from the Spence-Chapin Adoption Service. The really hideous thing about what has transpired here is that the Spence-Chapin Agency, in its alleged wisdom, decided not to tell the DeMartinos that Miss Scarpetta had changed her mind *only five days* after they obtained the baby. The "Baby Lenore" case never would have become a case if the DeMartinos had been advised of the true situation then.

Miss Daniels decides on her own that a lot of natural mothers change their minds but don't really mean it. Well, Olga Scarpetta meant it. Because she is the type of person she is, non-aggressive and non-assertive—she agreed to return for additional counselling from the same young, single girl. The counselling—or trying to get Olga to change her mind—effort accomplished nothing.

The Supreme Court of the State of New York said in clear and unambiguous language that the baby properly belonged to Miss Scarpetta. The DeMartinos are not related to this infant. They have not adopted Lenore in New York, in Florida or anywhere else. Because of this, we have contended that the DeMartinos had no standing to raise the "welfare of the child" issue. Besides, and most importantly, this issue was decided in Miss Scarpetta's favor in New York.

The DeMartinos get pretty emotional and teary-eyed—"my baby" and being a "mother and father," and every other appealing label they can think up. But this baby is here because of the strength and resolve of Olga Scarpetta, because the easy way out for a woman in this circumstance is to have an abortion.

This child is Colombian. This is her identity. This is her heritage, and she is going to be an adult a lot longer than she is going to be a child. She has a right to know her mother and her grandparents and her uncles and aunts. Miss Scarpetta admits that she made a mistake in signing the consent. She was crying so hard the first time she couldn't sign it and had to return days later when she was still sobbing.

But they were in New York and under New York law she had six months within which to change her mind. She changed her mind 23 days after signing the consent, and only five days after the DeMartinos obtained the infant. That horrible, foul deed; changing her mind. She signed the consent. Well, let's look at that in context.

She was alone. She was ashamed. She was fearful. Her family was in another country. She had no attorney when she was dealing with Spence-Chapin and she was talking with people who had a vested financial interest in seeing that the adoption was consummated.

Is it fair, or is it just to deprive this mother of her daughter for the rest of her life because of one mistake—a mistake that she has done everything within her power to rectify? Consider what this woman has been through in terms of her steadfastness —the time, the money, the effort, the embarrassment in fighting to get her baby back.

I remind you that all New York Courts decided that Miss Scarpetta was fit and competent and had the right to rescind her consent. Not a shred of evidence was offered by the DeMartinos to show that Olga Scarpetta was unfit in any way. Are we just going to ignore the decisions of a sister state and the full faith and credit clause of the U.S. Constitution?

The general law of this state and every state is that as long as the mother is fit, it is presumed that the best interest of the child is with its natural mother. The DeMartinos are seeking to establish a new theory—"adverse possession" in child-custody cases. They say, "We have had her this long. She knows only us, and therefore it would be against her best interest to take her away from us."

Miss Scarpetta is a college graduate with a master's degree who has a very responsible position with a vast international corporation. She speaks three languages and her work history has been that of helping others—teaching and advising. She is financially secure and she is able to care for the baby.

I have to assume, based on the Court's ruling, that you were impressed with the medical testimony on behalf of the DeMartinos. The only thing their medical testimony proved was the power and influence of Mr. Colson and Mr. Fuchsberg. I don't know too many lawyers who could get that many doctors from all over the country to come in to a Miami courtroom and testify out of the goodness of their hearts.

What did the doctors really say? They said that it wouldn't be good to remove a thirteen-month-old infant from her usual surroundings. Of course, as an abstract generalization, I agree. But we don't tear an infant from her mother permanently because there may be a difficult transitional adjustment.

Judge, a lot of things are not good. Divorce is not good when children are of tender years. It is frequently bad when a woman remarries and brings a new father into the home. It is bad when a husband and wife don't get along, and when they scream and fight in front of the children. Not one of their doctors could predict, based on reasonable medical certainty, the effect of a transfer on this particular child.

Do I have to remind this court that there are no guarantees in this world? There are no guarantees that because a child is brought up on Park Avenue or her parents are highly educated, that he or she is going to be a success. We have example after example of children who become dope addicts, children who commit suicide, and children who commit ugly crimes although brought up in the best of circumstances.

Conversely, we have children who were deprived, children whose parents were no good, children who were lonely and unhappy—who became captains of industry or community leaders who are admired by all. Most of us grow up to be relatively normal, functioning human beings in spite of the shocks of childhood.

To make the actions of the DeMartinos even more flagrant in disregarding the lawful orders of their state is the fact that Mr. DeMartino is a lawyer who knew full well that there was a six-month waiting period. He had previously adopted a child from this very agency and he handled adoptions for clients as well.

We can return to the jungle and to the swamp very quickly if each person is going to decide which laws to obey and which ones to disobey. Everyone who breaks the law has an excuse— "It is society's fault. I am poor. I have been deprived. I didn't know I was violating the law. Life has been unfair to me."

Nick DeMartino's excuse is that he is a "father" and Jean DeMartino's excuse is that Miss Scarpetta "gave her baby away." Well, Nick DeMartino is *not* Lenore's father because she has not been adopted. My client gave provisional and temporary custody of her baby to the Spence-Chapin Agency. She changed her mind, which she had a right to do, and this revocation has been unanimously affirmed by eleven judges in three New York Courts.

The period of grace is for the benefit of the prospective adoptive parents as well. It frequently turns out that a child at three, or four or five months will show signs of mental retardation, loss of hearing or some other defect. If the adoptive parents decide they want to give the child back to the agency, they have that right.

Not only is Mr. DeMartino in contempt of the courts of his home state, but he sat here and lied through his teeth about his real reason for coming to Florida. He said, "I have been thinking about coming to Florida for many years. I had my honeymoon here."

This is a couple who have lived all their lives in New York. I say that kind of answer is an insult to this court. The only reason he is in Florida is because he shopped for a friendly jurisdiction. Let them lavish their love on an unwanted baby. We all know there are enough of them in this country. Don't reward them for fleeing New York!

Let's suppose a person kidnaps a child, not because he is really a kidnapper but because he loves kids. That person drives through a poor ghetto area and he sees a sad, undernourished infant. He is rich and educated and can take wonderful care of that child. Say he does in fact take splendid care of the child, and thirteen months later the law catches up with him. His argument is that it would be traumatic to return the baby to its natural mother. He may even have a family unit, whereas the true mother is poor and alone, but obviously it would be ridiculous to rule in his favor.

Colson and Fuchsberg could get the same doctors to come in here and talk about psychic scars, but it wouldn't hold water. If Olga Scarpetta were not the type of woman she is, nothing would have been easier for her than to do what the DeMartinos did. Take the baby and go to New York. Legally, it is as impossible to kidnap your own child as it is to rape one's spouse. Once in New York she could thumb her nose at the world. But she didn't choose to do that.

The judge didn't say a word during my entire argument. He didn't look me in the eye once, either. It was obvious that he had no intention of changing his mind, and he said so. I had to go to my "ace in the hole"—the right of a natural mother at least to visit with her child. The very gracious and generous DeMartinos had this to say through their lawyers.

Mr. Colson: Mr. Rosenblatt didn't produce any medical testimony here today to show that visitation would be in the best interest of this child. If your Honor is going to consider that, we certainly would want medical testimony to be heard. I think visitation would create a medical problem.

This was complete rubbish. I responded:

Every judge in this building has granted visitation to parents who are bums, who are months behind in their child support payments and who obviously have been bad parents. But such visitation is granted on the basis that the erring parent, simply because he or she is a parent, has the right to see their own child. I am absolutely amazed that the DeMartinos and their attorneys are so certain what is in the best interest of this child. Lenore may tell them in several years that they were wrong, that she wanted her real mother.

Well, by that time the lawyers will be on different cases, of course, and they will undoubtedly tell the teenager how sorry they are. But being sorry at that stage won't be good enough.

To pretend that we can really be sure after one day of testimony of what is in the best interest of this child is just ludicrous. I say respectfully that under the circumstances of this case, to deny Olga Scarpetta visitation with her own daughter would be cruel and unusual punishment.

Mr. Colson: I think it still comes down to medical testimony, and I would suggest to him that he still hasn't shown anything except his opinion.

Mr. Rosenblatt: Here you have a New York lawyer, judge, in contempt of the courts of his own state who has not adopted this baby and he is saying to the natural mother, "You can't see your own child." On the petition for habeas corpus, you did not rule that the DeMartinos were the parents of this child; you simply ruled that our petition was denied and they did not have to give the baby to Miss Scarpetta. It would be unconscionable not to permit this mother to see her baby.

The Court: I am denying the motion for visitation.

On September 28, 1971, the Third District Court of Appeal affirmed Judge Cullen's decision. The opinion said:

We have and do give great weight and respect to the orders of sister states but we conclude, under the circumstances of this case, that the trial judge followed proper procedure and law in ruling that the best interests and welfare of Lenore were served by leaving her custody with the appellees. . . . We point out that the change in circumstances and passage of time giving rise to the relationship between the baby and the DeMartinos occurred in great part because of appellant's consent, through her New York attorneys, that the custody of Lenore remain with the DeMartinos during the pendency of certain New York legal proceedings.

Yes, Leo Durocher, "nice guys finish last." Olga Scarpetta and Joseph Zalk could have insisted after the trial court's decision in New York that the baby at least be returned to the adoption agency. Instead they went along with Judge Ascione's strong recommendation that Lenore remain with the DeMartinos during the appeals. Little did they dream that an attorney and lifelong resident of New York would flee the state.

On April 25, 1972, the Florida Supreme Court denied our petition for writ of certiorari, our last hope in a Florida court. They simply refused to hear or decide the case. The opinion of the Third District Court of Appeal, therefore, remains the last word in Florida.

In New York the baby belongs to Olga Scarpetta. In Florida the DeMartinos are legally entitled to Lenore although they still have not adopted her. The situation does little to engender respect for the law. The United States Supreme Court has refused to decide the case either from the New York Appeal taken by the DeMartinos or from the Florida Appeal taken by us.

In a *Life* magazine article, captioned "Two Cribs for Baby Lenore," Miss Scarpetta said, "I believe in the end I will have my baby, simply because she is mine and no one can take her from me. Even if they have her while she is growing up, when she is grown, she will come to me. She will know how to find me, and when she comes, her record will be all clear. I have saved all the news clippings in a scrap book and have taped everything said on TV. It is her story, and she has the right to know all the angles of it."

Many times a lawyer gets involved in a case only to wish that he was on the other side. Initially you hear one version of the story, and it can happen that after investigation and depositions you become persuaded that your client is wrong. At that moment your obligation is either to withdraw or to do your best regardless of your true feelings.

I have never felt that simply because I am a lawyer, I must represent anyone who seeks my services. There was no dilemma for me at all in this case, in spite of the public outcry, the deliberate misinformation given to the press, and despite the obvious fact that someone had to be hurt.

I never thought that the DeMartinos were bad people. I can even understand their motives. But as far as I am concerned, Miss Scarpetta was absolutely entitled to have her baby.

I strongly believe that blood is thicker than water. I believe that heredity, genes, and heritage are concepts that have meaning. I may be quaint, but I am glad I was not conceived in a test tube. Knowing that my mother is my own mother means a great deal to me as, I am convinced, it does to the vast majority of people.

It is fashionable to say that you could love another person's children as much as your own, or that you could feel the same toward adoptive parents as your own, but I do not believe it. There *is* a difference. Even though that difference may exist in the deep recesses of one's id, it is still there.

Lenore is six years old now. Someday she will read the full transcripts of the New York and Florida proceedings and I do not expect her to view the contents with equanimity. Only time will tell what was truly in Lenore's best interest, and the definitive answer will have to come from her.

Epilogue

We are in the midst of a revolutionary period in the entire field of civil jury trials. Some of those who reflexively welcome any expansion of government regulation, in the name of "reform," seek to abolish the jury system. The "no fault" automobile statutes are the opening wedge for this previously unthinkable concept.

The jury system is far from perfect but it is far superior to any alternative system of resolving disputes. The greatest virtue of the jury system is the difficulty of "fixing" or corrupting it. Citizens do not serve as jurors long enough to become politicized or predictable. They retain their independence since they are not "pals" of any of the participants. The real trial lawyers may retain their independence as well since they don't have to take part in the hideous ritual of fawning before judges or arbitrators.

The concept of "no fault," where theoretically everyone gets paid voluntarily regardless of fault, sounds good but it is a gigantic ripoff. It would abolish basic human rights and enrich insurance companies beyond all imagining. Gone would be the right to ask compensation for pain and suffering, mental anguish, lost earning capacity and the inability to lead a normal life. The quid pro quo for receiving "out of pocket" expenses would be that the injured person would not have to prove that the other party was negligent.

The drunken driver who sustained injuries and economic loss would be paid to the same extent as the innocent person who was rear ended while stopped for a red light.

There is a certain kind of mentality rampant in our land which seeks to bureaucratize everything. The more rules and regulations and forms to fill out, the better this ilk likes it. One of their phony rationalizations for abolishing civil jury trials is the assertation that it would free more judges to hear all the important criminal cases.

One-half of all criminal arrests in the United States are for drunkenness, disorderly conduct, vagrancy, and gambling. We have unenforceable laws against adultery, pornography, prostitution, and various consensual sexual acts. This preoccupation with victimless crimes is a root cause of our failure to solve real crimes like murder, robbery, rape, aggravated assault and burglary.

If we reserved jury trials for these serious crimes, we could cut the budget of our criminal justice system in half. The criminal trial and the full panoply of constitutional due process are luxuries we cannot afford for the ordinary trivial offense such as petty traffic violations. Likewise, not every fender bender which results in a minor "whiplash" should entitle the aggrieved person to a jury trial. The piddling cases—both civil and criminal—should be removed from the court dockets.

The jury trial is a fundamental bastion of freedom. It is the primary remaining forum for citizens to engage in participatory democracy. Sure, every now and then a jury is hoodwinked by great oratory. But the beauty of the adversary system is that it permits the jurors to hear both sides of a controversy—and in heavy civil trials, each side is generally presented by lawyers of comparable skills.

Of course, I have a selfish interest in all this. Jury trials often are exciting and dramatic, and they can even be fun. I would be bored to tears trying cases before judges or mediation panels. There is a pleasure to be derived from pacing in front of a jury of your peers, waving your arms, raising your voice, trying to get strangers to see things your way. There can be heartache in it, too, but at least you know you are alive and being pushed to do your best. The "no fault" proponents want to equalize skill, and talent and imagination. They want the courthouse to be as dull gray as the assembly line. They want their own mediocrity to go unnoticed.

Ninety percent of my practice involves jury-trial cases. The problem with judges or arbitrators is that they hear the same types of cases constantly. It is very easy for them to become jaded and develop fixed points of view. Ofttimes the evidence is a complete sham since the decider has his mind made up as soon as he learns the nature of the controversy.

The medical profession is screaming the loudest about the abolition of the jury system in malpractice cases. These free-enterprise hypocrites were always strongly against any type of governmental interference in their practices. Now that their insurance rates are being raised, they are begging governments at the federal and state levels to help them. Big government is fine so long as it saves them money. The medical profession and the insurance industry deserve one another, and they are both about equally dishonest in their pronouncements to the public.

Investigators for United States Senate Panel working to draft reforms of the Medicaid Program reported after a four-month study that as much as one-half of the program's fifteen-billion-dollar annual cost is wasted through fraud and mismanagement. These findings were made public on August 30, 1976. Ripoffs from Medicaid, which serves welfare clients, are even worse than medical ripoffs from Medicare, which serves those on social security.

The fraudulent techniques involve charges for patient

visits that are never made, charges for laboratory work never done or never required, faked invoices, and "ping ponging" of patients from doctor to doctor within particular Medicaid mills. Where is the outrage of the American Medical Association or state and local medical associations? How many licenses have been revoked? How many of these vermin have been prosecuted? The medical profession responds in the way it always has to such problems—it looks the other way.

Until about ten years ago, a successful medical malpractice case was just about nonexistent. Americans had been brainwashed to believe that every horrendous result was just "one of those things." Doctors were kings. No one asked them penetrating questions; no one examined their office records or their shoddy past performances. They wouldn't testify against one another.

Bad doctors, hospital screw-ups and unnecessary operations were all closely guarded secrets like the Latin mumbo-jumbo on prescription pads. Nearly always, even the good doctors looked the other way. No one wanted to rock the boat of impregnable virtue.

Even today the furor is not over incompetence and malpractice. No, it is over money—the high cost of insurance. I have absolutely no sympathy for a lawyer who undertakes a matter beyond his competence because he is too greedy to refer the case and pass up a fee. Obviously the professional cannot guarantee a successful result. But if death or serious injury ensues from a negligent act, he should damn well pay for it. Many physicians agree, and that is why some are willing to testify against their fellows.

One example of the medical profession's shortsightedness is their desire to regulate attorneys' fees. Are they so naïve as to suppose that bureaucratic regulation is a one-way street? They moan about the contingency-fee contract which permits a patient, a client of modest means, to hire a great lawyer. I, as well as every heavy litigator in medical malpractice, have expended hundreds of hours and thousands of dollars on cases and come up empty. *We* can't look to Medicare or client insurance policies for payment. What business is that of the doctors? Of course, there are some awful abuses with respect to contingency fees, and if the client has a complaint, *that* should be given attention.

Plaintiffs' malpractice lawyers have done more to improve medical practice than all the self-righteous doctor committees and insurance lobbies put together. The medical strikers have shown their true colors in this whole controversy. They are not worried about the patient, or the jury system, or strangulating red tape. No, they are worried primarily about their incomes and their images. When is the last time there was a doctors' strike because of deplorable hospital conditions?

It's all quite simple, really. The "malpractice problem" exists because there is so much damn malpractice. The doctors will groan all they like about dumb juries (in private) and greedy lawyers (in public), but people understand that the plaintiff has a heavy burden of proof in a malpractice action and that when the doctor loses it is generally because he did something wrong.

If not for "medical malpractice," Jerry Burke's death would have been swept under the rug. It would have been blamed on a heart attack, an embolus, or an allergic reaction to anesthesia. What layman has the expertise or the wherewithal to question these proclamations?

Beware of those who ask you to relinquish precious rights for a fistful of dollars! And a jury trial, however imperfect, is indeed a precious right. Citizens in a democracy should have the prerogative (with certain sensible limitations) to have their disputes decided by fellow citizens rather than by professional arbiters.

I intend to remain a trial lawyer as long as it is feasible.

"Lawyer" and "trial lawyer" are two very different concepts to me. I regard it as a badge of honor to be able to walk into a courtroom to do battle on behalf of individuals who have been maimed or killed by malpractice.

The human factor and the intangibles of community standards and common sense must remain part of the judical equation. If they ever depart, the computer will reign supreme and the technicians, with formulas in place of hearts and minds, will inherit the earth. The struggle must be joined now if we are to prevent such an eventuality.